WE ARE ALL AFRICANS HERE

Edited by Noel B. Salazar, University of Leuven, in collaboration with ANTHROMOB, the EASA Anthropology and Mobility Network.

WORLDS **IN MOTION**

This transdisciplinary series features empirically grounded studies from around the world that disentangle how people, objects, and ideas move across the planet. With a special focus on advancing theory as well as methodology, the series considers movement as both an object and a method of study.

Volume 10
WE ARE ALL AFRICANS HERE
Race, Mobilities, and West Africans in Europe
Kristín Loftsdóttir

Volume 9
LIMINAL MOVES
Traveling along Places, Meanings, and Times
Flavia Cangià

Volume 8
PACING MOBILITIES
Timing, Intensity, Tempo and Duration of Human Movements
Edited by Vered Amit and Noel B. Salazar

Volume 7
FINDING WAYS THROUGH EUROSPACE
West African Movers Re-viewing Europe from the Inside
Joris Schapendonk

Volume 6
BOURDIEU AND SOCIAL SPACE
Mobilities, Trajectories, Emplacements
Deborah Reed-Danahay

Volume 5
HEALTHCARE IN MOTION
Immobilities in Health Service Delivery and Access
Edited by Cecilia Vindrola-Padros, Ginger A. Johnson, and Anne E. Pfister

Volume 4
MOMENTOUS MOBILITIES
Anthropological Musings on the Meanings of Travel
Noel B. Salazar

Volume 3
INTIMATE MOBILITIES
Sexual Economies, Marriage and Migration in a Disparate World
Edited by Christian Groes and Nadine T. Fernandez

Volume 2
METHODOLOGIES OF MOBILITY
Ethnography and Experiment
Edited by Alice Elliot, Roger Norum, and Noel B. Salazar

Volume 1
KEYWORDS OF MOBILITY
Critical Engagements
Edited by Noel B. Salazar and Kiran Jayaram

We Are All Africans Here
Race, Mobilities, and West Africans in Europe

Kristín Loftsdóttir

berghahn
NEW YORK • OXFORD
www.berghahnbooks.com

First published in 2022 by
Berghahn Books
www.berghahnbooks.com

© 2022, 2024 Kristín Loftsdóttir
First paperback edition published 2024

All rights reserved. Except for the quotation of short passages
for the purposes of criticism and review, no part of this book
may be reproduced in any form or by any means, electronic or
mechanical, including photocopying, recording, or any information
storage and retrieval system now known or to be invented,
without written permission of the publisher.

Library of Congress Cataloging-in-Publication Data

Names: Kristín Loftsdóttir, author.
Title: We Are All Africans Here: Race, Mobilities, and West Africans in Europe / Kristín Loftsdóttir.
Other titles: Race, Mobilities, and West Africans in Europe Description: New York: Berghahn Books, 2022. | Series: Worlds in Motion; volume 10 | Includes bibliographical references and index.
Identifiers: LCCN 2021039736 (print) | LCCN 2021039737 (ebook) | ISBN 9781800733275 (hardback) | ISBN 9781800733282 (ebook)
Subjects: LCSH: West Africans—Europe—Social conditions. | Nigeriens—Europe—Social conditions. | Refugees—Europe—Social conditions. | Refugees—Niger—Social conditions. | Africa, West—Emigration and immigration. | Niger—Emigration and immigration. | Europe—Emigration and immigration. | Racism—Europe.
Classification: LCC D1056.2.A38 K75 2022 (print) | LCC D1056.2.A38 (ebook) | DDC 305.80094—dc23
LC record available at https://lccn.loc.gov/2021039736
LC ebook record available at https://lccn.loc.gov/2021039737

British Library Cataloguing in Publication Data
A catalogue record for this book is available from the British Library

ISBN 978-1-80073-327-5 hardback
ISBN 978-1-80539-714-4 paperback
ISBN 978-1-80073-328-2 web pdf
ISBN 978-1-80539-905-6 epub

https://doi.org/10.3167/9781800733275

This book is dedicated to my Nigerien friends participating in this research, some of whom live in Brussels, Milan, Paris, and in Niamey.

Contents

List of Illustrations   ix

Acknowledgments   xi

Introduction   Racialized Mobilities   1

Part I. Making Precarious Migrants

Chapter 1   Living in Divided Europe: The Theme Park and the Street   17

Chapter 2   "Enough of Refugees": Depictions of Precarious Migrants in Europe   31

Chapter 3   Into the Heart of Europe: Migrants in Brussels and Beyond   39

Chapter 4   Global Citizens and the Backstage   51

Chapter 5   Multicultural Europe: Invasions against European Values?   62

Part II. Entangled Histories

Chapter 6   This Is All in the Past Now: Niger and a Global World   75

Chapter 7   Nostalgic Colonialism: Different Kinds of Otherness   93

Chapter 8   Spaces of Innocence: Belgium's Colonial History and Beyond   106

Part III. Europe's Past and Future

Chapter 9   The Heart of Darkness: EUrope as a Concept   117

Conclusion   Welcome to the Future: Dismaland and Anxieties in Europe   134

References 145

Index 167

Illustrations

Figures

1.1. Demonstration in Milan against racism in 2018. © Kristín Loftsdóttir. 21

1.2. The Mexican side of the border town Naco in Sonora in 2018. © Árni Víkingur Sveinsson. 25

3.1. Looking out Ali's window to the city of Brussels. © Kristín Loftsdóttir. 44

4.1. Different comic strip murals are found widely around Brussels, celebrating the city's comic book artists. Photo taken in spring 2019 at Rue des Capucins, where the characters Blondin and Cirage are depicted. © Kristín Loftsdóttir. 53

6.1. A woman and her child in the town Tchintabaraden in Niger in 1996. © Kristín Loftsdóttir. 79

6.2. The author celebrating with young WoDaaBe girls in the pastoral area in Niger in 1998. © Kristín Loftsdóttir. 90

7.1. Gerewol dance. While the photo was taken by the author in Niger during 1997, it reflects a popular representation of WoDaaBe in the European imagination. © Kristín Loftsdóttir. 97

7.2. Selling jewelry at a music festival in Brussels in 2014. © Kristín Loftsdóttir. 101

8.1. The leopard man (Aniota) at the AfricaMuseum at Tervuren (photo taken in 2019), with iron claws and spotted-skin costume. The statue iconized the savagery of Congo for Europeans, and inspired Hergé in his making of Tintin in Congo. © Kristín Loftsdóttir. 109

8.2. Protest of Belgium's colonial heritage included strategic vandalism of King Leopold II's statues. © Jean-Marc Pierard / Alamy Stock Photo. 112

9.1. Visiting Mini-Europe Park in Bruparck, 2017. The author's son and the miniatures display. © Kristín Loftsdóttir. 121

9.2. Place de la Bourse in March 2016. After the attacks this was a gathering place to commemorate and pay tribute to those killed and injured. © Kristín Loftsdóttir. 130

10.1. Dismaland's Cinderella: the dream of a happy ending in disarray. © Guy Corbishley / Alamy Stock Photo. 138

Map

6.1. Map of the main African central and western migration routes to the European Schengen Area, used by undocumented migrants between 2008 and 2018. Source of data: Frontex and IOM. © Kristín Loftsdóttir, Ignacio Fradejas-García, and Jana Ohanesyan. 84

Acknowledgments

This book would not have happened if not for my Nigerien friends and interlocutors who generously spent time with me over the years, welcomed me during each visit, and were willing to share their stories with me. As you—my friends and interlocutors for this research—are in a precarious position I will refrain from mentioning your names. You know who you are. I want to thank especially my closest friends in Italy and Belgium, who helped me find others to talk to, and also those who generously invited me to their homes or out for ice cream or pizza, or invited me to transitional events in their lives, all while being extremely patient with my broken French and often naive questions and understanding.

I am extremely grateful for the kindness that I encountered in Niger a long time ago, which shaped my outlook on the world and taught me about the meaning of friendship, family, and solidarity. It helped me to understand with my heart, my interlocutors' emphasis on Niger as a place of peace, respect, and kindness, as well as understanding the importance of *munyal*, or patience necessary for all research. I also want to thank other friends in Belgium and Italy that I engaged with during the research, which I will not name either as many of you have been or are close friends with some of my interlocutors. Thanks for sharing your perspectives and stories with me and helping me to navigate and understand better Belgian and Italian society.

There were many colleagues who encouraged me to write this book or to not give up; who read over different chapters or assisted in other ways with its making. Thank you, Sonia Sabelli, Brigitte Hipfl, Sarah Lunaček, Kristján Þór Sigurðsson, and James Gordon Rice. I am especially grateful to Scott Youngstedt—whom I met a long time ago in Niger and have stayed in contact with ever since—for encouraging me to continue writing and for replies to endless questions regarding Niger. Thank you also Paweł Lewicki for your help in understanding some of the dynamics in Brussels better.

Noel Salazar's encouragement to write about this research during one of my fieldwork trips in Belgium was really inspirational during its early stages. Early on, Ashley Shelby gave me extremely useful comments on the manuscript, helping me to organize the discussion as well as pushing me to continue to write the book. I am thankful to all of these people. Chapter 10 derives partly from a paper that was composed for a conference, organized at the University of St. Andrews. Thanks to Daniel M. Knight and Rebecca Bryant for inviting me, and for providing valuable feedback on my presentation and pushing my thoughts on future aspirations. Anna Lísa Rúnarsdóttir gave me valuable feedback on the manuscript in addition to assisting with compiling it, and Ignacio Fradejas-García and Jana Ohanesyan created Map 6.1. on very short notice.

I am grateful to Berghahn Books, especially Tom Bonnington, assistant editor, for having faith in this manuscript and transforming it into a book. I want to thank the University of Iceland Research Fund for making the research possible with funding for data collection and fieldwork trips, and I also thank the Icelandic Research Fund (RANNIS) for funding for the project CERM (Creating Europe through Racialized Mobility, grant number 207062-051), which helped me to analyze and understand better the mobility issues at stake.

At last, I am grateful to my partner, Már, my three children, Mímir, Alexía, and Sól, and my parents, Eria and Loftur, for valuable assistance with making the research become a reality in personal and highly practical terms, as well as taking a part in some of the travelling that it involved. It was really rewarding to be able to bring together my personal life back "home" in Iceland and my Nigerien friends—some of whom I have known since I lived in Niger a long time ago.

Introduction
Racialized Mobilities

For someone from Iceland, Milan is hot in the summer. The air seems to hardly move, and the sun is high in the sky. The first days of my short work trip are filled with matters related to my research regarding migrants from Niger, where I conducted my PhD research almost twenty years ago. This time, I am accompanied by my early teenage children in an attempt to reconcile my academic and family life. The kids have been promised a trip to the Gardaland theme park as a special treat, but when we discover the rail service is on strike, our trip there seems impossible. Due to my schedule, we cannot change the date of our visit. To make matters worse, we were planning to meet relatives there, who are also traveling in northern Italy. So, we resolve to go by car and in the early morning, we visit a nearby rental car agency, only to discover that we had to book online. Feeling rather ridiculous, we step outside and reserve the car by phone. After further complications, we finally climb in our rental and are relieved to be able to keep the promise to our children.

After arriving at Gardaland, and after a joyful family reunion in the parking lot, we try out the rides and the wonders that this man-made space of entertainment has to offer. After strolling around for a while, I can relax on a nearby bench with my father in the shade. Sprinklers cool the air slightly, as we wait for the kids to return from the rollercoaster. It is all very pleasant, and I am relieved that the trip worked out, making it less stressful for me to continue with my research the next few days.

My dad and I watch the people walking by, most accompanied by children who run excitedly in front of them. He says quietly: "Do you notice how few Black people are here? Almost everyone is white." His remark strikes me. I observe the environment around me in a completely different light. There are certainly some non-white people around, but for the most part the bodies traveling through the park are white. White faces, hands, and feet moving around this space that is Gardaland: well-dressed people buying expensive ice cream, overpriced pizzas or hotdogs. I think about where our apartment in Milan is located and visualize the people I have seen around the neighborhood metro station Pasteur. The difference is striking. Not only is our neighborhood more diverse in terms of presence of people being defined as non-white, but it also exhibits much more economic variety.

As I start to look deeper into this ocean of white bodies that surrounds us at the park, I think of the strikingly diverse landscape of human bodies in Milan, and within it the precarious migrants from West Africa I have come to know. I remind myself at this moment of one of the luxuries of white[1] privilege; the tendency, as whiteness scholars have stressed, of white people to render their own whiteness invisible to themselves, which is itself linked to their privileged positions of power.

It is not that I have never thought about this. In fact, I have thought about it a lot. However, here I am removed from my safe space of anthropology, where I try to deconstruct and look critically at everything. Instead, I have stepped into a different realm—the everyday life of white privilege. Although I am here in Italy attempting to juggle my academic and personal life, it is clear that this privileged opportunity—to step out of the workspace—is far more readily available to privileged white scholars who do not have to encounter racism in their everyday lives (Carter 2018).

My father's comment was yet another startling reminder of the stark contrasts I have seen in the lives of people in Italy. For the duration of this research trip, I have been overwhelmed by the ubiquity and depth of these contrasts: while some people live on the street or embark on long and dangerous trips away from their families in the hope of creating a better future, others, like myself, take leisure trips just to spend their time somewhere different. We mainly encounter trivial problems, like needing to rent a car to go to Gardaland. This feeling haunts me during the research in different contexts again and again. As I sit with my father, enjoying a day with my family, I think about how Gardaland, with its high gates and admission fees, is one of many oases of whiteness. It is a space of privilege where whiteness can be enjoyed away from the more complicated arenas of racialization and class. There are no street people or beggars in Gardaland, no visible signs of desperate people from the Global South, and no evidence of the marginalized populations of Europe who have failed to "make it" in an increasingly neoliberal world.

I start this book with this reflection because it is relevant to the world of West African migrants. These individuals exist along with me in a world that criminalizes the mobility of some while celebrating the mobility of others. It is this idea with which I critically engage in this book, asking who can move in and out of Europe, and why. I focus on the mobility and immobility of differently positioned subjects through an examination of the aspirations of men from Niger who travel to European cities, where they seek short-term economic benefits or asylum. I seek to show that Europe as such is not part of their aspirations, contrary to popular media depiction, but rather they are actively using their ability to move between different places to improve the quality of their lives and that of their loved ones back in Niger.

My insights derive from long-term research and fieldwork, developed in different projects that intersect and inform each other. In the late 1990s, I conducted ethnographic fieldwork in Niger among WoDaaBe, a group of pastoral nomads. Globalization was a topical issue at the time and gaining traction. I was far from my home in Iceland and wanted to understand what globalization meant for different people. Shortly after the completion of my research, some WoDaaBe started embarking on short visits to Europe. Expatriates and previous tourists from Europe in Niger often helped these WoDaaBe get short-term visas, meaning that the association of WoDaaBe with the exotic in European colonial imagination facilitated their mobility. At that time, it was difficult to imagine that one of the unforeseen consequences of globalization would be a fortification of European borders against those defined as undesirable outsiders. In the late 1990s, increased and less-restricted mobility seemed to be the natural outcome of globalization, one that had been celebrated and symbolized by the fall of the Berlin Wall in 1989 (Fassin 2011). Instead, what lay in wait was the gradual fortification of Europe. Precarious migrant men seeking to improve their poverty-stricken lives became, along with other West African migrants, increasingly stigmatized as some of Europe's most undesirable strangers—Black, Muslim, and male. Rhetoric suggesting that Europe was "flooded" by migrants or Muslim "others" intensified. At the same time, the mobility of privileged people in the Global North—including myself as an academic and a tourist—expanded and was hailed as a positive sign of an increasingly cosmopolitan and interconnected world.

After fieldwork in Niger, I carried out a series of short fieldwork trips to European cities that focused on precarious migrants from there. At the same time, I was engaged in research in Iceland, where one of the key focuses was on whiteness and the transformation of Icelandic people into European subjects through their engagement with coloniality. This research helped me to deepen my understanding of the wider sociopolitical relations within which Nigerien migration to Europe takes place, as well as the historically constituted relationship between Niger and Europe as a concept and an aspiration.

These small fieldwork projects, for the most part conducted in Brussels and Milan, started as an investigation into the life of WoDaaBe in Europe, but later mutated to focus on precarious men from Niger in general, as well as mobility in and out of Europe. It became clear that WoDaaBe were not categorized as the dangerous "other," but as a different kind of "other," that is, exotic, exciting, and nonthreatening. Thus, some individuals benefitted ironically from racist and reified processes historically characterized by European depictions of them, as they were not associated with other African "economic migrants" or negative depictions of refugees or asylum seekers.

I realized as well that my research on "whiteness" in Iceland and the mobility of "white" subjects in and out of Europe was also relevant to research on Nigerien migrants, then as a part of the larger geopolitical context. A critical and ongoing inspection of my own position as a privileged subject bridged these research perspectives. In Iceland, refugees and asylum seekers had become a part of my own environment, echoing or resisting a wider discussion on European migration. So, while I prioritize Nigerien precarious migrants in this book, my discussion seeks ultimately to draw attention to diverse actors who are differently positioned in a geopolitical context, and how their different positions shape their movement. I highlight the asymmetry in discussions about mobility, contrasting the white experts with the migrant, as well as drawing attention to the silencing of Europe's imperial and colonial past in discussions of mobilities. How, for example, are subjects within the category of historically constituted "others" differentiated regarding class, religion, race, and their historical relationship with Europe? How are these categories created and maintained?

Recent debate about asylum seekers and refugees has intensified questions of Europe's colonial past and, consequently, what that past means for the future (Hipfl and Gronold 2011: 29). The depiction of Europe as a constant and unified whole forced to push back against the flow of external "others" (Ponzanesi and Blaagaard 2011) draws on specific interpretations of the past where Europe is seen as consisting of clearly bounded national entities.[2] Despite the celebration of increased global fluidity, Europe's borders have become more fortified through various measures, as immigrants are constantly projected as threats and increasingly subjected to intensive practices of securitization and surveillance (Balibar and Collins 2003). Further, scholarly discourses of mobility often take place in separate spheres, where discussions of economic migrants, expatriates, or tourists occur in isolation from one another (Salazar 2011).

The concept of cosmopolitanism is a case in point, often seen in the European imagination as facilitating European integration and embracing diversity (Baban 2013, Bhambra and Narayan 2017), while other kinds of mobilities and identities are simultaneously perceived as incompatible with the European cosmopolitan project. These "problematic" mobilities include Muslim migration to Europe from poorer parts of the world (Edmunds 2013), which tend to be discussed not as part of a burgeoning cosmopolitanism but instead in the context of immigration or refugee studies. Recently, the 2020 protests across Europe and the US in the aftermath of George Floyd's killing also drew attention to continued racialization and exclusion of certain populations within Europe—including citizens of Europe—and how the colonial past continues to matter in various ways.

My analysis in this book is based on two key intersecting streams of theoretical debates, which have most often been theorized separately. The first key stream consists of theoretical discussions about multicultural society and critical race studies. A "crisis of multiculturalism" has become a framing device used in public discussions in many European societies (Lentin and Titley 2011). This idea intensified thanks to increased numbers of asylum seekers and refugees which mutated into a "refugee crisis." The idea of a "crisis of multiculturalism" is in itself based on ahistorical notions of Europe as consisting earlier of "pure" cultural spaces, as well as a complete disregard for the effect of colonialism on transnational movements. Discussions about the "refugee crisis" are also marked by these shortcomings. Here it is particularly urgent to analyze the changing landscapes of racist practices and identities, as scholars have stressed that racism is more difficult to target in the present because it is coded under different labels, such as culture and religion (Balibar 1991).

Racialization has, of course, always involved a mixture of cultural and biological features, in addition to being entangled with ideas of gender, class, and modernity (see McClintock 1995; Garner 2009). But with extreme nationalistic and populist parties gaining more currency in political debates in Western Europe, religion has become a "privileged marker of racial and absolute difference" (Fortier 2007: 110; see also Werbner 2007). In current rhetoric, religion and cultural characteristics are incorporated within discourses based on a slip between notions of culture and race (Abu El-Haj 2002). Racialized images that intersect or surface with reference to culture or religion also take on stark gendered representations, such as those revolving around the "oppressed Muslim woman" and the "male Muslim terrorist" (Abu-Lughod 2002). More recently, there has even been a merging of the image of "the terrorist" with "the Muslim" (Bhui 2016).

When the intersection of race with other categories of difference is emphasized, a more nuanced and complex picture of the persistence of racial classification can emerge, one that illustrates the way racial classifications touch on other categories and interact with them. This book utilizes this approach to draw attention to how Europe's cosmopolitan aspirations become complicated, due to their intersection with the multiple identities of particular subjects, and with Europe's colonial and imperial past.

Within discourses of migration, categories such as Muslim, immigrant, or African signal particular subjective categories that are historically negative in Europe. My research in 2013 indicated that WoDaaBe were, however, primarily seen in Europe as "exotic others," disregarding their identities as Muslims and migrant workers. As such, they received assistance from local people in applying for Schengen visas, as well as with housing and other expenses. By comparing WoDaaBe experiences with other racialized subjects from Niger, including those who have not occupied the "exotic" category in Western writing and discourses, I ask what kind of bodies are categorized as "others" and investigate the continued relevance of "exoticness" in contemporary Europe. My discussion also asks what subject positions these migrants feel they take once in Europe, as they encounter the different manifestations of the "other" that exist in Europe today.

In discussing racialization and the so-called multicultural society, I use the phrase "precarious migrants." While the term "precarity" is often theorized in relation to the labor market—in some cases only as referring to neoliberalism or post-Fordism changes in labor relations (see discussion in Vickers et al. 2019; Paret and Gleeson 2016: 279; Lewis et al. 2015)—I follow here Priya Deshingkar's understanding of precarity as an "ontological stage of 'life,'" as entangled with local histories and global conditions (2019: 2638). This means that its analytical usefulness is interlinked with how it situates inequalities as having to do with social structures and historical conditions, as well as drawing attention to "multiple forms of vulnerability" (Paret and Gleeson 2016: 280), that characterize the lives of certain migrant populations. As argued by Paret and Gleeson:

> migrant existence is often precarious in multiple, and reinforcing ways, combining vulnerability to deportation and state violence, exclusion from public services and basic state protections, insecure employment and exploitation at work, insecure livelihood, and everyday discrimination or isolation. (2016: 281)

Precarity is not intrinsic to these men as individuals but rather points toward structural conditions that are produced globally, and which shape their lives. Theoretical discussion of precarity also importantly touches on agency and the ability to exert agency (Paret and Gleeson 2016: 282). Most of the men I spoke to would not see themselves as passive victims as they actively try to change and enhance their lives. My use of the term "precarious" in connection to the term "migrant" seeks to draw attention to the multiple ways of being a migrant, where some mobilities of migrant populations are made more precarious than others, while those in precarious migrant positions are not only those migrating from south to north but also those migrating within Europe or their country of origin (see discussion in Vickers et al. 2019). This means as well that not all migration from south to north is or should be seen as precarious. West Africans are welcomed into Europe as, for example, medical doctors and football stars, which does not necessarily exclude racism and exploitation (Darby, Akindes, and Kirwin 2007; Hagopian et al. 2005; Jiwani 2008). In Brussels, people from sub-Saharan African countries come for different reasons, including to pursue lives as students, artists, and diplomats (Lo Sardo 2013: 313; Kagné and Martiniello 2001). People from Niger thus go to Europe for a longer or shorter time due to an array of reasons that this book does not cover.

The second stream of theoretical discussion informing this book focuses on mobility and immobility. As suggested earlier, discussions of multiculturalism and migration, both on the scholarly and popular level, often seem to assume that there was a prior state of immobility, which calls for an historical perspective on mobility as crucial context to any such discussion (see the criticism in Glick Schiller and Salazar 2013: 184; Salazar and Smart 2011). The use of the term "migrant" in migration studies has been criticized for its presumption that people move between two points, that is, their country of origin and a destination country (Schapendonk 2020), working from the framework of "departure-movement-arrival-integration" (Schapendonk, Bolay and Dahinden 2020: 2). The reality is far more complex, as Joris Schapendonk stresses in regard to African mobility to Europe, where "relations and notions of belonging change along pathways of movements," with people engaging in multiple forms of mobility (2020: 4). Similarly, scholarly and popular discussions of racism also presuppose a particular kind of mobility, that is, that the mobility of precarious subjects is creating the racism directed at them. It is necessary to contrast and juxtapose different kinds of mobilities to avoid the assumption that racism is somehow the consequence of recent migration to Europe, and to recognize racism as constitutive and embedded in modernity itself (Grosfoguel 2011). Here I stress the need to place the aspiration of cosmopolitanism as a positive European virtue alongside contemporary discourses of who belongs and who is welcome in Europe, and in so doing to reflect Europe's continued struggles with "colonialist and imperialist attitudes" (Ponzanesi and Blaagaard 2011: 4). The term "regimes of mobilities" draws attention to how the state, international regulations, and various security and surveillance mechanisms affect and shape who is mobile and in what ways, making regimes of mobility inherently interlinked with power (Glick Schiller and Salazar 2013: 189). It also draws attention to the importance of understanding mobility in relation to immobility: to ask critically whose movement is disallowed, and why? (Salazar and Smart 2011).

Finally, cutting across these two theoretical streams is my interest in "crisis" as a concept (see Loftsdóttir and Jensen 2014; Loftsdóttir, Smith, and Hipfl 2018). Crisis traversed the lives of my interlocutors in ways that became evident as my research unfolded, especially as European conversations about mobility were often framed as different kinds of crises. The "crisis of multiculturalism" became the "refugee crisis." Muslims as a category became a "terrorist crisis." My interlocutors' travels from Niger's constant social and economic crisis as one of the poorest countries in the world became a part of a humanitarian crisis due to the civil war in Libya, where they had sought new lives. Furthermore, their lives became shaped by Europe's economic crisis and the growing sense of precarity among those living in Europe. Now as I write this book, the crisis has become linked to the global pandemic, which has affected their lives extensively.

While this book anchors its discussion in the experience of the Nigerien migrants, it also reflects on wider questions about migration in Europe in relation to racialization and different ways of othering. It asks how this space, Europe, is configured by those outside of its sphere of privilege (Herzfeld 1989, 2016: 72; Ponzanesi 2016) and what kind of transnational and historical connections become evident if the lives of precarious migrants in Europe are used as a reference point. Of particular relevance here is the intersection of racism, gender, religion, and culture in the lives of migrant men as it interacts with their position as former colonial subjects of European powers. This draws attention to past-present relations and the "after-effects of colonialism" (Ponzanesi and Colpani 2016).

Niger demonstrates the continued need for such a perspective. The ongoing political, social, and economic instability in Northern Africa has affected Niger in many ways, such as with the collapse of the tourist industry with rebellions in the country (Grégoire and Scholze 2012; Snorek 2016), and a large influx of refugees arriving from neighboring countries with Niger becoming both a hub for West African migrants in transit and a site of refugee centers (Larémont, Attir, and Mahamadou 2020; Veronese, Pepe, and Vigliaroni 2019). In addition, with the end of Gaddafi's regime in Libya, small arms and weapons became dispersed and thus more accessible in the Sahara and Sahel region, creating a situation of political uncertainty as the region has become a place of weapons, drugs, and human trafficking (Danjibo 2013: 19, 31). Niger has as well been dragged into the US-led "war on terror" (Elischer and Mueller 2018) and become an important part of the externalization of Europe's borders (Idrissa 2019; Brachet 2016; Larémont et al. 2020), as well as shaped by other conflicts, some of which relate to the foreign exploitation of Niger's uranium (McGregor 2007; Afifi 2011). These circumstances profoundly affect people in Niger, increasing the precarity of already precarious lives.

In this book I will occasionally refer to examples from my own intimate environment of Iceland, because my research on mobilities in Iceland informs my insights of how discourses of migrants, refugees, and asylum seekers informs popular views across Europe. The example of Iceland serves as a further illustration to elaborate what it means to be European and what means to be non-European.

Research

As the previous discussion suggests, this book scales back and forth between a larger perspective on Europe and the experiences of these precarious Nigerien men, as well as moving between different geographical sites. The research was conducted at several locations in Belgium and Italy, especially in Brussels and to some extent in Milan. Brussels is often depicted as the capital of Europe, while Milan is one of the focal points of Europe's migration crisis. In 2004, 2011, 2012, and 2016–18, I conducted ethnographic work in Belgium, as well as in northern Italy from 2016 to 2018. While brief, these persistent field trips allowed me to acquire significant insight into the migrants' lives in these localities.

In my analysis, I reference earlier research I conducted in Niger from 1996 to 1998 on mobility and globalization. My interlocutors in the research presented in this book are from different areas in Niger, and mostly aged between thirty and forty-five, though I also interviewed some younger and older individuals, as well as some individuals who were not from Niger. Most of the men I talked to were married, having left their families behind; they came from conditions of extreme poverty and had only minimal or informal education. There were also a few individuals with long formal education who had for the most part left Niger due to political prosecutions. My interviews were with Nigeriens from diverse ethnicities, including not only WoDaaBe and Tuaregs but also other ethnicities such as Hausa, Zarma, Fulani, and Toubou, and also a few individuals from neighboring West African countries. The names used in this book are pseudonyms, but in some cases I also changed the background of some of my interviewees to further mask their identities. For example, in order to protect the identity of some research participants, I sometimes treat individuals who are Tuaregs or WoDaaBe as belonging to the same ethnic group, even though this is a gross simplification as in Niger these are quite different groups in terms of history and self-identification. I chose to do this because I learned from my initial research among WoDaaBe that their limited numbers in Belgium make it difficult to hide their identity, even when pseudonyms are used. For the context where I do this, it matters that Tuaregs in Niger have historically held a similar place as WoDaaBe in the European imagination.

As stated earlier, the discussion in this book is also informed by debates about migration and refugees in Iceland, where I live and where I originated. Initially, I debated whether Iceland was relevant to this book, but soon saw that referring to migration and other transnational movement in Iceland informed and enriched my research on West African migrants, in particular concerning the transnational character of certain practices and ideas. Additionally, as a part of Europe and of the Global North, Iceland draws from and contributes to larger discourses about migration, asylum seekers, and refugees.

The research is shaped by my academic upbringing in anthropology, where ethnography has not only been a key research method but a source of theoretical inspiration and way of communicating research results. Within anthropology, discussions of *what* ethnography is, have continued to a be a fruitful way of thinking about research methods and how to engage with the present. Researching mobility has revealed new methodological challenges, including questions about how to analyze a planet in "flux" (Salazar, Elliot, and Norum 2017: 3). Multi-sited ethnography has become particularly important in this regard (see discussion in Salazar et al. 2017: 10; Xiang 2013: 283). My approach can be defined both as multi-sited and multi-scalar. In regard to migration, scholars have stressed the need to focus on migrant experiences as well as actions in regard to policy making, where "how social phenomena, such as transnational migration, are constituted through actions at different scales" (Xiang 2013: 284; see also Fortier 2006).

While these perspectives are important there is a long tradition within anthropology of conducting research among objects and people "on the move" (Salazar et al. 2017: 5) and to emphasize a holistic perspective, where different spheres of society are not only seen in conjunction with each other, but where the analysis scales between more localized experiences and larger political and historical context. Thus, for a long time, anthropologists have dealt with the complication of, what Xiang phrases, "small observable details and big generalizable critiques" (Xiang 2013: 283).

My methodology for capturing mobility can be understood as a combination of multi-sited and multi-scalar participant observation and interviews. I scale back and forth from a wider historical perspective where Europe is a central concern toward the experiences of individual Nigeriens in Europe. Part of understanding the broader power structures and historical inequalities that shape the lives of these men are my occasional insertions of Icelandic debates and concerns as a small country in Europe. I see this approach as providing deeper insight into how mobility is racialized as well as bringing the interconnected lives of those racialized in different ways more sharply into perspective.

In trying to capture this story that I want to tell, I am inspired by anthropologist Anna L. Tsing's (2011) observation that ethnography constitutes a methodology that pulls in salient bits and pieces here and there, using the term "patchwork ethnographic fieldwork." As Günel, Varma, and Watanabe (2020) point out, the term seeks to capture these irregularities of fieldwork as well as how "home" and "field" are no longer separate entities but intersect in various ways. For my own fieldwork, patchwork ethnography also involves trying to patch together different commitments to the people I worked with, to my workplace, and importantly also to family members. When looking back, these were not simply disruptions to the research but also sources of insight.

Organization

Throughout this book, I jump between different locations and different moments in the research in an attempt to capture interlinked spaces and lives. Furthermore, by placing different kinds of migrants, that is, the less and more privileged, side by side, the racialization of mobility becomes more clearly visible.

The first chapters of the book, in Part I "Making Precarious Migrants," focus for the most part on individual stories of migration, while acknowledging the context of a wider recent discussion of migration. Chapter 1, "Living in Divided Europe: The Theme Park and the Street," begins with a brief insight into the lives of precarious Nigeriens in northern Italy, who generally see themselves in transition. The chapter focuses on the global inequalities of mobility and how borders work toward a racialized classification of people into "beings" and "nonbeings." The chapter also demonstrates how similar stories of migration can be seen across the Global North, wherein racism and dehumanization become almost mundane in their repetition across different spaces. Chapter 2, "'Enough of Refugees': Depiction of Precarious Migrants in Europe," provides a wider context of discussion of migrants in the European contexts, especially in relation to asylum seekers and refugees in 2015. In Chapter 3, "Into the Heart of Europe: Migrants in Brussels and Beyond," the discussion moves from the borders of Europe and more abstract discussion of migration toward Brussels, where we are introduced to precarious Nigerien migrants living in the city. The concept of Europe is the subject of Chapter 4, "Global Citizens and the Backstage," where the discussion scales toward a different wider context by examining and aligning their particular mobilities within the broader spectrum of mobility in general in Belgium, but also more widely in questioning what are desirable and undesirable mobile subjects. In Chapter 5, "Multicultural Europe: Invasions against European Values?" the focus is on the positionality of these Nigerien migrants within discussions of multiculturalism in

Europe, where I draw attention to how precarious migrants in Europe are familiar with and engage with media discussions of migrants as criminals or dangerous others.

Part II "Entangled Histories" is composed of Chapters 6, 7, and 8, which anchor the subject matter into the history of colonialism. Chapter 6, "This Is All in the Past Now: Niger and a Global World," starts with a brief discussion of Niger's history as a shared history with Europe, as well as its current embedment in global politics. Modernity takes on a particular form in Niger, which cannot be separated from wider global context nor its shared history with Europe. In Chapter 7, "Nostalgic Colonialism: Different kinds of Otherness," I scale down to the experience of particular types of migrants from Niger, who arrive with a visa into the Schengen area. The chapters show how new and not-so-new meanings of exotic otherness can become an important commercialized resource and where particular kind of "strangers" are welcomed in Europe, even during times of intense fortification at its borders. In Chapter 8, "Spaces of Innocence: Belgium's Colonial History and Beyond" the gaze moves toward Belgium's colonial history, and how across Europe colonial legacies are very much ignored. The chapter also reminds us of movements against the present glorification of this brutal past.

Chapter 9 and the Conclusion in Part III, "Europe's Past and Future," focus more deeply on what the preceding discussion means in term of future anticipation of migrants and others living in Europe. Chapter 9, "The Heart of Darkness: EUrope as a Concept" draws attention to the concept of Europe, as well as these men's desire for a "livable" life, and their struggle to reconcile Europe's association with humanitarianism with the harsh response to the migration crisis. The last chapter, "Welcome to the Future: Dismaland and Anxieties in Europe" focuses on crisis and migration in relation to future anticipation. I juxtapose the migrants' stories with broader narratives of loss in Europe, including the loss of a particular vision of the future, and draw attention to how such narratives are used to mobilize hate groups and anti-migration sentiments.

Taken together, I aim with these chapters to draw attention to how people live within the same shared discourse, even while being positioned differently within it; elucidating the mobility of racialized images and ideas, and how they translate into practice; and how the discourses that take place in wider Europe and which shape the lives of these Nigerien migrants, are expressed in different locations. Spaces across Europe, such as Gardaland, are endowed with racial meanings, reflecting structural and historical relationships that tell a larger story of colonialism and enduring discriminations.

NOTES

1. In line with critical research on race and racism, "white" and "Black" are used here as social classifications. Recently, anti-racist mobilizations have called for capitalizing "Black," partly to recognize the persistent salience of racism (Weeber 2020). There have been debates regarding whether or not "white" should be capitalized as well, as it constitutes a social construct just as the term "Black" does. The uneasiness of capitalizing "white" derives from fears of reifying whiteness and giving legitimacy to white supremacy (Weeber 2020; Daniszewski 2020). I decided not to capitalize it in this volume, although I remain conflicted about whether that is the best decision.
2. This interpretation selectively "forgets" Islam as a part of Europe's history, where it is discursively constructed as an external force (Özyürek 2005).

PART I

Making Precarious Migrants

CHAPTER 1

Living in Divided Europe
The Theme Park and the Street

I stand in front of Central Station in Milan. People are on the move all around me. Men and women in business suits hurrying to and from the station; young people with backpacks walking slowly but steadily; tourists pulling their lightweight suitcases behind them. Also walking across the plaza are souvenirs salesmen. They approach the other people, and even though I do not hear what they say, they are obviously trying to sell some of their merchandise, with disappointing results. I imagine that many of them come from West Africa and have, as my interlocutors from Niger, entered the country under precarious conditions—some probably hoping for asylum, others to earn money to create a more secure economic future. Perhaps some of them came from Libya, as most of those whom I have talked to have, migrating from their countries of origin in the hope of accumulating good money by working hard for some years. After the Arab Spring and the civil war in Libya in 2011, the African migrants working there, fled via the sea route to Italy, often in the hope of being able to go further north. "Europe" had not been their destination, rather some felt themselves forced to take that path. As Delf Rothe and Mariam Salehi have shown, for many migrants coming to Europe from Libya, Europe was not their first choice, some being driven out of Libya (2016: 90).

As Elena Fontanari (2017a) has documented, a state of emergency was declared for a short time, but soon many migrants in Italy found themselves on the streets without humanitarian assistance, attempting to find places where there was work. This meant moving between different Italian cities, lacking permission to work elsewhere in Europe. Their mobility within Italy was often facilitated by the social networks these individuals had established during their earlier migration (Fontanari 2017a: 40). The lives of these African migrants traveling across the world in search for work, can be characterized as cosmopolitan, though they are not generally recognized as such in European discourses (see discussion Theodossopoulos 2010: 3). The tourists around me in Milan are—however—generally seen as a part of Europe's cosmopolitan population; their mobility is celebrated as economically important, as creating jobs and making the wheels of economic prosperity turn. Volunteer groups of young people in distant countries also constitute a part of this cosmopolitan "clan," along with expatriates working in international aid and other fields. And I am myself part of this group, as an academic on the move.

Despite this inequality in who qualifies as cosmopolitan, cosmopolitanism is seen as something that embraces and celebrates diversity (Baban 2013: 217). This captures the inequalities in how we conceptualize the world: as mobility is celebrated in popular versions of cosmopolitanism, various technologies have been developed to create or strengthen borders in order to keep particular kinds of mobile people out (M'Charek, Schramm, and Skinner 2014: 473). June Edmunds (2013) shows that this involves not only migrants coming from what is seen as outside of Europe but also certain groups within Europe who are seen as somehow less European. Disparate groups across different European countries, such as Muslims and Eastern European migrants, are perceived as incompatible with the European cosmopolitan project (Edmunds 2013: 784). Edmunds's (2013) observation on how cosmopolitan aspirations of different groups are perceived differently captures how the cosmopolitan project involves particular subjects, and thus particular types of mobilities. Ruben Andersson points out that precarious migrants in general are not a part of "the dream of a mobile world," meaning that they are a threat to the image of free mobility (2014a: 4). Andersson also contends that faceless migrants "haunt the rich world," even though it is usually unclear who these migrants are or why they produce such fear (2014a: 4).

There is no doubt that racism plays a role in these fears, but racism has never revolved around "color" classifications only. It is also strongly embedded in ideas of culture, ethnicity, and civilization (Smedley and Smedley 2005; Fekete 2009). Different terminologies have been used by scholars to capture how racism is essentially based on dualistic classifications of people. I find particularly useful here the flexible depiction of racism offered by Ramon Grosfoguel, Laura Oso, and Anastasia Christou, who see racism as a "global hierarchy of human superiority and inferiority," that is produced politically, culturally, and economically (2015: 636). This hierarchy, as

Grosfoguel et al. point out, separates those seen as superior human beings from those seen as inferior: those considered full human beings with access to rights and those who have their humanity denied or neglected and their access restricted to certain rights (636). Within these two zones of being and nonbeing the intersection of different identifications is articulated in diverse ways, which creates further stratification (637).

In a similar fashion, Shohini Chaudhuri adopts the term "un-people" from Mark Curtis, which she applies to those whose lives are seen as expendable and worthless. Curtis links these people to the "savages" of the past who were deemed disposable in the pursuit of modernization and power (Chaudhuri 2011). Likewise, Giorgio Agamben's (1995) identification of "bare life" captures how some people's lives are stripped of political status and worth and are consequently reduced to their elemental biological basis. All these definitions capture how certain groups today have been dehumanized and deprived of basic rights as human beings, while other groups enjoy these rights as universally given. These categories overlap with race, but also with class and geopolitical location.

This dualistic thinking is also found in the context of migration, with the movements of some being rendered natural, easy, and nonproblematic, while the movements of others are criminalized or demonized. Physical, man-made borders, Elena Fontanari reminds us, have become powerful instruments for governments to "sort populations" into these different forms of hierarchies (2017a: 27). Within popular and political rhetoric, many of the individuals with whom I engaged in my research would be classified as "illegal." In such a depiction, illegality is in the body of individuals, rather than in their actions as understood within a legal framework (R. Andersson 2014a: 17). The term migrant, as Ruben Andersson (2014a) points out, is in fact usually reserved only for those who are poor and whose movement is "problematized" while other terms such as the expat is reserved for mobility seen as more prestigious.

Research on migration has shown the necessity of looking at the racial consequences of legalized or institutionalized frameworks. Such a perspective illustrates how racism is not solely a product of individuals' thoughts or desires but is also reproduced through various practices and regulations of institutions and governments. Steven Garner (2007) points out the racial consequences of the policies of the European Union (EU), where migrants coming from outside of the EU are subject to much tighter immigration control than those moving within its borders. These stricter visa controls are aimed at people from poorer countries and, ironically, often at those from countries that share history with Europe as former colonies (see also Fox, Moraşanu, and Szilassy 2012). In this same vein, Anthias and Yuval-Davis (1983) stress the need to recognize institutional racism as something that involves practices and structures that effectively produce exclusion, exploitation, and subordination of certain people grouped in particular ways. Institutionalized racism, Fox et al. claim, can be described as "exclusionary institutional practices, routines, and cultures that both draw on and reproduce a logic of racialized difference" (2012: 684). Border controls are one important example of policies that distinguish between what kinds of bodies belong within the space of Europe and which should be kept out (Loftsdóttir et al. 2018: 13). Indeed, the Mediterranean Sea off Italy has, in recent decades, been transformed into a deadly border, instead of its historical role as an arena of mobility and commerce with North Africa (Sorge 2018: 199).

I meet Karim for the first time at a small coffee shop close to Milan's Central Station in 2016. Nigerien and in his forties, he has refugee status in Italy. I arrive early at the station because I did not know how long it would take to get there. While I wait, one of the street vendors comes to me and tries to sell me a bracelet. He addresses me in Italian, which I do not speak. When I reply to him in French, he seems pleased and tells me that he is from Senegal. I say a few words in Fulfulde that I learned while living in Niger, and he politely compliments me. When he sits down next to me, he takes care not to sit too close to me, perhaps due to his awareness of negative images about Black migrants and their association with criminality. We say nothing for a few moments. Then he puts his face in his hands and complains about the heat. We make brief small talk about Milan, how large the city is and how hot, and he tells me that souvenir sales are difficult, with so many people selling and so few interested in buying. The conversation is superficial and polite. We sit silently for another moment, and then he nods and leaves. We are just two strangers whose lives happen to converge, strangers from North and South, differently positioned in a deeply unequal world, with dramatically different opportunities, while sharing in the moment the same space and time.

When I arrive at the coffee shop, I find Karim is already there. He is sitting at a small table but stands up when I enter. He shakes my hand firmly. I have met him before, as we have been put in touch by a mutual Italian friend. When we sit down again and start talking, he tells me about how tired he is of living in Europe. I learn that he migrated to Italy after leaving Libya, the boat landing in Sicily. While he has gained refugee status, he wants to return to Niger. "People don't want to move. No one really wants to leave, no one in this world. People usually prefer to stay in their area and age there, see their children growing up, stay and die in their own land. We in Niger, we are also like that. But there are no opportunities for us to stay in our own country."

Figure 1.1. Demonstration in Milan against racism in 2018. © Kristín Loftsdóttir.

Karim is simplifying, of course. As elsewhere, people in West Africa do not only migrate due to necessity, but also for enjoyment and adventure, a fact that also applies to precarious migrants (Schapendonk 2011: 20). There is a risk of reducing migrants in precarious positions to passive victims, which ignores the strong transnational character of the lives of many West African people (Schapendonk 2017: 395). However, Karim's point that many of those who migrate to Europe have no desire to do so is important, and one that I hear repeated over and over during the span of my research. Agency is important here, an attempt to change one's position. David Rain has pointed out that in the context of the West African Sahel in general, sometimes "people have been left with no resource but to pick up and leave" (1999: 17); he draws attention as well to the fact that such a decision in itself is a political expression. Noel B. Salazar (2011) stresses, furthermore, that the power of imagination must be considered when discussing migration, with the media and consumer goods facilitating dreams of life in other places. Rain's and Salazar's emphasis on the agency of migrant populations reminds us of the necessity to move beyond narrow conceptions of "push" and "pull" factors. Individuals make choices, even though these choices are not made in isolation from the political and social environments that surround them. As we will explore in Chapter 6, this applies to precarious migrants from Niger whose mobility is connected to a long tradition of mobility in West Africa. Their present-day mobility contains agency, as it did in the past, as they attempt to select the best path available to them and their families. Karim's emphasis on necessity is still an important one as it draws attention to a situation of desperation and injustice that he and many others experience.

I meet another Nigerien, Amir, a few days later in a park outside of Milan. Like Karim, Amir originally came to Sicily by boat from Libya. He had traveled to Libya from Niger with hopes of building some economic security for himself and his extended family. He stayed in Sicily for a month before moving to Milan, where he remained briefly before moving to another city where we meet. We were originally introduced by another Nigerien friend, and this is our second meeting. Amir does not really want to recall the journey to Italy. He explains to me, however, that around one hundred and fifty people started the journey on a small rubber boat, and during the four days at sea, forty died. He was told that there was nothing to do other than to drop the bodies into the water. He looks at me intensely when he says this; the memory is painful. But his eyes also seem to be asking me if this does not also sound crazy, as if he is searching for confirmation in my expression that he is not alone in finding this experience shocking.

After the dangerous journey, Amir's life in Italy is difficult and frustrating. He has problems getting work and discovers there are very few opportunities for him to earn an income. He sleeps here in the pocket park where we meet, along with a friend, who is also from Niger. He points to the sports bag that he keeps next to him. "I sleep here, you see, this is my bag." He notices that I have placed my bag on the ground by the bench and reminds me that it is safer to hold it close to me, due to theft. They both look at me with sympathy, as if tolerant that of course I cannot know better. This kind comment toward me reminds me of the precarity in his life and others in the same situation, and the differences between their life experiences and mine.

As we continue talking, Amir tells me that people in northern Italy often tell him to go back to where he came from. He offers me an example from a recent occasion when he went to wash his clothes at a laundromat and a man approached him and said that he should go back to his country. Like Karim in Milan, Amir's story contains frustration, seemingly at how little these people know. "You know the Nigeriens do not want to come to Europe," he says. "They don't want to. And how are we going to stay here in Italy? No, no, we cannot stay here." As studies have shown, undocumented migrants in Italy are as elsewhere not only excluded from the wider society but are exploited and vulnerable in the Italian labor market (Giudici 2013: 66).[1]

In the days that follow my meeting with Amir, I reflect on his story and the way he searched my face for a sign that I, too, found the details of his boat journey horrifying. Forty people's life stories and experiences ended on that boat. Forty people dropped into the deep sea, each one an individual who had hopes and aspirations for the future. Amir is right. Stories of the borderland are stories of mobilities that are difficult to understand. What makes this even more horrifying is the fact that for most people living in the Global North, such as myself, stories like Amir's are nothing new. They have been a constant presence in the media over the last few years. *Migration Data Portal* states that more than four thousand fatalities on migration routes are reported annually worldwide since 2014 when they started collecting this data. They also point out that this number represents the *minimum* estimate, since the majority of precarious migrant deaths are not documented anywhere ("Migrant Deaths and Disappearances" 2020). In 2017, 3,139 died while crossing the Mediterranean out of the 6,279 that are reported dead or missing. For most of the 3,139 who are presumed dead according to this statistic, no data exists about their origin. The available data indicates, however, that the largest group is from sub-Saharan Africa ("Migrant Deaths and Disappearances" 2020). The numbers were even higher the year before with 5,143 dying in the Mediterranean ("Migrant Deaths and Disappearances" 2020). Amir's experience is thus nothing unique, but just a part of the reality of our world today.

Stories of migrants' suffering and dehumanization are everywhere. While in some cases they have evoked sympathies and compassion, often they seem to create fear and anger toward the migrants themselves. It is almost as if there is a "war on migrants," or against those perceived as having a migrant background, rather than the so-called war on terror so intensively produced over the last two decades, especially by the United States, but also with the participation of European states. Everywhere, there are stories that teeter on the edge of the absurd relating to border protection, mainly accounts of efforts to keep out undesirable populations.

In Iceland, I read a story about a man named Mahad Mahamud in the newspapers, who lost his Norwegian citizenship 2017 after moving there in 2000. An anonymous tip delivered to Norwegian authorities claimed that he was from Djibouti, not Somalia, as he had stated when seeking asylum. He was only fourteen years old at the time he sought asylum, but over the next seventeen years, he educated himself, became a medical laboratory technician, and, at the time the tip was called in, was working at the Ullevål hospital. Mahamud was deported from Norway and sought asylum in Iceland in 2018. Because of the Dublin regulation,[2] however, the decision was made to simply send him back to Norway (Ísleifsson 2017; Sigurþórsdóttir 2018).

Media interviews with Mahamud reveal his hope that he would find help in Iceland, but not only was his application for asylum never processed, he was also forced to report to a police station every week, a requirement usually reserved for people who are seen as threatening and dangerous in some way (Ámundadóttir 2018). I ask myself, where is the logic in this story? How does it make sense?

There are other stories, different stories. Examples of stories like Mahamud's abound in my small island-environment, but also in other parts of the Global North; the extent of their similarities and their prevalence are startling. As part of my privileged mobility, not only as a tourist but also as part of the global clan of mobile experts, consultants, expatriates, and academics, in 2018 I visited Tucson, Arizona, where I studied for my PhD. My proximity to the US-Mexico border strikes me intensely. A detention facility used to hold migrant children after they have been separated from their parents is situated close to Tucson. The Department of Homeland Security's implementation of a "zero-tolerance policy" is responsible for the presence of such detention facilities, which operate even though they have no centralized system to identify, track, and reconnect the children with their parents (US Department of Health & Human Services 2019). This policy meant the detention of everyone who crossed the borders unauthorized, and that instead of being sent to detention centers, people were placed in federal prison. This meant that they were separated from the children accompanying them. The lack of record-keeping led to the inability to find the parents of hundreds of kids, where some of these parents had even been deported without knowing anything about their children (Frye 2020: 354; Dickerson 2020). While the policy was ended in 2018, due to strong public criticism, the separations continued (Aguilera 2019; Jervis and Gomez 2019).

But there are less-extreme cases that demonstrate the craziness of this fear of migrant mobility. I visit Bisbee during the same year, an old mining town in the beautiful surroundings of southern Arizona, and from there I take a short trip to the nearby border town of Naco. There is nothing exciting about this trip and there is even a part of me that feels guilty about reducing my kids' experience of visiting Mexico to a "border" experience. As we drive from the Bisbee mountains toward Naco, we see a brown line in the ground in the distance, almost like a scar or a wound in the landscape. "Is this the border?" I whisper aloud, and my children, startled, repeat my question. When we get closer, we see the brown line we saw is actually a wall stretching endlessly in both directions.

I know that this wall should become a part of the massive wall that former President Trump repeatedly promised to build. While physical structures delimitating the space between Mexico and the United States did not exist until 1911, different walls certainly existed before Trump's election, most of which were built after the mid-1990s (see Flynn 2014; Miller and Nevins 2017). The cost in human lives has been extensive (Smith et al. 2020). Furthermore, US border practices have long been externalized to other countries south of the border, making the wall only "one part of a gigantic enforcement regime" (Miller and Nevins 2017: 145). *National Geographic* mentions this particular wall in Naco in a 2009 article, describing it as four meters high, with the Border Patrol station being the largest building in this little town (Bowden 2007). The brown color we see is rust on the iron composing the wall. On the American side of the border are empty buildings that obviously used to be restaurants and shops. My American friend, Lori, tells me that when she lived in Bisbee in 2000, people used to go back and forth over the border to shop for fruit and vegetables or alcohol. Now, the town seems empty. We park the car, cross the border, and walk in the space between Mexico and the United States, which is located beneath barbed-wire fences and the large Border Patrol building.

The absence of communal life I see at the borders in Naco is the result of the securitization of the Mexican and US border since the 1990s, which has created intense insecurity for the locals living there (Basok et al. 2015: 66; Miller and Nevins 2017). Boyce and Williams draw attention to the violent death at the border by the US Border Patrol agents, pointing out that it is ironic that "in many border towns, Border Patrol agents present a threat far greater than that posed by the drug traffickers, unauthorized migrants, or potential terrorists that are used to justify securitization efforts" (Boyce and Williams 2012). Their article cites cases such as in Nogales, near Naco,

Figure 1.2. The Mexican side of the border town Naco in Sonora in 2018. © Árni Víkingur Sveinsson.

in 2012 where a sixteen-year-old boy was shot seven times in the back by a Border Patrol agent, who was standing on the other side of the fence. The boy was throwing rocks.

Lori, my friend, is shocked by the changes in the community that has taken place during the twenty years since she last visited Naco. As we walk into Naco on the other side of the border, we find there are some people around, including a group of children running on the sidewalk playfully and individuals passing us going about their daily business. We come across a man who is trying to sell his small puppy for $20. He tells us in excellent English—and with much less of a foreign accent than me—that he used to work in California as a mechanic. One day, two policemen came to have a tire changed. They asked him about his papers, and when he was unable to produce them, he was jailed for a couple of months. He looks down when he tells us about this experience, and it is easy to see that he feels perplexed and humiliated.

Going back over the border to the American side, we pass tired immigration officers who look at our blue passports and allow us back into the country. I am reminded of our trip to Tombstone a little earlier, where every car was stopped after leaving the town, even though we were not crossing a border. It is proximity to the borders, one American friend explained to me, somewhat embarrassed, and thus here it is necessary to have one's passport close at hand. All the cars that passed through were stopped at a small station, creating a line that moved slowly toward the officers whose job it was to check papers and passports. The line was not exceptionally long, but it moved slowly.

While I sit in the front seat, a dour-faced Border Patrol agent approaches the car, holding tight to a German shepherd, which strains against the leash, as if trying to run toward its prey. It was a scary sight. Was this simply a display of power aimed at evoking fear in us as we sit in our cars waiting for our passports to be scrutinized? Another officer looks through the window of my car and nods to my partner, who sits behind the steering wheel. With a flashlight, the man in uniform looks to the back of the car where my three children are sitting quietly, and then signals that we can move forward. He does not even look at our passports. When we drive away my son says, dryly, what we were all thinking: "So I guess we were white enough for him."

There are other stories around me in Arizona that illustrate the complexities of mobility. On my way to the zenith of American consumerism, the retail store Costco, I came across the story of Crystal Mason, a forty-three-year-old woman with three children who was sentenced to more than five years in prison just for casting a ballot in the 2016 presidential election. Encouraged by her mother, who told her that, as a Black American woman, it was important that she participate in the democratic process, Mason was determined to vote. She discovered that her name was not on the register, so she cast a provisional ballot. Tiny print on the form explained that American citizens who had been convicted of a felony could not vote under Texas law. Mason had previously been convicted for tax fraud, which removed her right to vote. As a result, her vote was discounted. But that wasn't where it ended: Mason was also sentenced to prison. Texas is one of the strictest states in terms of voting law, and, perhaps unsurprisingly, also has one of the worst voter turnout rates in America (Pilkington 2018). What is important here is that Mason is not a migrant. She is an American citizen. Even though most Black Americans have been in the United States longer than white Americans (Berlin 2010),[3] their presence is still problematized by the wider society, they still seen as the Other by white racist logic.

While these stories do not all revolve around Europe, they do tell of precarious people made into criminals, and of the production of fear. Even those who are educated, like Mahamud, or citizens, like Mason, can apparently never be sure about their position as rights-bearing citizens. These stories tell us that migration and criminalization take place systematically in different places and locations, and that Otherness does not begin and end with migrants.

As I will explore in Chapter 2, we often see migration from the South presented as if Europe were under attack from uprooted and displaced populations from North Africa and the Middle East. In these narratives, West African countries are portrayed by the international media as places that breed terrorism and Islamic radicalism (Walther and Retaillé 2010), which further enhances the sense of a Europe under siege by outside forces. Ghassan Hage (2016) speaks of how the feeling of being "under siege" has become increasingly important in the Global North, with the sense that "dangerous others" are pressing against the borders of civilization.

The term "regimes of mobilities" draws attention to how both the state and various security regimes affect and shape who is mobile and in what ways, and how current mobilities are not governed by the state alone. International regulations, agreements, and surveillance administration are important as well (Glick Schiller and Salazar 2013: 189). Leo Lucassen (2018) critically addresses how such regulations and surveillance produce fear and a sense of the other, while also pointing out that the recent surge of asylum seekers in many European countries is not dramatically different from other historical cycles. The total numbers of asylum seekers in Europe during 2011–15, Lucassen notes, were lower than in the first half of the 1990s, with Bosnians and Croats fleeing the civil war in Yugoslavia, followed by refugees from the Middle East and the Horn of Africa (Lucassen 2018: 4). There was no sign that an "indifferent mass of poor migrants from the

Global South had been unleashed" (3); but the migrations in most cases came from a small number of war zones in Afghanistan, Iraq, the Horn of Africa, and Syria (3). One reason for feeling that current numbers are much higher, Lucassen highlights, is how increasingly difficult it has become to cross the borders of Europe. In the 1990s, people could travel more easily by land over Eastern and Southeastern Europe, rather than taking the extremely dangerous routes to Italy's shores or to the Greek islands. Similarly, Majcher, Flynn and Grange point out that the refugee peak in 2015 was followed by a drop already in 2017 when arrivals gradually become more like pre-2015 levels (2020: 4).

It was in November 1993 that the Convention on Controls on Persons Crossing External Frontiers made it necessary for those in Asia and Africa to apply for a visa prior to leaving their country. Even before stepping foot over the border of their country, these people could now be refused access to buses, airplanes, and ships (Lucassen 2018: 391). These regulations, based on an early nineteenth-century US idea called "remote control" (390), intensified the pressure experienced by those working for carriers, such as airplane staff, who were forced to "act as immigration officers" in order to minimize the risk that their airlines would face large fines or expenses for transporting people without proper papers (Philip 1994: 177–78). Organizations working with refugees and asylum seekers expressed concerns with these new regulations (177–78), but as Lucassen states these "paper barriers," as he terms this approach, took considerable time to implement and thus lacked visibility for most people until recently (2018: 390).

Liz Fekete talks about these processes being formalized in the Tampere European Council in 1999, effectively turning the Global South governments into "immigration police for western Europe" (2009: 24). Individuals within the Global South who have "education" or some skills that are deemed useful to the Global North can enter, while others are refused entry. This creates what Fekete labels a new kind of "social Darwinism" where it is not only the "gene pool" but the "skill pool" that is the "key" (2009: 27).

In the years that followed, the Arab Spring and the subsequent war in Libya led to an increase in migrant numbers arriving on the coasts of Italy in 2011 (see for example Fontanari 2017a, 2017b; Giudici 2013: 64; Rothe and Salehi 2016). The countries on the margins of Europe in the south, like Italy and Greece, are entry points for many of those trying to enter Europe without the necessary documents. The Dublin Regulation (the dictate that resulted in Mahad Mahamud being denied asylum in Iceland), states that "people who have obtained international protection in one of the European member states—the first one in which they arrived to—have the right to work and settle in that state alone. They can move within the European Union for only three months, as tourists, but do not have access to the labor markets of other EU member states" (Fontanari 2017a: 39–40).

For those migrants who make it to Italy, Milan is one of the most common destinations, due to the relatively friendly social system and since many migrants consider the city to be a stepping-stone for further migration into northern Europe (Fontanari 2017a: 41; 2017b). Elena Fontanari (2017a) argues that this social system, based on services provided by various social service actors, fulfils the migrants' basic needs but does not provide them with the means for an independent life. Furthermore, because these services are scattered around the city, many migrants spend their time moving between shelters, public showers, soup kitchens, etc. (Fontanari 2017a: 41). Being made to wait, while also kept on the move between locations, creates in these individuals the sense that they are not in control of their lives and that they are in a constant transition period (see Fontinari 2017a: 33). That does not mean that they do not actively attempt to take control of their lives through any means possible; they still actively try to shape and act on these conditions.

According to Daniela Giudici (2013), most of those who arrive in Italy without having claim to asylum, arrive legally with a visa, and proceed to remain in the country after it has expired. In some cases, people do not so much overstay their visa as lose the grounds for continued permission to stay, such as being fired from their job suddenly (Giudici 2013: 66). In Europe, people overstaying their visa permission have also been the majority of those who are undocumented, contrary to popular depictions of "illegal" populations pushing against European borders (see R. Andersson 2016: 7). European border controls do not leave much room for those seeking asylum to gain that status through legal channels. This means that in Europe, like those seeking to enter the United States through Mexico, people have to endure dangerous journeys and engage in various illegal activities, such as using false documents, just to exist in the space to which they have traveled (Giudici 2013: 61; Fekete 2009: 22).

As many others, Amir risked much to eventually get to the small Milan park where we meet. Crossing borders is an act that is at once deeply personal and universal. These acts, as Andersson reminds us, consist of: "'illegal immigrants' crammed into unseaworthy boats, squeezed into rusty trucks trundling across the Sahara, walking through the distant deserts of Arizona, or clinging onto Mexican cargo trains" (R. Andersson 2014a: 2). How can we make sense of the disparities that seem to exist in different worlds with the cool spraying of water to relieve the guests at the Gardaland amusement park due to the heat and these life-threatening experiences that the so called illegal migrants endure? Placing these narratives side by side captures the consequences of sorting of people into hierarchies.

After my research trip to Milan, my family and I take a short vacation further south along the beautiful Ligurian coast. We stay in an apartment near the beach, with a fresh breeze blowing in through our windows, shielding us from the heat. We walk to the peaceful beach, toss a blanket on its rocky surface, and rest our brightly colored cooler box filled with water bottles. The sea air is refreshing, and in the distance, I see the waves coming in and breaking gently on the beach. I laugh with my kids and watch their little bodies running excitedly toward the waves that gently lap at the rocky surface of the beach.

But I cannot stop thinking of the desperate people who could be somewhere out there at sea, too far for me to see, on a small boat or a raft, hoping to reach a new life full of possibilities. They are drowning in the same water we are playing in.

NOTES

1. The official statistics for the number of Nigeriens in Milan is extremely low, with only around fifty to sixty individuals estimated as staying in the wider Milan territory each year between 2017 and 2020 ("Resident foreigners on 1st January—Citizenship: Lombardia" 2021). This statistic is unlikely to capture the actual number of people staying in the city.
2. The Dublin regulation is explained later in the text but revolves, briefly, around that those seeking international protection can be sent from a European country that they are seeking asylum in to the first country of entry.
3. Berlin (2010) points out that majority of Black citizens in the United States can trace their ancestors back to the seventeenth and eighteenth century while most white US citizens are the result of more recent waves of migration.

CHAPTER 2

"Enough of Refugees"
Depictions of Precarious Migrants in Europe

While I was writing this book in 2020, my partner, shocked, showed me a Facebook invitation from an old classmate. It was to join a group called "Er ekki komið nóg af flóttamönnum?" which roughly translates as "Is this not enough of refugees?" When I looked at the text, I felt an intense sense of sadness. But I thought that actually the text was quite right: there should be no more refugees; no more people needing to escape intolerable situations, fearing rape, murder, genocide, facing an inability to provide for their families, or being driven away from their homes. We know, however, that this is not what this group was about. Rather, it was about excluding people from seeking international protection; turning away from the plight and the reasons that some people seek shelter or international protection in Europe. The real crisis seems ironically often not to revolve around the circumstances of people seeking international protection or fleeing extensive poverty, persecution, or violence, but the inconveniences to those who live in more secure conditions.

In this chapter, I will map out some of the recent discussion in Europe over the past two decades concerning precarious mobility. Most recently, refugees and asylum seekers have been at the center of the discussion on migration; these concerns often revolve around questions of whether or not they are in "reality" economic migrants rather than people in need, as if these were mutually exclusive categories. Questions of refugees and asylum seekers thus shape the debate on migrants in general. While I dealt with policies and regimes of mobility that shape migration to Europe in the introduction and chapter 1, I want here to focus on this topic in the context of the wider European discourse about migration. This is due to its relevance for understanding some of the wider context in which the mobility of my Nigerien interlocutors takes place, as well as serving as a backdrop to my discussion about unequal mobility of people.

The "Crisis of Multiculturalism"

Already in 2001, things took a dramatic turn with the bombing of the New York World Trade Center on September 11, which not only cost a high number of innocent people their lives but also demonstrated the power of the media in shaping public perception and delimitating certain groups as enemies. This is nothing new of course, but for many, the intensity of the flow of images within different mediums was striking, even horrifying. It demonstrated the strong intertextuality of images and intensity in the then relatively new age of globalization. Perhaps this sense was intensified by excitement for a new millennium that had characterized 1999, which many imagined could be the beginning of something fresh and exciting. According to the BBC, Tony Blair, then UK Prime Minister, said that the "'confidence and optimism' about the new Millennium should be bottled and kept forever" ("2000: World Celebrates New Millennium" 2000).

After September 11, 2001, religion became a "privileged marker of racial and absolute difference" (Fortier 2007: 110; see also Werbner 2007) where Muslims as a category were seen as potential terrorists and a threat to the West (Grosfoguel 2012: 18). As argued by Elgenius and Rydgren (2019), September 11 became a turning point in the sense that criticism of Islam became an alternative to expression of openly xenophobic views, where expression of anti-Islam views was now acceptable. Lila Abu-Lughod's 2002 article entitled "Do Muslim Women Really Need Saving?" captures well the gendered stereotypes advocated widely during this time against Muslims as a uniform group. Abu-Lughod (2002) shows how simple stereotypes of Muslim women as passive victims were used to justify military actions in the war against terror and warned against culture-based explanations.

The growing discourse of the "crisis of multiculturalism" in the new millennium by politicians and public media reflect that Abu-Lughod's concerns were right on target, as this discourse revolved around Muslims' presumed incompatibility with Europe. This discussion centered on the view that multiculturalism had "failed" in Europe, that there existed multiple parallel societies of migrant communities that did not "integrate" (Werbner 2007; Lentin and Titley 2011). Alana Lentin and Gavan Titley describe this discourse adeptly a "backlash against 'multiculturalism'" (2012: 124). This discussion flourished around diverse issues such as wearing burkas or veils and their alleged incompatibility with European or particular national values (with France banning the veil in 2004, and Belgium and Spain following soon after) (Barát and Sungun 2012); debates on the presence or ban on constructing minarets in public spaces in Switzerland and beyond (Lentin and Titley 2012); as well as specific events such as the Muhammad cartoons in Denmark in *Jyllands-Posten* in 2005 (Eide, Kunelius, and Phillips 2008). Belgium and the Netherlands had debates about the veil, and about the refusal of some Muslim women to shake hands with the opposite sex (Fadil 2009). Such incidents, taking place in different European countries and historical context, became instantly transnational media events, widely seen as demonstrating the existence of a "shared European crisis" (Lentin and Titley 2012: 127), thus suggesting a particular condition "that transcends national particularities" (Titley 2009). Some of these controversies, such as, the anxieties about the veil in France, encompassed a larger sociohistorical story (Barát and Sungun 2012). In the context of a wider, shared discourse on multiculturalism in crisis, such debates were extremely powerful as they found support and meaning in other equivalent narratives spreading throughout the Global North. Also, allegations that multiculturalism had failed were strongly supported by people in power, including prominent European leaders (Papastergiadis 2013). It was during this environment of intense depictions of multiculturalism as a failure in Europe that an act of terrorism took place in 2011 in Norway killing seventy-seven individuals; the killer saw his victims as contributing to increased multiculturalism in the country (Bangstad 2014; Papastergiadis 2013; McIntosh 2014).

This discourse about unassimilated others or their incompatibility with European values was made possible, as shown by Lentin and Titley (2012), by another persistent idea: that the Global North had moved toward post-racism, where racism was no longer an issue. Racism became reduced to a narrow understanding in line with late nineteenth-century classifications of human diversity (which were in reality much more complex). This meant that behavior or speech of individuals could be recognized as racist in this post-racial society while the larger structural aspects of racism were ignored. Scholars had then already stressed for some time how racism had become more difficult to target, as it had become coded under different labels, such as culture and religion (Balibar 1991; Bangstad 2018), as well as how the discourse slipped effortlessly between "culture" and "race" (Abu El-Haj 2002). The context of "crisis of multiculturalism" made, however, these essentializing notions of culture particularly evident and powerful. Lentin and Titley stress (2012) that culture became the "hegemonic language for discussing difference when 'race' is a taboo" (2012: 131). As observed by Matti Bunzl (2005), discourses about Muslims thus centered on their presumed incompatibility with Western culture rather than claims of racial inferiority. Bunzl states that nevertheless the result was that: "Islamophobia, in other words, functions less in the interest of national purification than as a means of fortifying Europe." (2005: 502).

The "Refugee Crisis"

If the "Crisis of Multiculturalism" was the catch phrase for the first decade of the new millennium, the key term for the second decade was the "Refugee Crisis." First, the media attention was on the migration to Europe from the Middle East increasing in 2011 due to the uprising after the "Arab Spring" (Seeberg 2013) and then migration in 2015 and 2016, which accelerated due to the continued humanitarian crisis in Syria. In the second half of 2015, the portrayal of the migrant crisis was dominated by images of people arriving from Syria, Afghanistan, and Iraq (Crawley and Skleparis 2018). The economic crisis starting in 2008 was still being felt in Europe and as Nina Glick Schiller and Noel B. Salazar (2013) have stressed, mobility is often seen as especially threatening during times of economic crisis, while immobility becomes naturalized as normal and secure (2013: 184). The strong emphasis on "refugee crisis" led many European countries to shift to harder line policies from emphasized reduction of detention of migrants and asylum seekers into increasing them. This was made easier by prior changes in EU legislation and policy (Majcher et al. 2020).

A map from Frontex's website which I saw in 2017 vividly captured how this migration was presented publicly. European countries were presented in dark or light gray in accordance with their status as part of the EU or not and migration routes were shown with bold arrows pointing from the South into the gray area signifying Europe. The arrows were brightly colored almost as if to highlight the danger to the continent, thus visualizing and making risk real through "abstract arrows" (R. Andersson 2012: 9). I don't know when this visual presentation appeared first on the Frontex website, but as argued by Ruben Andersson, Frontex has helped to redraw the frontiers of Europe, as well as providing the language "to make sense of and operationalize this frontier in terms of migration" (2012: 9; see also van Houtum and Lacy 2020). In 2018, possibly due to criticism, the arrows that I saw on the website had been replaced by dots. *The Economist* published in 2015 a map—based on Frontex data—with the headline "The Way In" in large letters and then below in smaller letters "Main European Migration Routes, Detection of Illegal Border Crossings, January–July 2015" (2015: 22). The phrasing of the "way in" rather than the "way to" clearly captures this hegemonic discourse where Europe is depicted as under attack. The rhetoric of "collapse of control" frequently discussed in different mediums, created a sense of the nation state as unable to control or otherwise manage migration into its territory (Kasparek 2016; see also Rosen and Crafter 2018). Words used in the media and public documents referring to "flows, waves, torrent or streams," evoked an image of something that is almost an uncontrollable phenomenon (Kasparek 2016: 67).

Presentations of Europe as "flooded" by migrants were often mingled with discussions of migrants as a "drain" on resources (Rosen and Crafter 2018), where, as discussed earlier, Europe and the West as a whole seemed to be under siege in different mediums in the Global North. Hage cites headlines from widely read newspapers to exemplify this, drawing attention to the fact that these were not only conservative or far-right newspapers but a consistent discourse on the "invasion of migrants," "floodgates," and "Europe under Siege" (2016: 39). Rachel Rosen and Sarah Crafter's research on the UK tabloids in 2016 shows how unaccompanied children were increasingly presented as "large faceless groups," rather than as individuals, and a threat waiting at the border to cross into the United Kingdom. As well, the tabloids increasingly questioned the authenticity of the children, suggesting that they were all much older, thus associating them with illegality and "bogus" migrants (2018: 75). This discussion of unaccompanied children migrants thus moved steadily toward concerns with legality, threat, and either undeserving or deserving migrants. As mentioned in Chapter 1, the anti-migration agenda mobilized by different European populist parties (Fekete 2018) has not solely been directed against new migrants in European countries but also against citizens (Bhambra 2017).

This discourse of the "refugee crisis" can be described as what has been called "categorical fetishism" (cited in Apostlova 2015 from Crawley and Skleparis 2018). The categories "asylum seeker" and "refugee" are legal categories assigning some people rights, resources, and protection while excluding others. Simultaneously, they are based on binary distinctions between "legal" and "illegal" populations (Hall 2012: 9). Economic migrants *become* illegal, migrating to Europe for the wrong reasons, while the "true" refugee becomes the subject of pity and sympathy. The asylum seeker becomes a boundary position between those seen as documented and thus legal and economic migrants seen as undocumented and thus illegal (Giudici 2013: 62). Goodman and Spear claim that, in the media and the public sphere, all asylum seekers become suspect, regarded as possible cheaters, and are thus treated with doubt and suspicion (Goodman and Spear 2007: 179). The categorization of some people as "real" refugees and others as not (usually economic migrants) thus ultimately aims to distinguish between those who deserve compassion and respect, and those who do not. As the Facebook invitation that my partner received reflects, discussions of the "refugee crisis" was seen primarily as the crisis of those European countries that received refugees instead of what the refugees were experiencing (De Cleen et al. 2017). As Alessandra Sciurba (2017) notes, instead of speaking of the refugee crisis the focus should be on "right-to-asylum crisis."

More often, these legal categories actually don't make sense as people are not always escaping directly from their countries of origin but have been in precarious situations for years, and the motivation of different individuals can fit into various categories; they can be escaping war and intolerable situations, and simultaneously hoping for better economic security elsewhere (Crawley and Skleparis 2018; see also Ingvars 2019). As reflected by my Nigerien interlocutors, many of the migrants escaping the war from Libya were unable, due to the war, to go back to their country of origin, sensing that it was relatively safer to migrate to Europe (see also de Haas and Sigona 2012; Rothe and Salehi 2016).

Spaces of compassion and activism were certainly visible regarding the refugee crisis. In that regard, it is also clear how the coverage of certain events has shifted the discourse (Koca 2016). One important media event in this regard was the 2015 image of a Kurdish-Syrian toddler, Aylan Kurdi in 2015. The little boy drowned in the Mediterranean while trying to reach Greece with his parents and the image of his small body provoked a public outcry widely across Europe and the world (Rosen and Crafter 2018). Solidarity campaigns proliferated across Europe, along with demands for change in policies. The march of refugees from Budapest to Austria that took place in August during the same year was another powerful media event. The sympathy generated by Kurdi's death probably led to a much more positive response to the march. Those marching had been prevented from boarding the trains leaving from the train station in Budapest and those who had already boarded the trains were told to get off. The images of hundreds of people walking over the tracks were particularly potent as a contrast to the predominant images that depicted those seeking asylum as docile agents (Benli 2017).

Different turning points quickly followed, with other events heavily covered by the media. The November 2015 massacre in Paris, where 130 people were killed and several hundred wounded, was seen as a direct succession to the Charlie Hebdo shootings that had taken place in January 2015. These tragedies were then further contextualized within other terrorist acts in Europe, including the attacks in Brussels in March 2016 (Brancato, Ricci, and Stolfi 2016; Lüthi 2017). Also affecting the more sympathetic media climate was an event on New Year's Eve of 2015–16, widely called "the terror of Cologne," where women near the cathedral in Cologne were assaulted by a group of men who were said to be refugees or North African migrants. This event renewed the focus on sexist and racist presentations of Muslim and North African men—here grooming or assaulting white women—which were quickly adopted by groups hateful toward migrants (Boulila and Carri 2017). For some, this event was used to claim that "the" Islamists were declaring a war on the West, suggesting that these men were weapons being used to destabilize the West (Lüthi 2017). Such depiction of refugees and asylum seekers as a source of danger to white innocent women and girls were disseminated widely across Europe (see for example Virkki and Venäläinen 2020).

Sumiala et al. draw attention to the complexities of contemporary media events defining them as "multi-sited, multi-temporal, multi-actor and multi-voiced phenomena articulated by a simultaneous connectivity of a variety of communication processes" (2016: 100). This insight can, furthermore, be connected to what Ponzanesi and Leurs (2014) refer to as "digitalized connectivity," stressing the shared media experiences between those who are migrants and those who see themselves as residents (Ponzanesi and Leurs 2014). An example of the complexity and fluidity of the media are narratives which Cathrine Thorleifsson (2019) calls the "idea of Swedish dystopia," centering strongly on the need to protect Swedish women from dangerous migrant men. These have been taken up widely by populist groups in Europe (Thorleifsson 2019) and by Donald Trump, the former president of the United States (Jezierska and Towns 2018).

This "mediascape" that migrants and citizens within Europe are a part of has thus become increasingly complex. Various counter-media outlets seek, for example, to discredit the conventional news media, aiming to "reinform" the issues at hand (Pyrhönen and Bauvois 2019). Pyrhönen and Bauvois point out that a conspiracy story can be seen as an "enticing format for advancing reinformation, relying upon counter-media as the 'alternative,' anti-establishment source of information" (2019: 721). Also, as Adam Klein explains, the new media technologies have created new avenues for hate groups to distance themselves from accusations of racism and legitimate their message as belonging in mainstream society (2012: 431). Klein uses the term "information laundering" to show how hate groups regularly frame hateful rhetoric as educational and even academic (2012: 432). Emotional responses to actual tragic events have thus, for example, as discussed by Mattias Ekman (2018) in the context of Sweden, been appropriated by populist far-right groups in order to justify violence directed at refugees.

My research, scattered over a relatively long period of time, did not specifically focus on these media events, nor especially on the media. These discussions and debates on migration, however, shaped the wider environment and the conversations that I had with my interlocutors because they were interwoven with actual events and discursive regimes at the time.

This wider context of discussion of migration in Europe is also not simply relevant due to the inhumanity that accompanies various border control mechanisms and interactions, or the structural racism that the current regime of mobility is based on. It is important as well to ask about the multiple effects of deportations and classifications of people into legal and illegal, where being Muslim and/or refugees automatically signifies a terrorist threat for the majority population living in Europe and beyond. How does the combination of structural aspects and media depictions facilitate the creation of a certain type of people—un-people to use Mark Curtis's phrase—whose lives are characterized as worthless and expandable (Chaudhuri 2011: 192)? As Fekete draws attention to, some of these individuals are locked up in private profit orientated prisons, not because they have committed crimes, but for the "administrative convenience of government" (2009: 14; see also Majcher et al. 2020).

In this context we need to ask what the effects are of routine news reports that dispassionately announce the deportation of these and other individuals into the unknown—notably, deportation of individuals who are racialized in different contemporary discourses and historically. How do these media depictions create a sense for particular types of people who do not deserve to be "here"?

CHAPTER
3

Into the Heart of Europe
Migrants in Brussels and Beyond

Youssouf knocks on the door of the small apartment I am renting in downtown Brussels, close to the Midi train station. It is spring and our mutual friend, Ardo, has arranged this meeting. When I open the door, I see Ardo with Youssouf standing silently next to him. Compared to Ardo, Youssouf is large and muscular. His narrow beard and the dark-blue gown indicate that he is a Muslim. Ardo reminds me that he is meeting someone else, and now that he has shown Youssouf where I live, he must leave. I shake hands with Youssouf who smiles politely, but his eyes seem to me hard and rather cold. After Ardo says goodbye, I invite Youssouf inside, wondering if this interview will come to anything.

Inside, I make tea and we sit down at the little kitchen table holding our steaming cups. A moment of awkward silence, which is broken by my teenage son and partner entering the kitchen to say goodbye to us so I can conduct the interview undisturbed. Youssouf seems a little surprised and stands up. Greeting formally is important in the Nigerien context, and Youssef shakes their hands politely. While Youssouf exchanges words with my partner, he seems particularly keen on talking to my son. The pleasant conversation lingers on, and I get a little stressed, not knowing how long Youssouf will be able to stay. When they leave, Youssouf asks more about my family and life back in Iceland. Perhaps his interest is because his own family is in Niger, as is the case with all of those with whom I speak for this research.

Youssouf's story, once he begins to tell it, is somewhat familiar. He tells me that he is Hausa, and left Niger to work in the hopes of being able to send back money and also to save funds for a more viable future there. However, unlike the circumstances of most of the other men that I have talked to both in Milan and Belgium, Youssouf comes from a family that used to be relatively well-off. But, after losing his parents as a young man, he had to quit school to take care of his younger siblings. He now has a wife and two children back home in Niger.

In Brussels, Youssouf takes on whatever job is available. He tells me that even though it would obviously be better to have a steady income and more security, he is able to make enough to send money home regularly. Usually these jobs are at restaurants, chopping vegetables, cleaning up, or washing dishes from mid-morning to late into the evening. Sometimes, he explains, he gets ten hours of work every day for a few weeks, and then perhaps only five hours a week. As he tells me this, I visualize the bustling tourism sector in town, the scene at different restaurants and bars. I ask if he meets some of the tourists. Youssouf shakes his head and explains: "I never see them, because I do not go to those areas. I am someone that does not go out much. If I am not working, I just stay in the room that I rent. That is what my life here in Brussels is like." Youssouf of course goes to these areas on his way to different places where he works, but his reply draws attention to that he does not really engage with tourists or seek to visit the parts of Brussels where they stay.

For anyone interested in migration and the different conditions under which people undertake migrant journeys, it is probably difficult to find a more compelling place than Brussels. As my discussion with Youssouf indicates, the city reflects the movement of people for different purposes, but it is also home to segregation and hierarchical ranking according to origin and class. Youssouf is one of many migrants in the capital of the multilingual and ethnically diverse Belgium, a metropolis that hosts some of the most important institutions of the EU. Brussels has been proclaimed the "center of European culture," as the city's official tourist site (Brussels.info. n.d.b) makes clear and considers itself the *de facto* "Capital of Europe" (Jansen-Verbeke, Vandenbroucke, and Tielen 2005: 119; Blainey 2016: 481).

For others, Brussels stands for an "institutionalized Europe" (Blainey 2016: 490), which hints at its association with a rather uninteresting civil service culture. This reinforces the generally held perception of the city as "dull and bureaucratic" (Jansen-Verbeke and Govers 2009: 143; Thedvall 2007). Yet many find downtown Brussels attractive, even seductive, as it captures some of Europe's past with its buildings from medieval times and its charming streets with quaint shops that recall older times.

Cutting across these images is the immigrant presence in the city, representing a multicultural Europe. As Youssouf's circumstances illustrate, many immigrants are segregated by living in low-income neighborhoods and through their association in the European imagination with "multiculturalism" and, increasingly, with discourses about "security." As we saw in Chapter 2, these individuals have increasingly been seen as a threat to Europe's future. At the same time, Brussels' association with the EU marries the city to aspirations of shared tolerant European values and Europe's cosmopolitan future.

This chapter moves from borders and media representations of migrants into the "heart" of Europe, offering glimpses into the lives of my interlocutors in Brussels, ones that are characterized by solidarity and precariousness. Brussels is shaped by different kinds of mobility, as I discuss in Chapters 4 and 5, and in that vein, I see Brussels as a place that exemplifies the different aspects of being mobile and the different conditions under which people are mobile. The city can also be viewed as a multivocal symbol: it constitutes not only a destination of many economic migrants, but for others it also embodies aspirations for a unified Europe.

Simultaneously, the city is one of many sites where Europe's dark history—including a brutal colonial history and an ongoing denial of its significance—is a part of the landscape. In Brussels we see stratification of different sets of people; stratification which I spatially try to capture with the concepts "backstage" and "front stage" in order to draw attention to the inequalities at play globally, where some people are visible while others are hidden behind the curtain.

From Niger to Brussels

According to the Brussels Institute for Statistics and Analysis (BISA), there were about 2200 individuals born in Niger living in Belgium in 2018[1] ("Population." n.d.). These Nigeriens make up only a small portion of the sixty-three thousand West Africans living in the country and comprise an even smaller fraction of the nearly half a million Africans then living in Belgium (Eurostat n.d.). Most of these Africans live in the Central Brussels area, mainly in the neighborhoods clustered around the western section, that is, Anderlecht, Molenbeek but also in Schaerbeek, and Bruxelles ("Population." n.d.). According to one estimate, the Nigerien population in Brussels in 2010 was roughly 1,000 people, of which 75 percent were men (Lo Sardo 2010: 39). Information from Statbel, the statistic agency in Belgium, shows that in 2018, a little over 800 people in Brussels were born in Niger, 477 were men and 330 were women. Out of these, 583 had Nigerien citizenship (Statbel, personal communication, 2021). The actual number of people who are from Niger in Brussels is higher of course due to the many undocumented individuals, but these numbers still give some indication.

Ardo, who I met in Niger nearly two decades ago when he was a young teenager, lives in one of these neighborhoods. He was the son of a friend with whom I lost contact when I moved back to Iceland. When I meet him in Antwerp many years later, I don't recognize him at first, but he reminds me of our earlier encounter in the pastoral area in Niger. Ardo helped me with my research for its duration, and this long bond between us allows him to speak more openly about the difficulties of staying in Belgium and the pain of leaving one's family behind.

His experiences have been difficult. He has been in Belgium for more than ten years, mostly in Brussels. He rents a small room that he shares with two other men. There are three mattresses on the floor and one small window. Each man keeps his clothing packed carefully in a medium-size sack. Everything is well organized, probably a necessity when three people share such a small space. Ardo and his roommates have access to a bathroom and a cooking space, which they share with other tenants of the house who also have a migrant background. One of Ardo's roommates has asylum status, but the other has no papers, like Ardo. None of them has a secure income and each came to Europe in the hope of securing an economic future back in Niger. As with most of the migrants I spoke with in Brussels, I don't see Ardo as having much prospect of transcending his life of poverty. Prior to arriving in Europe, the continent seemed to embody for many, including Ardo, a hope for a better future, not necessarily in Europe but as a vehicle to make life back home better.

With his cell phone in his palm, Ardo turns the screen toward me to show me the newest photo of his son and his daughter. He smiles and gazes at it. I ask myself, as I have done so many times before, what Ardo is doing here after so many years away from his family, wife, and children about whom he speaks so often? Why doesn't he go back? Despite our long friendship, he evades this question every time, no matter how carefully I phrase it. His replies echo the replies of Ali, another Nigerien friend who has stayed a long time in Brussels and who tells me regularly that most of all, he wants to go back to his child and wife. "But you know the situation in Niger," Ali explains to me, just as Ardo has done. "There is nothing for me to have there."

For irregular West African migrants in general a sense of failure and shame is one of the central components preventing them from returning home, despite the unemployment and other economic difficulties which characterizes their life in Europe (Esson 2015: 523; Leman 1997: 28; Lo Sardo 2010: 38). That shame probably shows in their unwillingness to share the real reasons for not going home.

The only person who admitted this humiliation to me was someone I met by coincidence, when I was out with Ali to get a bite to eat. Ali had greeted a Tuareg man who seemed to be in his late forties. He introduced himself to me as Mohammed and, as with other Nigeriens I meet in Europe, is deeply impressed that I have been in Niger. "Perhaps it could be interesting to you to speak to him?" Ali said suddenly. "He arrived in Brussels a short time ago." Without waiting for my reply, he turned toward Mohammed and asked if I could ask him questions. After a moment's hesitation, Mohammed, clearly surprised, said carefully, "Yes, I think I have time." I explained that I was conducting research, hoping to make it easier for him to decline if he wanted to, but he seemed genuinely interested, telling me that he would really like to talk to me.

The three of us sat down at a coffee house and Mohammed shared a narrative that had become painfully familiar. People had warned him against coming to Europe, but he had not listened. He thought he could turn things around for his family by going to Europe and working really hard. He arrived in Brussels less than a year earlier, at that time in 2015, but had found work was scarce, given the economic crisis in Europe then. After Ali left us to run some errands, Mohammed used the opportunity of us being alone to share his frustrations, as if relieved to finally have someone to share it with. Almost in a whisper, he told me that he felt trapped—unable to stay but equally unable to go back home to his family with nothing. Ironically, those I speak to in northern Italy imagine that those like him in Belgium and Northern Europe have succeeded in finding better future possibilities.

Some of those I have interviewed have arrived with legal papers and have overstayed, as is common with those who are undocumented in Europe (see Mau et al. 2015; Giudici 2013: 66). Most, however, came first to Italy, acquiring papers that allowed them to work Europe-wide. Oumar, however, went to Brussels from Spain, where he had worked for several years, with a few other West Africans in the wake of the 2008 economic crisis. He explains to me, as have others I have spoken with, that they were "just looking for a place where we can stay in peace and find work, and then work regularly to support our families back home. That's why we came here to Brussels."

It may seem surprising that people continue to stay in one European country like Belgium, or navigate between different ones, when they feel that the effort is not leading to the benefits that they expected. Regardless of the shame it can also make sense from an economic standpoint. As explained to me by another Nigerien friend, the difference between staying in Belgium and Niger is that in Belgium you have the "chance to get something. It is not necessarily what you had desired in the first place, but a little something that can help people back home in Niger." This friend meant that even though it is difficult, at least in Belgium he is able to find work and earn some money. To strengthen his points on both the precarity of people in Niger in comparison with Europe *and* the importance of solidarity in Niger, he says: "We don't have insurance in Niger. The insurance in Niger is really your family, everything that you have is your family, so if you don't

Figure 3.1. Looking out Ali's window to the city of Brussels. © Kristín Loftsdóttir.

have family member who can send something, you are in some sense lost." Yakobo explains, "If we go back home, we have less than before we left. You just close your eyes and tell yourself that one day this will change."

Most of those I talked to came to Europe, however, through Libya after the war broke out in 2011. As discussed by Ines Kohl (2002), reform policies by Gaddafi in the 1970s and 1980s led to a "modernization boom" in the country and Libya changed from being one of Africa's poorest countries into one of its richest with a relatively strong social security system. Many Nigeriens were drawn there for work possibilities and good salaries. After Libya's collapse, as Ali has explained to me, Nigeriens went to Italy where there was no work to be had and then to France, Belgium, and Germany where it was also difficult to get work.

Youssouf migrated to Libya in 2009 in the hope of providing a better life for his growing family. "The salary was good," he tells me, "for some people the salaries would not have been high, but this was fine for me as I never spent any money. I sent all that I had to Niger." Youssouf stayed in Tripoli, Libya's capital until 2012 but decided then that he needed to leave. He recalls the fear saturating the atmosphere during the NATO-led coalition's 2011 intervention in Libya.[2] "We ran out to the street when the bombs started raining over the city. We were really afraid to be buried alive under the fallen buildings."

Babouli, in his late 30s, stressed to me when I met him in Brussels in 2016, that life was good in Libya for those coming from West and North Africa. When the civil war broke out, the route back to Niger became dangerous and like many others he felt that the best option to escape the war was to take a boat across the Mediterranean Sea to Italy. He traveled with two other Nigeriens in the same situation and their boat landed in Lampedusa. From there he went to Naples and sought asylum in Europe. Like the others I talked to, he firmly stressed that he is not living in Europe because he wants to, but because of the lack of other options. He stresses that even though it is difficult to find work in Brussels, it is even harder in Niger. Many of those who went back to Niger after the war faced the situation of unemployment in Niger, mourning, like Babouli, the end of Gaddafi's regime (Puig 2015).

For my interlocutors Libya represented a dream of a better future that is now shattered, or as one of the homeless asylum seekers in Milan tells me: "Libya before the civil war, was better than Europe. Much better than Europe, there is nothing here while . . . Libya, Libya before . . ." He trails off and adds sadly ". . . not Libya now. Now it is nothing but a hassle. Now there is just a war there."

Trajectories of mobility have to be seen as shaped and entangled with diverse and intersecting aspirations, social capital, and regimes of mobility (Schapendonk et al. 2020). France and parts of Belgium are attractive destinations for Nigeriens because of the shared language, since France colonized the western part of Africa. Language communities and common educational systems are often seen as variables that make former colonial powers attractive as destinations for African migrants. In addition, it can be useful to connect with cultural elites from one's own country in a new place (Castagnone et al. 2014: 224).[3] For my Nigerien friends and interlocutors, the presence of a Francophone community was an important factor in their decision to stay in the French-speaking part of Belgium. As Mohammed explained to me, "I prefer to stay in Brussels because I understand the language. Because of that, I can take my chances here to get work." Oumar expressed similar sentiments: "The fact that you speak French directs you toward areas where people speak French."

However, it would be an over-simplification to cite language as the only variable shaping these individuals' choices to migrate to Brussels or to other places in the northern part of Europe. Most of those I spoke to had learned some Italian while waiting for an opportunity to move further north and some spoke English; it is common in Niger to navigate through several languages. It would have been easy to stay in Italy if language were the only variable at play. However, after increasing numbers of refugees began arriving in Italy in 2015, it became much more difficult to find jobs in Milan. This was further complicated by racism, as explained by one of the men I spoke to there: "There's a lot of. . . how do I say this? We don't give a Black person a job; we don't want to give a Black person refugee status when we have Italians without jobs." His words were probably shaped by increasingly hostile discussion toward migrants in Italy (see discussion Larémont et al. 2020: 362–63).

The desire to migrate north, however, was not merely a reaction to these circumstances. Those I spoke with prior to 2015 also indicated a much stronger desire to be in Northern Europe than in Southern Europe. The desire to go "north" seemed to be connected with the desire to go to what they saw as the "real" Europe. Here it is important to keep in mind the power of imagination of particular places in shaping people's mobilities, as Noel Salazar (2011) has stressed. I was told by Nigeriens in both Brussels and Milano that Italy has nothing; that it is a place to pass through to the northern part of Europe, where they were more likely to get good jobs and salaries, to have a livable future. In fact, every precarious migrant I spoke to in northern Italy did not see Italy as his ultimate destination but rather as a stop on the way north. Andrea Muehlebach points out, with regard to minors arriving at Lampedusa in 2014, that they did not see Italy as the "promised land" but more as a place that you arrived at to go somewhere else where they envisioned would be more potential for future of stability, and from where they would be able to send money back to their relatives (2018: 143).

This desire to get to the "better" parts of Europe reflects of course the economic disparities within Europe, where some countries have faced high unemployment and economic precarity, especially after the economic crisis of 2008 (Glorius and Domínguez-Mujica 2017), in addition to taking in many of those seeking international protection in the 2010s. This idea of Northern Europe also echoes old and persistent narratives where European countries are placed within a particular hierarchy of "better" and "worse," where those in the southern part of Europe have been racialized as being lesser, almost African. In Italy, the division of north and south can be traced to the late 1800s when the country was unified and consequently reified and racialized, with southern Italy characterized negatively, as more African and darker (Muehlebach 2018: 139).

For my Nigerien interlocutors, Northern Italy had, however, more racism while they felt that Southern Italy's precarious economic status created less racism toward them. Racism was less felt there, several told me, because they are after all "just like us the Africans."

Being Nigerien and African in Europe

The photos that Ardo regularly shows me of his children on his phone tell a story that is larger than his longing for his family. It shows that technologies have transformed people's mobility and the reality of those who leave their loved ones behind. These men can, through digital technology, stay constantly connected both locally and with friends and family back in Niger. Texting and sharing photos or videos have become the most important ways cell phones are used in the sub-Saharan region (Poushter and Oates 2015), creating intimate links between families and other networks. Scott Youngstedt's (2004b) research on the diasporic community of Hausa from Niger shows how the creative use of the internet, telephones, and wireless transfer allows diasporic communities abroad to stay in touch with family in Niger (see Youngstedt 2004b). Inexpensive phone apps, such as WhatsApp, provide my interlocutors with what Vertovec has called "social glue," connecting people across the globe (2004: 220). As emphasized by Youngstedt (2004b), in the context of his research in Niger and the United States, many Nigeriens are extremely resourceful and creative in their use of these technologies; even those who lack formal education do not let that stop them.[4] Within globalization literature, technology tends to be glorified for bringing extreme changes but, as De Bruijn stresses, these changes should not be seen as automatically transforming social relationships, but should instead be recognized for facilitating continuity in social relationships across different continents (2014: 332).

The phone serves another, equally practical purpose: connectivity with other Nigeriens and West Africans within Brussels is crucial for successful job hunting. During most of my interviews in Brussels, my interlocutors were constantly on the phone, either texting or receiving phone calls from home and from nearby people, thus staying constantly engaged with networks of family and friends within Brussels and Niger. Idrissa, one of my interlocutors, is having a cup of coffee with me. He is different from most men that I spoke with in that he has a university education. He has been in Belgium for about three years. He explains the importance of the network in this way: "There is solidarity among us Nigeriens in Brussels. So, if someone earns good money, he will give part to his Nigerien brother. There is a solidarity, and if you don't have legal documents, if you don't have work, then this solidarity matters. It makes life a little easier." Idrissa's use of the word "brother" to refer to fictive kinship between all men from Niger, should not be taken as only referring to their common origin within the same nation state. It also indicates that despite being of different ethnicities and from different parts of Niger, many of them—even those with formal education—are in the same position of precarity when in Brussels.

When I tell Idrissa that I do not understand how people get by when work is so scarce, he agrees that it is challenging. "Without work it is difficult to eat and difficult to take care of yourself, but people are always looking for whatever opportunities on the black market. If your friend has work, he will give you something. If you rent a small place you rest there with your friends, you sleep there one night, and then next day you look for something else. This is what life is like." He adds, proudly: "There are people here who sleep on the street, but never any Nigeriens, because of the community of Nigeriens here." Though I don't say this to Idrissa, I have known Nigeriens who had to sleep on the street. However, much more frequently I have witnessed many of my friends assist someone who was on the street find a place to stay.

The emphasis of these men on solidarity also extends to women. A few of the Nigerien men I talked to, especially my long-term friends, emphasized that due to this solidarity, Nigerien women never have to resort to prostitution. Ousseina Alidou, however, has mentioned in her writing, the presence of Nigerien trafficked prostitutes in European cities. Just like the men I talk to, these women send money back to their families, and in some cases can finance the education of their siblings (2005: 194). The failure of my interlocutors to mention this aspect of their lives is probably due to idealized views of Nigerien identity, and a lack of interest in disclosing to an outsider what they possibly see as a humiliating exception.

This stress on the importance of being Nigerien is somewhat different from what I encountered in Niger two decades earlier, when minority groups especially, like the WoDaaBe, would strongly stress their ethnic identity, even though, as Alidou (2005) notes, boundaries between different ethnic groups are not rigid, but dynamic and contextual. Still, in everyday life, ethnic identification is an important part of solidarity and interaction; this was strongly emphasized to outsiders, like myself, when I lived in Niger.

In Brussels ethnicity was relevant, but much less so than in Niger. Sébastien Lo Sardo's (2013) research on Hausa in Brussels emphasizes the strong ties between Nigerien Hausa and Zarma-Songhay communities on one hand and Tuareg-Fulani on the other, which reflects the social relationships in Niger (Keough and Youngstedt 2019: 86–87). This reflects how people are a part of overlapping communities, where they are Nigerien in one context but Hausa or Fulani in another. Furthermore, as Scott Youngstedt draws attention to in his research in the United States, many West African immigrants feel a sense of solidarity through their shared adherence to Islam, which intersects with their sense of belonging in other communities (2004b: 45).

Without being prompted, Idrissa explained: "It does not matter if there are few from particular ethnic group because we the Nigeriens, have solidarity. We don't think in terms of Hausa, Fulani, or Tuaregs. Niger equals Niger. In our country, ethnicity matters, but in Europe our ethnicity does not matter." When Idrissa emphasizes to me the importance of this solidarity in getting by in Brussels, he again uses the French word for "brother" (*frère*) to refer to all Nigeriens. Interestingly, it is not only ethnic categories that seem to have less significance in Brussels. Even nationality seems to have become secondary to continental solidarity. "We are all Africans here," Ardo explains to me on more than one occasion. "It does not matter where you are from. Here in Brussels, it becomes irrelevant."

Ali not only likes to show me images of his family on his phone but he also wants to view pictures of my children and parents and even occasionally to show them to his friends. He has met all of them, and thus they become a small part of his lifeworld as well.

When I visit Ali in October 2016, my recent stay in Paris also becomes a photo-event to be shared. As I am sipping Lipton tea in his small room, he comes in with another man, one that I have never seen before. Ali explains to me that he had to bring him to see me because this man, a West African like himself, had eagerly been following Iceland's success in European football and wanted to see a real person from Iceland.

We shake hands and the man observes me smiling and he compliments Iceland enthusiastically for beating the United Kingdom as well as putting up a good fight against the French. Ali is also excited; I sense that knowing me is giving him some social capital at this moment. When Ali shows him the photos that I took at the Stade du France during the Iceland-France match, the man looks at me, astonished. There is no hint of envy, more an acknowledgement of how lucky I was to be there. I have no interest in football. It was a coincidence that I was in Paris at the time and even a bigger one that I was able to get tickets to the game with my partner and children. The fact that we were able to take advantage of the situation and buy the tickets had nothing to do with luck in that sense, but everything to do with my privileges in a world of inequalities.

NOTES

1. According to Eurostat there were little more than 1900 people (see Eurostat n.d.).
2. For critical discussion on civilian casualties see Human Rights Watch 2012 and Milne 2012.
3. Castagnone et al. (2014) point out that even though there has been a strong pull, especially for those better educated, to go to the former colonizing countries, these migratory patterns along with others have been rapidly changing.

4. At one point, Ardo gently but firmly takes my phone out of my hand and downloads WhatsApp without asking me. He explains that it less expensive for me to stay in contact with my family in Iceland this way, rather than phoning them through the Icelandic phone company.

CHAPTER
4

Global Citizens and the Backstage

On one of my first trips to Brussels, I stayed at a downtown hotel belonging to the NH chain. When I entered my room, I saw on my bed an application for the NH's loyalty program. I picked it up and observed the brochure's cover with interest before I read the text. It featured pictures of a suitcase, a compass, and a globe, objects that reminded one of leisure tourism and explorations. There were also items shown suggesting a more privileged life of the "Eurocrat," including a personal computer, books, and a man's tie. Inside the brochure, the "loyalty program" promised to make me feel like a "global citizen."

This chapter focuses on mobility within Brussels in a broader sense, demonstrating how the migration of my interlocutors is only a small fraction of mobility in a city that can be defined by migration; they live in a city that is quite diversified and stratified in terms of mobility and socioeconomic status. The chapter seeks to draw attention to different kinds of "strangers" in the city, that is, the economic migrant, the tourist, and the expat, using these examples to reflect on different kinds of desirability of mobile populations.

The Complex City in an Even More Complex Country

Belgium exemplifies mobility as characteristic of Europe and the complexity of Europe as a space. The making of Belgium was a painful historical process, as attested by abundant references to the country as the "battlefield" of Europe with its history of multiple annexations, as well as its horrible position in the World Wars (Jansen-Verbeke and Govers 2009; Blainey 2016).

Belgium was once a part of the colonizing Dutch empire, which maintained colonies and trading posts at different times across the world, such as in Indonesia and Suriname.[1] In contemporary discussions of the borderlands that are seen as protecting something called "Europe," it is easy to forget how diversified and contested different spaces within Europe have been (see Ponzanesi and Blaagaard 2011). The development of the "Belgian" space vividly captures the various intersecting identities and their shifting meaning and salience over time, with the state both strengthening and destroying identities (Ceuppens 2006: 149).

The development of a southern Dutch identity developed in relation to Catholicism, and eventually led to the establishment of Belgium as a separate country (Jansen-Verbeke and Govers 2009: 144). Today, Flemish speakers, who constitute the main linguistic community in Belgium make up roughly sixty percent of the Belgian population, while the French-speaking population is about forty percent. There is also a small minority of German-speaking Belgians in the south of the country (Blainey 2016; Swyngedouw and Baeten 2001: 837). The two main linguistic communities in Belgium mirror the principal division of the country into the Flanders area (with Flemish as the main language) and the Wallonia area (with French as the main language), in addition to the small German-speaking enclave.[2]

While the French-speaking population constitutes a minority in terms of number of people in Belgium as a whole, it constitutes a strong majority in the Brussels capital region (Mielants 2006: 315). This reflects that following Belgium's independence from Dutch rule, the French-speaking elite in the more prosperous part of Belgium at the time established French as the official national government language, making it necessary for the Flemish-speakers to learn French if they wanted to participate in broader public life (Blainey 2016: 487; Jansen-Verbeke and Govers 2009). Blainey argues that this rendered the Flemish de facto second-class citizens in Belgium (2016: 487). During the second half of the twentieth century, postwar economic growth in the Flemish part of Belgium led to more demands among Flemish-speaking Belgians with regard to the Flemish language (Blainey 2016: 487; on the complication of these debates see Ceuppens 2006). Today, Brussels is officially a bilingual city (Blainey 2016: 481). However, the split between the two main groups remains, and often it is so intense that anxieties remain about whether the country could potentially break up into "two separate countries" (Blainey 2016: 488; Ceuppens 2006: 169–70). It is into this fraught social and historical context that privileged and underprivileged migrant populations arrive.

If we define migrant populations as those with foreign citizenship, then in 2019 Belgium's migrants made up twelve percent of the country's population. Of this twelve percent, however, almost eight percent come from other

Figure 4.1. Different comic strip murals are found widely around Brussels, celebrating the city's comic book artists. Photo taken in spring 2019 at Rue des Capucins, where the characters Blondin and Cirage are depicted. © Kristín Loftsdóttir.

EU countries, with most in 2019 coming from the neighboring countries France, the Netherlands, and Italy (Eurostat 2020). But if we define migrant populations, however, as being made up of those who are foreign-born, then a full seventeen percent of Belgium's population is of migrant origin, with eleven percent born in Morocco (Eurostat 2020).

In Brussels, this diversity is even more salient, because one-third of the population is of "foreign nationality" (Humblet et al. 2015: 5). These outsiders do not always come from the places one might expect. For example, even though Congo was a Belgian colony, there was no extensive out-migration of Congolese to Belgium at that time, as I discuss in Chapter 8. Instead, the largest group of non-EU migrants in Belgium originates from Morocco and Turkey (Manço and Kanmaz 2005: 1107), in large part due to an effort on the part of government and private sector policies in the 1960s and 1970s to stimulate migration from these countries. Most of those immigrants worked in jobs that native Belgians shunned, such as mining, manual labor, or construction work (Mielants 2006: 314). As argued by Eric Mielants, there were few objections to the influx at the time, which he suggests could be due to that they were seen as *Gastarbeiter* or guest workers, and thus perceived as short-term workers (2006: 314). However, the economic recession of the 1970s spawned negative views of these workers, followed by new efforts, put in place in 1974, to restrict immigration into Belgium. The paradigm of "zero migration" replaced the earlier recruitment of these individuals (Martiniello 2003: 225). After legislative changes in the 1990s (1991, 1995, and 2000), it became easier to gain Belgian citizenship (Mielants 2006: 314).[3]

Asylum seekers in Belgium are shaped by similar legal constraints faced by those in other European countries; the debates that take place within Belgium on asylum are similar to debates taking place elsewhere in Europe (Martiniello 2003: 225; on diversity between Belgium and other European countries in terms of legal rights of asylum seekers, see Bank 2000; Majcher et al. 2020). As Martiniello has pointed out, the lengthy processing time of asylum applications means that people have been deported after waiting up to two years for a decision. Meanwhile they had settled in Belgian society (2003: 228). For the last few years, Belgium, like many other European countries, has been characterized by a "hardening" of both immigration-related policies and public attitudes, reflected for example, in the allowance of detention of families with children and increased emphasis on detaining migrant populations in detention facilities (Majcher et al. 2020: 361–62). The detention of asylum seekers in detention facilities has been criticized by various human right bodies, including the UN Committee on the Elimination of Racial Discrimination (Majcher et al. 2020: 377). Also, as elsewhere in Europe, including my native country Iceland, asylum seekers in Belgium are often associated with crime and suspected of not being "true" asylum seekers (Blommaert 2001: 416).

Another mobile population—that is the economic migrants segregated from the rest of Brussels' population—are the more privileged migrants who work in the EU and other intergovernmental and private institutions, ranging from NATO to the WEU and Eurocontrol (Swyngedouw and Baeten 2001: 839), plus various NGOs, as well as a myriad of consulting firms (Gatti 2009: 6). But these "migrants" are generally referred to by a different term, "expatriates." This term has been criticized for its elitist and racist application because it is most often used in place of "privileged white migrants" (see Guðjónsdóttir and Loftsdóttir 2016; Leinonen 2012; Kunz 2020). Emanuele Gatti shows that this community tends to use "expat" to define themselves; they are targeted as such by public and commercial organizations that have a heavily invested interest in promoting the city and offering a panoply of services to expats (2009: 7). These interested parties produce a particular rosy image of expats in Brussels as cosmopolitan and as a real community (Gatti 2009), which recalls the brochure at the hotel that I mentioned at the beginning. The expats generally distinguish themselves from other migrants by noting their higher education and professional level and that they do move due to professional reasons (Gatti 2009: 3). They also separate themselves from the general category of "migrant" (Gatti 2009), as research has shown to be the case with other privileged migrants (see Guðjónsdóttir and Loftsdóttir 2016).

This sense of exclusive community is further intensified by the occasional use of the term "Bruxpat" (Gatti 2009: 9) to refer to expatriates in Brussels. In other cases, the term "expat" has been refined to "Eurocrat," which mainly includes only people of European origin. "Eurocrat" has been loosely defined as referring to "European citizens working temporarily in Brussels, and/or attending meetings in Brussels on a very frequent basis" (Jansen-Verbeke et al. 2005: 110).

Gatti (2009) points out that the use of the term expat in the rhetoric of promotional materials creates a sense of community, familiarity, and a sense of belonging to an exclusive club. Within the expat community, there exists a strong hierarchy, as Paweł Lewicki (2016, 2020) has shown, in which reproduction of older hierarchies within Europe flourishes, such as between South and North Europe, as well as between East and West. Polish expats can thus be perceived by the members of the older member states, as "a different category of EU officials" to use Julia Rozanska's (2011) phrase. Here it is useful to remember that precarious migrants can also be people migrating from other European countries. Research has shown that, for example, prior to Poland joining the pan-European labor market, Polish migrants featured highly in discussions about "illegal" migrants in Brussels (see Leman 1997: 27). Lewicki's (2020) research on EU institutions in Brussels reflects the various unspoken ongoing negotiations in regard to clothing and other body markers, between citizens of the newer and older member states in terms of what is to be European, shaped by different shades of whiteness and notions of secularism.

Although internally differentiated, the expat community in Brussels constitutes in many ways a sphere separated from other migrants and from long-standing residents. They distinguish themselves from other migrants not only by the terms described above but also through various practices: such as when house-hunting, they are told by estate agencies and long-term expats to avoid areas where lower-salaried migrants live, that is, districts associated with people of African descent (Gatti 2009: 3).

Another issue, critically pointed out by Mielants (2006), and one that tells a story about the value assigned to these different groups of migrants, is that much of the expat population in Brussels, particularly diplomats and those in international institutions, are exempt from local and national taxes in the city. Despite this, many are still eligible to vote in the local elections, thanks to agreements made between the federal government and other EU member states. Contrast this with the tough reality that other migrant families—who often have a much longer history in the city than the "Eurocrats," and who pay taxes—are not eligible to vote in these elections. Mielants also pays attention to the political tensions when claiming that Flemish politicians were reluctant to give the right to vote to EU citizens, due to fears that these individuals, who live mainly in the Brussels region (where Francophone speakers are more numerous), would be biased in favor of French-speaking candidates over Flemish ones (2006: 315-16).

Living alongside this mobile population in Brussels are the "native" Belgians, who can be divided into the "elite" native Bruxellois and the less-well-off locals. Despite its role as administrative headquarters of the EU, Brussels suffers from significant structural unemployment along with substantial social inequality (Humblet et al. 2015). Despite the presence of well-paid expats in the city, the average income in Brussels is twenty percent less than in the country. It has been estimated that at least one third of the population of Brussels lives in poverty (Humblet et al. 2015: 6).[4] According to Gatti, native Belgians see expats as "privileged and high-salaried people" (2009: 3). They resent the changes in the city of Brussels, with massive EU buildings radically transforming certain areas of the city, as well as the increased property prices (Gatti 2009: 3).

The more affluent "natives" live in the suburbs while the aging or less privileged natives who cannot afford the outskirts live with the Muslim population and other more precarious migrants in the less privileged parts of town (Manço and Kanmaz 2005: 1107). Distribution of income reflects this: in most city center neighborhoods, the average income per inhabitant is below the average for Belgium as a whole, while in the outskirts of Brussels, especially in the affluent south, income is considerably higher than the national average (Humblet et al. 2015: 6). The neighborhoods that surround the city center and form a part of it used to be working-class neighborhoods but can now be described as forming an "area of poverty" (Mazzocchetti 2012: 3; see also Deboosere et al. 2009).

Brussels' Backstage and Front Stage

Populations in cities such as Brussels are divided internally, containing different kinds of intersecting subjectivities that do not necessarily fall into neat categories of migrants or non-migrant, or white natives and non-white others.

The ideas of "backstage" and "front stage" are, to me, useful tools to think through the social landscape of Brussels and the sharp separation of spaces in the city that are occupied by different kinds of migrants, ranging from tourists to Eurocrats to asylum seekers who coexist with the "native" population. In her analysis of the film *Dirty Pretty Things*, Gibson (2006) sees the hotel as a place where different mobilities are brought together. "The hotel becomes the interface between these strangers," she writes. "The cosmopolitan global mobile elites and the 'invisible people' who clean up after them and service them" (700). To capture the performance aspect of human interaction, Gibson links her analysis to Erving Goffman's (1959) idea of a "front stage" and "backstage." The backstage at the hotel, Gibson points out, is often a door marked "staff only." Behind the door are undocumented workers and other precarious migrants working at various mundane, poorly paid tasks, like my friend Youssouf. The front stage is the space where those living more precarious lives in Brussels and the privileged migrants such as tourists, Eurocrats, and other expatriates meet, while the backstage is kept out of view. These metaphors, "backstage" and "front stage," are notably only tools to capture particular divisions and in no way capture the complexity of the city, nor the self-perception of people living there. Rather, these terms are a way to draw attention to how certain aspects are proclaimed by the state and others—and made visible for tourists and EU officials in multiple ways—while other parts are more hidden.

We can characterize Brussels' front stage—we could also call it a façade—as composed of beautiful old buildings, not only echoing Europe's medieval culture and Belgium's faded and tainted glory as a colonial empire but also highlighting its tourist presence and multiple opportunities for luxury consumption. The historical marketplace "Grand Place," which is at the geographic core of the tourist zone and remains a main tourist destination in Brussels (Jansen-Verbeke et al. 2005: 114, 117), occupies a prominent place on the front stage. Also, on Brussels' front stage would be the EU quarter, which, as some have observed, is fundamentally segregated from the rest of Brussels (Blainey 2016: 497), with thousands of "Eurocrats" and expats living lives largely separated from the local population (Jansen-Verbeke et al. 2005: 110). The buildings that house these institutions are concentrated in the "European quartier," of which Leopold Park is a part, and host different institutional bodies associated with the EU. Their architectural style aims to create an association with modernity and rationality. Both ideas are usually conceptualized as originating within Europe and evolving most progressively within it.

Backstage are the neighborhoods where those in more economic and socially vulnerable positions live. Many of them cluster around the tourist core in the downtown area. Halal restaurants can be found here, and butcher shops, along with storefront businesses and mosques (see also Manço and Kanmaz 2005). When I navigate these areas, I am struck by the complete absence of tourists in these spaces, which are occupied by people going about the mundane everyday tasks of carrying groceries, by children coming home from school, or by teenagers whispering secrets to each other. To my interlocutors, their neighborhoods are a space of sociality and familiarity. When I walk with them to different places within their neighborhoods, they constantly greet friends and other Nigeriens. In one of these neighborhoods associated with migrant communities, Anderlecht, we even enjoy dinners at a pleasant Nigerien restaurant. It is full of people, and we share a large plate of meat and rice, eating with separate spoons like we would in Niger. The Heyvaert area in Brussels, between Anderlecht and Molenbeek-Saint-Jean, where many Nigerien Hausa live, has a vibrant trade in used cars that are shipped to West Africa. Businessmen visiting from West Africa come here to do business, indicating the energetic nature of these neighborhoods (Lo Sardo 2013: 316) as a meeting place of different mobilities. Lo Sardo describes, however, that in the eyes of other inhabitants of Brussels this area is perceived as "dark and desolated area, almost a no-go zone" (2013: 315).

While these areas are spaces of vibrant social interactions, it is difficult not to notice the trash on the street, the shoddy infrastructure, and the many run-down apartment buildings. Research by Jacinthe Mazzocchetti (2012) among adolescents from African migrant backgrounds living in neighborhoods in the poorer part of Brussels vividly demonstrates how deeply segregated the city is along lines of race and class. Similarly, Patrick Deboosere et al. (2009) speak of "invisible boundaries" between communities with different socioeconomic backgrounds who have little interaction in their everyday lives, while some neighborhoods are certainly characterized by more mixing in terms of people's background. Mazzocchetti (2012) points out that while the formulation of "ghettoes" has not taken place in Belgium, as it has in the US inner cities, there are still aspects of "ghettoization" in certain Belgian neighborhoods. For example, school segregation is present with the so-called elite schools and ghetto schools, as shown by Mazzocchetti, which results in substantial performance gaps between students of foreign origin and those of native background (2012: 6). In some cases, the living space of young people in these neighborhoods is confined to just a few streets, leading to a strong sense of marginalization and a sense that they are confined to it. They experience their own neighborhood as rundown and dirty, coupled with feelings of social injustice. In some neighborhoods, Mazzocchetti tells us, these young people must go through regular humiliating police identity checks (2012: 5), which target especially North Africans, where they are interviewed or asked for ID (Hebberecht 1997: 166).

In contrast to the adolescents Mazzocchetti (2012) writes about, the migrants I interviewed in Brussels generally seemed to have a positive view of their neighborhoods. Most did not often leave it, unless it was necessary, because they felt everything they needed was there.⁵ However, my interlocutors' experiences are different from these youths because they are without their families and do not envision their future in Brussels. It is equally important to note that they do not identify themselves as Belgians and did not necessarily anticipate themselves as making a future life in Belgium.

I want to return to the brochure that I noticed on one of my first visits to the city. The next morning, as I walked into the hotel's breakfast room, it lingered at the back of my mind and I asked myself: To whom did this brochure speak? Who qualifies as "global citizen"? Once in the breakfast room, I looked around for clues. The hotel certainly looked like a business hotel—stylish but not overly so. The individuals enjoying their breakfast next to me would, as I would, for the most part be identified as white, with Northern European backgrounds. Judging from their attire, many seemed to be traveling for business. Regardless of how they might be classified in terms of ethnic origins or race, all the guests staying here are probably part of a population that can move between the places they want to go to with relative ease. This ease of mobility puts them in a privileged group that includes "Eurocrats" attending meetings, tourists experiencing the cultural uniqueness of Brussels, and even academics like myself. This population has access to easy travel—their disposable cash can buy things like taxi rides, tourist packages, priority passes to avoid lines, and comfortable hotels with good Wi-Fi connections.

I begin to realize that what is bothering me about the brochure is the unspoken fact that while tourists like me are welcomed into and even recruited by the hotel chain's loyalty program, other individuals, such as the asylum seeker and the illegal or other marginal immigrants, who are equally mobile and just as desirous of moving between different parts of the world, are unlikely to be invited to be part of this marketing scheme. Just as the children interviewed by Jacinthe Mazzocchetti (2012) experience, these mobile individuals do not have the same opportunities to enter the exclusive ranks of NH's "global citizenship," as it is presented in the pages of my brochure.

NH Hotels' invitation to join the ranks of "global citizenship" engages with the notion of cosmopolitanism. Scholarly debates about the concept of "cosmopolitanism" reflect a lack of agreement of what it means and how it can be used theoretically (Wardle 2010). The uses of the term are too numerous to parse out here, but they are often entangled with scholarly aspirations of the future that include more "openness" to diverse cultural experiences, an acknowledgement of universal humanity, as well as referring to emic descriptions of individuals' aspirations to be "cosmopolitans" (see discussion Wardle 2010: 384; Beck 2012). Gurminder K. Bhambra and John Narayan critically draw attention to how the EU is often seen as embodying the cosmopolitan ideal, with its emphasis on preserving peace, as well as a model of "post-national democracy which the globe can learn from and emulate" (2017: 4).

In some cases, ideals of cosmopolitanism are linked to mobility in a way that ignores power relations and class (Glick Schiller and Salazar 2013: 186; Lewicki 2016; Bhambra and Narayan 2017). The term's theoretical weakness has to do with how it is used both as a "moral project" and as an analytical concept (Wardle 2010: 384).[6] In this particular context, it tends to reflect long-lasting European aspirations of Europe as a source of civilization, liberal values, and not only of tolerance for difference but an active embrace of diversity. Gibson's (2006) discussion of the hotel acting as a metaphor for an unequal world clearly draws out that in a cosmopolitan space, such as the hotel, the bodies of "strangers" are classified into desirable bodies and undesirable bodies. The term "cosmopolitan" revolves thus certainly around mobility—but the right kind of mobility of privileged subjects.

Europe's embarrassing colonial past pops up in various contexts, reflecting how it continues to influence the present (Dzenovska 2013), including our understanding of what kinds of bodies are desirable and which ones are not. It is necessary here to draw from theories of intersectionality, which emphasize converging categorizations of various groups or divisions of diversity and identification, such as the Muslim, immigrant, gender, sexuality, and the exotic other. Noel Salazar and Alan Smart stress (2011) how the decision to be mobile is itself entangled with power, in a world where not all are able to choose freely between mobility and immobility (also Abram et al. 2016).

Here is where the idea of Brussels' backstage comes into play, because its rundown buildings provide a clear reflection of the economic marginalization of the population living there in contrast with the normally bustling tourist spaces, with restaurants and various consumer items at every corner. Backstage, where many of my Nigerien friends live, their daily reality is divorced from that of the expatriates and the tourist population. The backstage has created its own kind of sociality—not one composed of tourists or expensively dressed people rushing to appointments, but one with a strong sense of community, with real people living their lives, children playing, and neighbors talking on the sidewalks, enjoying each other's company. The front stage is still where many of my interlocutors work. While invisible to tourists or others who enjoy fancy hotels and restaurants, they stay in the back, cleaning, chopping, and peeling vegetables. They usually know the front stage well, in that they are my tour guides, explaining which sites are the most popular to visit and enjoy.

When making my way by train from Brussels Airport on one of my first visits, I experienced this gap. I had made an appointment with one of my old friends, Bermo, from Niger, who had migrated to Brussels. He had offered to come to the train station, and we could then go together to my NH Hotel downtown. I had never been to that hotel before and hardly knew Brussels. On the train, I started wondering if the hotel was close enough to the train station to walk or if I should take a taxi or some other transport. I asked a friendly woman on the train showing her the name and location of my hotel, if it was close enough to walk. She told me that it is not very far from the station but advised me to not walk through the neighborhood around the train station as it could be dangerous. Bermo waited for the me at the station and we walked peacefully to the hotel. I noticed that there were some Muslim women and men on the street—it is the backstage in the terminology that I used above—and I realized then that that this is probably what made her see the neighborhood as dangerous for me. In her eyes, probably my strong Icelandic accent, light skin and other cultural markers, made me as alien in this space, just as Bermo felt himself to be at the NH hotel once we arrived there.

NOTES

1. Many of these colonial projects were in the hands of independent companies, including the Dutch East India Company and Dutch West India Company.
2. Marc G. Blainey (2016) points out that this division runs across the map of Europe from the West to East, where the division of Germanic and Latin speaking parts of Europe correspond partly with the division of Europe into North and South (2016: 480). As Blainey argues, the Flemish region of northern Belgium still forms an exception to the North-South divide of Europe due to the fact that the Germanic countries in the North are generally Protestant or secular, while Belgium is both Germanic and Catholic (2016: 494).
3. A detailed historical analysis of policy in Belgium toward those defined as "aliens" is provided by Frank Caestecker (2000), which also shows the shifting meanings of concepts such as "guest worker" and "refugees."
4. In 1993 it was only two percent lower (Humblet et al. 2015: 6), which tells a larger story of widening economic inequalities than can be told here.
5. This corresponds with Sébastien Lo Sardo's (2013) findings in regard to the Nigerien Hausa living in Heyvaert.
6. If we follow Ulrich Beck's (2012) suggestion and remove the term from its elitist connotations, its theoretical utility becomes questionable, in my view, along with its distinction from other terms, such as transnationalism and globalization.

CHAPTER
5

Multicultural Europe
Invasions against European Values?

In the metanarratives of "multiculturalism in crisis" and the "refugee crisis," there are no large ships. We do not see the ships that carried people for hundreds of years to be sold in slavery nor do we see those that carried vast wealth from colonized parts of the world elsewhere. Instead, only small boats—even rafts—are visible, carrying refugees and other migrants across the Mediterranean Sea.

As we are sitting at the kitchen table in a small flat in Brussels, Youssouf and I are both strangers in this land, Belgium. Whether we like it or not, we are a part of an interlinked history that shapes our own countries and our lives. After I finish with my questions, we linger at the kitchen table. He wants to hear even more about my life in Iceland, about my parents and my children. We flip through the family photos in my phone and in his. He misses his children but says he does not want to bring his family to Europe, because there are important qualities of life in Niger, such as the strong sense of community, families, and friends. He tries to work as much as he can to create a better life for them there, hoping that later they will be together.

When he stands up to leave, I stand up to walk with him all the way outside, as is customary both in Niger and Iceland. We wait together for the small elevator that will bring us to the first floor. When the elevator door opens on the ground floor, I see one of my neighbors collecting his mail. He is watching Youssouf and me closely as we step out of the elevator. He telegraphs a mixture of fear and suspicion. We both greet him, and he politely greets us in return. I have seen this man several times with his little dog. I know he is at home at lot because his wife is seriously ill. As he observes Youssouf with a cold and somewhat frozen expression, I wonder what he is thinking, what he really sees.

In this chapter, I use the experiences of my Brussels interlocutors as a gateway to look at multiculturalism in Europe, searching how their experiences "fit" into the narrative of multicultural Europe. Many of those seeking asylum in Europe are from countries where Muslims make up a majority, and with the so-called migrant crisis the conflation of the categories of asylum seekers and Muslims has increased greatly (Bhui 2016). The category "Muslim" has become primacy as the ultimate Other in European and American discourses (Westin 2010: 24; Fortier 2007). As I noted earlier, there is nothing natural about this. When tracing the historical development of asylum seekers in Europe, Lucassen (2018) has pointed out in reference to Bosnian refugees in the 1990s that even though a majority of them were Muslims, they were regarded as Europeans. This chapter also examines the shared mediascape of migrants, those who welcome migrants, and those who resist them, in a context where Muslims are demonized even as the idea of Europe is associated with equality and human rights (Ponzanesi and Blaagaard 2011).

The Unassimilated Ones

I interview Salim in his modest room, which he shares with another man. The small bedroom holds only two mattresses and a chair. Different from other Nigerien migrants that I know better, Salim does not want me to sit on the mattress. Instead, he borrows a chair from another room in the building, which has been divided into small spaces for rent to people in similarly precarious positions. The floor space in Salim's shared room is so limited that we sit rather uncomfortably close to each other. As there is no table, I hold in my hand the glass of water that he has offered me.

Salim's story, like those of so many of the other Nigerien migrants I have heard, is painful to hear. His desperation is clear from his body language. As Idrissa, Salim is different from most others I have spoken to due to the fact that he received good formal education in Niger. Despite this advantage, he felt compelled to leave because of poverty, no job prospects, and his sense that there was no future for him in Niger.

When Salim tells me again and again that he is well "assimilated" into Belgian culture, with a persistence that bears witness that he has tried to do all the right things in order to get permission to stay here, he echoes a familiar story. The use of the concept "multicultural" society has long been criticized by anthropologists for its reifying assumptions (Baumann 1999).

Of course, the concept "multicultural" is also often used to positively acknowledge and embrace the plurality of society, but the problem with the term lies in how it prioritizes ahistorical notions of "culture," and how it often becomes a racial marker. "Integration" is the bureaucratic term used to explain how people from different cultural backgrounds adapt to mainstream society. However, despite sometimes being explained as going both ways, in reality the term is often used like "assimilation," assuming specific problems among migrants—especially migrant Muslims (Rytter 2019). I lose track of Salim soon after this conversation, but I find it hard to forget his frustrations and sense of puzzlement over why people like him, just wanting simple things like work, are so unwelcome.

When considering how the history of Europe is encapsulated within the metanarrative of multiculturalism, that is, Europe with a pristine, static past where everyone, until recently, had their place, I find Daniel Knight's and Charles Stewart's (2016) coined phrase "re-stitching of time" useful in tracing how crisis often shapes perceptions of time. In this "re-stitching of time," colonialization, as part of the fabric of time, is cut out, dismissed, or forgotten, along with past mobility throughout history within and outside this space we refer to as Europe. The question of who does and who does not belong within Europe continues to be contested (Ponzanesi and Blaagaard 2011). We see this in the extreme nationalistic parties that gained more currency in political debates in Europe after the 1990s (Westin 2010: 24), with the public mantra of the crisis of multiculturalism (Lentin and Titley 2011). Using an ahistorical notion of Europe as consisting of "pure" cultural spaces prior to the present, this idea disregards the effects of colonialism on transnational movements.

These ideas of migrants' integration also came to my mind when talking to Amado a little earlier. I meet him at the apartment of a mutual friend. He shakes my hand shyly, smiling almost to himself. He is very young and, in my eyes, only a little older than my own teenage son. As a Fulani, he speaks Fulfulde, which I learned during my time in Niger, but our common friend remains because Amado finds it more comfortable.

Amado's life has been eventful and dangerous. He left his parents at sixteen and went to Libya, as there was ample work there at the time. His reasons for leaving were basic: poverty and the hope that he could better support his family through migrant work. In Libya, he worked in construction and quickly learned many different skills. Because of the war in Libya, he went to Italy, stayed there for few years, and then came to Belgium. At first, he was alone, but quickly established friendships with other West African migrant workers. The skills he learned in Libya became extremely valuable in Belgium, allowing him to take all kinds of assignments relating to home renovations, constructing floors, and fixing electrical problems.

In the beginning, Amado explains, it was difficult to find work, but now he tells me with a smile, people know his work and contact him often. Thus, he is able to do what he set out to in the beginning, which is to send his parents money regularly to assist them. For many West African countries such remittance is important (Adeniran 2020: 23). All of Amado's work is, of course, done on the informal labor market, most of it in the neighborhood where he lives. I hear pride in his voice when he shares with me that "today there are many who ask me regularly to work for them."

When I look at Amado, I see a young man, who embodies the immigrant often referred to in European discourses, the one who has not integrated or assimilated. He speaks hardly any French and certainly not Flemish; he works outside the formal economy; and his life seems to take place in this one neighborhood. Here are his friends, his work, and all the services that he needs. He has built a solid reputation among those who know him; he works hard; and he supports his parents. Once again, I ask myself what it really means to "integrate" in a particular society.

A Muslim in a Multicultural Europe

Muslims are important targets of anti-immigration rhetoric in Belgium. Mielants (2006) points out that in the context of the recession of the 1980s, the Vlaams Blok political party gained traction by employing considerable anti-immigration rhetoric, even parroting racist anti-Semitic slogans from the 1930s in the context of Muslims. Vlaams Blok party members also declared that immigrants in Belgium should be forcibly returned to their country of origin, starting with all criminals, illegals, and the unemployed immigrants, followed by first-generation immigrants, and then second- and third-generation immigrants (see Mielants 2006: 318–19).

This is perhaps not too surprising when considering results from a survey conducted in the late 1990s: 22 percent of Belgians described themselves as "very racist," while 33 percent said they were "fairly racist." In addition, 41 percent of those under twenty-five years old felt that there were too many foreigners in Belgium (see discussion in Mielants 2006: 321).

According to Manço and Kanmaz (2005), Islamophobic views became somewhat less evident in the early 2000s in Brussels, due, in part to Muslims' diverse labor force participation and their high visibility in various associations, which contributed toward a more positive image of Muslims in general (2005: 1110). Emblematic of this is the relatively high political representation of Muslims in elected offices, such as in the Parliament of the Brussels-Capital Region (Zibouh 2011). Still, Belgium was one of the first European countries to issue a national ban on veiling in 2011 (Fadil

2014: 252). As pointed out by Nadia Fadil, a large consensus behind the ban emerged on behalf of the newly elected federal chamber after an institutional crisis on the federal level divided the Francophone and the Flemish political elite (2014: 252).

In analyzing the views of those who are identified as "native" Belgians, scholars have highlighted the differences between the Flemish- and the French-speaking populations, some even claiming that there is "no such thing as a unified Belgian debate about asylum and migration" (De Cleen et al. 2017: 59). More positive views of immigrants were found in French-speaking parts of Belgium (Manço and Kanmaz 2005: 1111), while there are stronger anti-migration attitudes among the Flemish part of the population (Rochtus 2012). Further, according to some scholars, racist attitudes are less prevalent in Brussels than in cities like Antwerp (the largest city in the northern part of Belgium), which has a larger Flemish population (Schuermans and De Maesschalck 2010). As Mielants argues, it is perhaps ironic that in the Flanders, where there are better socioeconomic conditions and fewer migrants, there seems to be more support for xenophobic far-right political parties (2006: 316). Regardless, racism toward those seen as "outsiders" is complicated and does not only work on the line of Flemish being racist and Wallonia non-racist. As Ceuppens stresses, attitudes intersect with class and various internal differentiations as indicated previously (2006: 158).

Synthesizing contemporary discussions on asylum seekers and refugees in the Flemish part of Belgium, Benjamin De Cleen et al. (2017) claim that the "refugee crisis" narrative was assimilated into much older culturalist and essentialist portrayals of migrant communities in Belgium. Flemish discussions on migration about Islam before the "refugee crisis," were thus important in framing the "refugee crisis," meaning that older essentialist concerns about the unsuitability of the culture of the migrant Others were adapted to this new crisis format.

The refugee crisis also strengthened gendered ideas about migrants, revolving around the importance of defending the nation state against especially Muslim men and the liberation of Muslim women from their own cultural environment. Similar to other European countries, De Cleen et al. (2017) maintain, the refugee crisis was primarily presented as a crisis for the Belgian people and Europe, where right-wing anti-migration discourse highlighted the need to help those "really" in need and who respect the established asylum process, while stressing as well that these needs should be subordinate to Belgium's cultural and security needs.

In the right-wing extremists' rhetoric, different cultural values of Muslims and Flemish people are generally portrayed as the core of the problem (Mielants 2006: 318). This rhetorical approach has found fertile ground in

Antwerp, with the second-largest Muslim population in the country (after Brussels), most of whom are concentrated in a few neighborhoods. The city has, in recent years, been associated with the success of the extreme right in Belgium. Anti-immigration rhetoric is entangled with the politics of Flemish and Wallonians, where the right-wing extremists in Belgium have simultaneously normalized Flanders' separation from Belgium and anti-Muslim hatred (Mielants 2006: 318). Among some politicians in Brussels, the Flemish-speaking minority in the city has, however, been seen as equally "non-assimilable" as the Muslims (Mielants 2006: 315). An example of this dynamic is that the French-speaking Belgian youth of Belgian ancestry consider being called "Fleming" (Flemish) by youngsters of Moroccan background a "racist insult" (Dirk and Rea 2007: 9). Also, as described by Ceuppens, Vlaams Blok's rhetoric goes between different categorization of the Other ranging from "Muslim immigrants and asylum seekers to Francophone Belgians" (2006: 164).

When trying to understand Islamophobia in a localized context, I find Nadia Fadil's observations about Muslims in Belgium particularly relevant. She points out how public outrage over issues such as veiling works toward enforcing a certain sense of "we-ness" in a nation with already highly diversified "white" majority (2011: 86–87). Her insights draw attention to an internal division of Belgium between a Dutch-speaking Flemish population, French-speakers, and the small minority that is German-speaking. Her observations also highlight the economic disparities within Belgium itself, which creates a stronger need to create a coherent common enemy. Debates about Muslims as a "problem" thus create a "we-ness" among the white majority, which is itself fractured along the lines of ethnic identity, language, and income.

Despite all this, most of my respondents from Niger did not see racism as a big problem in their daily lives in Brussels and in its surrounding environment. This probably is partly due to how they live in segregated communities and most do not engage with non-migrants. Mohammed, who has lived in Belgium for only a year, tells me that before he came to Antwerp, he had heard that it was racist and home to many extremists. However, he tells me that the only thing that he experienced while living there for a few months and trying to get work was that not being able to speak Flemish made things difficult. "And this . . ." he says, "I think this is not racism. This is just normal." He adds, "it is just like if you come to Brussels and you don't speak French then you will not get job there. If you would speak only Icelandic, for example, they would not hire you. This is just normal that the Flemish say that you have to speak the language to get a job."

But then he tells me of an encounter which clearly indicates racism was involved. He had gone to the post office to pick up a package. A postal worker pushed a paper to him and said *"handtekening."* He explains to me: "I tried to ask 'What is *handtekening*? I do not understand what is *handtekening*. I don't speak Dutch, please.'" The man asked him why he had come to Antwerp when he could not speak Dutch. Mohammed says, somewhat painfully, "I thought that was not fair."

Idrissa states firmly: "Here in Belgium there is not much racism, not against those who are Black, nor toward foreigners, not against Muslims. However, if you do not speak the language . . . I, for example, speak French, but I don't speak Flemish. If I would speak the language, then they would not . . . That is not racism, but it is like that. But if you have papers, then you are equal. Equality and justice and human rights. Because of this, there is no racism in Belgium." Often these claims of Belgium as a space of non-racism are still contradictory and contextual. Even though Salim begins, for example, with stating that there is no racism in Brussels, he emphasizes later when talking about his difficulties in getting permission to stay in Belgium, that this is racism. This is in line with research stressing the structural racism embedded in border controls. Salim explains that honest people like himself are not asking for anything from the state; they are just trying to get by but are treated as criminals due to their lack of a visa. He asks if this cannot be considered as a form of terrorism, at least a psychological one?

Research also shows that the perception of Belgium as existing outside racism is unfortunately incorrect. Research from the late 1990s has, for example, indicated that police officers in Brussels associate young people with migrant backgrounds with delinquency and migrants in general with crime (Hebberecht 1997: 166). Many police officers target young people especially, using verbal racism (Hebberecht 1997: 167). Mazzocchetti (2012) speaks of the dual stigmatization in Brussels of youth with immigrant backgrounds from North and sub-Saharan Africa, due to on the one hand their "skin colour, which locks them in an irreducible otherness," and on the other sociopolitical and socioeconomic discrimination. While skin color makes them visible as targets of discrimination, the sociopolitical and socioeconomic discrimination makes them invisible political and rights-holding subjects (Mazzocchetti 2012). In fact, when I read other works on racism in Brussels, I start to wonder if my interlocutors' lack of extensive experience with racist insults or comments constitutes primarily a reflection of their social isolation from mainstream society. As indicated, many of those I interviewed live in highly secluded environments and are careful not to step out of their milieu unless necessary. They keep to the back of the "hotel," to use Sarah Gibson's (2006) metaphor, doing the hard labor that others do not want to do, but staying out of the way and out of sight. When Youssouf tells me that he never goes to the tourist areas in Brussels, I ask: "So your whole life is here in Anderlecht?" He smiles and repeats, "All my life is here in Anderlecht."

Fearing the Muslim Other

As we have seen in previous chapters there is a strong negative metanarrative on precarious mobility from South to North, reflected in the emphasis of politicians and the media on statistics of migration "flows" (Fekete 2009), the crisis that this mobility causes for Europe (Lüthi 2017), and the vivid vocabulary used to describe these individuals as a "mass" and "hordes" (Fekete 2009: 24).

For my interlocutors, current electronic globalization links them with each other and with their communities back home, while it also makes it possible for them to recognize the place they occupy, within a larger complex global mediascape as male migrants from Africa. The strong insistence of these men that they are not interested in Europe, indicates how our conversations are unavoidably embedded within a larger global media discourse (the topic of Chapter 2), that is, the framing of Muslims and migrants as possible terrorist threats and how Muslims in general are seen as a threat to Europe. This mediascape must be understood as institutionalized, commercialized, and claimed by different subjects (Baker and Blaagaard 2016: 1; Sumiala et al. 2016). In our conversations, these Nigeriens are speaking against these assumptions and addressing larger global media discussions that form an intense part of their intimate environment, as it does mine. These are discussions where migrants from Africa are portrayed as a collective danger pushing at Europe's border, desiring nothing more than to seize the native population's hard-earned and taxpayer-funded benefits.

Thus, these men were often replying to questions that I had not asked, as if I had unwittingly entered in the middle of their conversation with someone else. Their strong reification of "Europe" in conversations with me indicates an awareness and employment of the same discourse predominant in the current mediascape, in that they are responding indirectly to these depictions of themselves as Black Muslims and African men invading Europe. One example is when they feel the need to state that they were not migrating to Europe to initiate some kind of violence against its occupants. The issues that they decide to discuss with me can thus be seen as one form of resistance to current images of migration, Muslims, and Blackness.[1]

What is also significant is that through their discussions of Europe, which included comments such as "not wanting to be in Europe," or in their emphasis of "Europe" as contributing to Niger's poverty, "Europe" becomes a "tangible" construct. This is similar to what Herzfeld argues in relation to the nation-state: It becomes real through critics and supporters talking about "it" (2016: 6). By referring to "Europe" when talking about their different experiences in European cities (e.g., Brussels, Naples, and Milan), these men participate thus as others in Europe, in the framing of "Europe" as a "real" and solid construct, even though Europe is addressed critically. Europe is still not a uniform place but is hierarchically ranked. As stated earlier, when I talk to migrants in northern Italy, some of them hold on to the hope of better lives by believing that if only they can work in Northern Europe then their lives will be better, as if their precarity is due to that they are stuck in the southern part of Europe.

The voices of these men expose some inherent weaknesses of the meta-narrative of migration from South to North and of Europe as a destination invaded by migrants wanting to settle there. Again and again in my interviews, different individuals emphasized that if things were not so difficult back home in Niger, they would prefer to live near or with their extended families. Most of my interlocutors have left behind families, usually wives and children but also in some cases parents and siblings. Almost everyone I spoke to explained their stay in Belgium as primarily due to necessity, not because they had an interest in Europe or Belgium per se. I heard the same in Italy. They stressed that they left Niger for two simple reasons: poverty and lack of opportunities.

I was asked in nearly every interview, even by those with whom I had spoken many times before: "You have seen the conditions in Niger, yes?" This was not a question so much as a reminder that as someone who had in fact once lived in Niger, I really should be able to understand the reasons for their departure. When I asked Youssouf about Niger, for example, he started, as others have, to speak about the corruption and poverty in Niger, and then added how Niger is really a rich country in terms of its resources but still the people who live there are stuck in pervasive poverty. "My country Niger; we have so many resources. Who takes them? The French do. How many die because they don't have anything to eat?"

Youssouf goes on to explain that not only foreign government and corporations are to blame for this situation but also corrupt Nigerien politicians. "If you are a politician, you just take the money and take it to a European bank, such as to Switzerland, and keep it for your own family." He adds, "Niger is not a poor country. There is no justice in this, there is just no justice." I can hear the anger in his voice. He stops talking and then smiles again. "I am really sorry," he says. "I just get really upset when I go into this."

In Ardo's room, I again meet the young Hausa man, Mohammad, whom I have met a few times before. He has told me previously, that he came to

Europe in 2010, by paying smugglers to take him from Libya to Italy. He stayed in Italy for a few years, but the economic opportunities were scarce, so he decided to migrate further north and ended in Belgium. When I ask him about his family, he tells me that his parents died a few years back and avoids further questions on his family circumstances back home. I always seem to find him in a good mood, even when he is struggling to find work. This time, he is on his way out to follow up on a possible job, and we exchange just few words: "Did someone tell you that they found gold in Niger recently?" he asks me. "Well, not that it matters much. Some European company will take the profit and the people of Niger will not get anything. This is why I must go to Europe. Because Europe takes everything from us with only poverty remaining." He laughs and tells me, smiling, "You see all the wealth of Niger goes to Europe and thus I just go. I followed the wealth to Europe." He adds more seriously, "we have to go to Europe to have a future."

The stories of Youssouf, Ardo, and others become particularly salient as they emphasize an inherent contradiction in the way in which they are depicted in the Western media: poor African migrant men desiring Europe's wealth as they try to escape their home countries, which have somehow failed to develop or have taken longer to develop than we have in the North. Or so the story goes. What then about this place they come from? What about Niger? Are the migrants' countries of origin relevant to their story of mobility and migration?

NOTE

1. Other forms of resistance would include an emphasis that in coherence with being Muslims, they try to treat others with respect in spite of all these difficulties they have to endure, as well as more direct engagement with these depictions through direct activism.

PART II

Entangled Histories

CHAPTER
6

This Is All in the Past Now
Niger and a Global World

When I came to Niger in 1996, it was considered the poorest country in the world, as three years earlier it had been ranked last by the Human Development Index[1] (United Nations Development Programme [UNDP] 1996: 29). Nearly thirty years later, Niger was still placed on the bottom of that list (United Nations Development Programme [UNDP] 2020).

Traditional theories of modernization would see this as a sign that the country was located outside modernity and behind the flows of history. While such stories of people living outside of history have long ago been rebuked by anthropologists and historians, they persist in popular and political imagination. These ideas provide the subtext to media stories focusing on migration from Africa to Europe, where it is assumed that people are migrating due to an ahistorical condition called "poverty." Current depictions produced by international development organizations and corporations help to sustain such images, through stories of people in Africa who "have to be taught" how to do this and that, in many cases failing to address how this poverty has been produced. Similarly, contemporary narratives of African men in the Global North often ignore the continuous involvement of Europe in Africa (Bakewell and de Haas 2007).

Although Niger is just one of many countries where precarious migrants in Europe come from, I find it necessary to briefly review parts of its history, particularly in the context of persistent stories of migrants "invading" Europe, by making visible the shared histories of what we generally see as different parts of the world. As the stories of my interlocutors reflect, Niger today cannot be understood without the historical context of colonialism, even though it cannot also be reduced to that history. Further, migration through and from Niger also cannot be understood without this historical and contemporary context.

If we understand modernity not as something singular but as multiple or parallel phenomena, as several scholars have theorized (Englund and Leach 2000: 227; Larkin 1997), then the kind of modernity that we see in Niger has to be recognized as related to modernity in other places. When I listened to Nigeriens like Karim, what came to mind was Laura Ann Stoler's (2008) concept of "ruination." Ruination draws attention to continuous processes of colonialization and imperialism that not only filter from the past into the present but continue to take new shapes and to be a part of people's lives in some places. How, Stoler asks, are "the effects of empire . . . reactivated" (2013: 11), while also being reformulated in new forms of governance in people's lives? What kind of ruination continues?

Part of the process of reducing economic migrants to faceless and ahistorical subjects is to exclude their histories of origin and their background, which also works toward the imagination of Europe's current and historical innocence in regard to world inequalities. This is another reason why I find it important to include a brief discussion about Niger, the country from which my interlocutors come and the place around which their aspirations for the future revolve.

Niger, Mobility, and "Developscape"

I do not remember ever having seen in Iceland any news on Niger, unless connected to poverty, corruption, or misery. In the Global North, Niger appears as yet another West African country stuck in ahistorical poverty and a premodern past (see Mann 2015). However, the history of people living in this region, that we now call Niger, is one of great empires and kingdoms (see for example Lenshie and Ayokhai 2013), involving active and dynamic interconnections with other parts of the world, one that has been a part of wider historical processes.

Mobility has been particularly important for people living in this area, due to its location as a part of the Sahara and the Sahel zone where rainfall is scarce and unpredictable. In fact, mobility has constituted an integral part of West Africa's history and its population's survival in these constantly changing Sahara and Sahel environments. So rather than constituting something entirely new, migration from West Africa to Europe is a continuation of older migration patterns, by people endowed with resilience and innovation (Bakewell and de Haas 2007; Rain 1999; Adeniran

2020). Migration today, however, is also shaped by West Africa and Europe's shared past through colonialism and imperialism even though that is often forgotten in contemporary discussions (Bakewell and de Haas 2007).

In 2019, Niger's population was estimated at twenty-three million ("Population, total—Niger" 2019). The overwhelming majority—about 95 percent—are Muslim, with most people living in the south of the country and most people subsisting on small-scale farming, cattle herding, or fishing. As my interlocutors emphasize to me, even though Niger is one of the poorest countries in the world, it is still a "rich" country in terms of its natural resources, having, for example, one of the world's largest uranium deposits (Afifi 2011: 96). Niger relies heavily on international aid, where according to Afifi writing in 2011, half of the governmental budget is provided from foreign donors (Afifi 2011: 96).

Niger is inhabited by Hausa, Zarma-Songhai, Fulani, Kanuri, Tuareg, and Toubou, in addition to smaller ethnic groups (Alidou 2005: 11). Colonial government in Niger emphasized, as elsewhere, the rigid listing and organization of ethnicities and culture into distinct groups, drawing clear boundaries between different ethnicities. Anthropologists have long criticized the reification that was involved in ethnic categorization during colonial times (Wright 1999). In the context of Niger, Ousseina D. Alidou stresses the danger of reifying different ethnic categories, pointing out that the reality is dynamic and complex; ethnic and cultural blending is not an exception, but a constant (2005: 8). Alidou uses the term *brassage Sahélien* to capture this dynamic reality of the Sahel region. Additionally, by 1977, Nigerien historian, Djibo Hamani, warned against essentializing different ethnicities in Niger. When Hamani pointed out the tendency to see light Tuareg and dark Hausa as completely distinctive and separated ethnicities, he was probably to some extent addressing the racism that has long been embedded in the colonial classifications in Niger (Hamani 1977: 2–3).[2] At the same time that the colonialists reified ethnicity, they did not hesitate to draw different territorial boundaries dividing French and British colonial possessions so that they cut across the existing states, as was the case with the Hausa people who now live in northern Nigeria and southern Niger (Rain 1999: 46).

The French colonial government ranked ethnicities in accordance with their own European racist categorization. They were, for example, much more interested in the Tuaregs than in the Hausa, having respect for the former but almost a contempt for the latter (see Roberts 1981: 196). The case was similar for the Fulani, who were cast in Europe as both distinctive racially from the Hausa and as superior to them (Loftsdóttir 2008). While exoticizing nomadic groups, the French colonial government actively worked toward suppressing the Tuaregs and other mobile populations in Niger. The colonial government actively tried to reduce or erase the mobility of pastoral people, which they believed should disappear with modernization (Loftsdóttir 2008). Deycard argues that late nineteenth-century colonial accounts of the area that now is Niger reflect the "ambiguity between the fascination and the will to annihilate any form of Tuareg political control over these territories" (2012: 55). The division of the Sahel and Sahara into different nation states, with fixed borders, meant that land and resources of Tuaregs in the north of Niger became divided between several states, which hindered their mobility considerably. This also meant that members of this diverse ethnic group became scattered in different countries, which imposed on them new national identities (Alidou 2005: 173; Snorek 2016). For nomadic Tuaregs, as for most pastoral populations in Niger and in the world, extensive mobility is not only a way of using certain ecological resources and conditions but integrated into their identity.

When Niger gained independence in 1960, it retained, as did most other African countries, the administrative structures set in place by the colonial government (Alidou 2005: 174). Rural farmers and pastoral people remained economically marginalized (Alidou 2005: 174). Meanwhile, uniform peanut production spread quickly in the Sahel area, as Franke and Chasin (1980) have discussed, first due to the emphasis placed on this crop by the colonial government, which then continued in independent Niger with international development assistance. From 1961, the development of new varieties led to an even greater expansion of peanut production into areas where it had not been possible to cultivate before (Franke and Chasin 1980: 65–66; see also Roberts 1981: 204–5). This pushed pastoral societies further north closer to the arid regions of the Sahara which increased the risk of drought to nomadic and sedentary populations alike.

Once Niger shook off colonial rule, self-sufficiency in staple food grains became an overriding national goal. This effort was supported by significant amounts of development assistance and was supposed to be initiated through the promotion of more intensive rainfed agriculture, based on "new or modified agricultural techniques" (Painter 1987: 149). But by 1984, it was evident that the increased production of rainfed crops was not the result of greater yields per hectare, but due to larger areas being cultivated. As Thomas M. Painter's discussion shows, these projects were based on "standard" solutions that were not well adapted to the conditions faced by peasants in Niger (Painter 1987: 150). This ill-fated drive to multiply agricultural productivity was shared with other Sahel countries, all of which saw disappointing results despite the large investments (Painter 1991: 1).

Serious drought in the area in the 1970s, and then again in 1984 to 1985 led to famine and massive population displacement. Large development institutions, however, generally ignored the historical and political reasons for herders' increased difficulties and saw Niger's problems as stemming

Figure 6.1. A woman and her child in the town Tchintabaraden in Niger in 1996. © Kristín Loftsdóttir.

from the herder's inability to adapt to evolving conditions (Franke and Chasin 1980: 212). In the aftermath of the droughts in 1968 to 1974, many people who had earlier been engaged in pastoralism or rural agriculture migrated to the city (see Beauvilain 1977: 191; Swift 1984: 489). The drought forced many young Tuareg men to migrate to Libya and Algeria, many of whom returned to Niger in the 1980s after the government promised to assist with their resettlement. The failure to deliver on this promise further increased the sense of isolation felt by many Tuaregs within the Niger state (Afifi 2011: 105; Snorek 2016).

Like many of its neighboring countries, Niger was obligated to accept Structural Adjustment Programs (SAPs) imposed by the International Monetary Fund (IMF) in the mid-1990s. These programs demanded privatization of national industries and the extreme reduction of basic social services, such as health care and education, in addition to food subsidies (Youngstedt, Keough, and Idrissa 2016; Keough and Youngstedt 2019; Olivier de Sardan 2011). The consequences of these measures in Niger were extremely severe, leading to an increased gap between social classes (Alidou 2005: 193) and an increased dependency on aid (Olivier de Sardan 2011: 33). The SAP's policy increased poverty with diverse and multiple effects on the local population. Scott Youngstedt et al. point out, for example, that SAPs resulted in water no longer being a state-owned resource. In 2001, the multinational corporation Vivendi Water (which later changed its name to Veolia Water), with headquarters in France, bought a fifty-one percent share of Niamey's water utility (Youngstedt et al. 2016; Keough and Youngstedt 2019).

Further, Alidou points out, due to the SAP's policies many young Nigerien women resorted to prostitution, to survive or support their families. Clients were not only local men, but also expatriate workers from various international organizations (2005: 193).

It was in the context of this extreme poverty that the people I knew in Niger in the late 1990s lived. What struck me most at that time was the integration of the country into what I viewed as a "developscape" (Loftsdóttir 2009). In creating this term, I relied on Appadurai's (1996) classic identification of globalization as a process of disjuncture which creates different and to some extent separate "landscapes" of people, money, images, and technology. As such, the developscape consists of the tangible and intangible elements associated with progress and development, such as billboards advertising the success of various projects, buildings, and cars, all of which are embedded in ideas of modernization.

The developscape also has to do with the mobility of experts from the Global North that come to "fix" these various problems. Gregory Mann demonstrates that the role of NGOs has become so intense that after the Sahel drought in the 1970s, the NGOs in the West African Sahel, had become "new forms of governmental rationality" (2015: 2) often taking over decisions normally made by the state or governing alongside them (2015: 244). These experts along with those from international or national institutions—which often are "white" and Western—drive around in large and powerful jeeps or SUVs and organize and execute various policies within countries like Niger that shape people's lives in multiple ways, but also contribute to creating different subjectivities that take on racialized forms. Mann (2015) captures their visual effects and power well when referring to the check points at highways between administrative districts; where those waiting to be allowed through or sitting at the side of the road watch the NGO's vehicles pass easily through or as phrased by Mann: "It's the NGOs that are on the move. They are visible, powerful and appear unstoppable" (2015: 166).

In the more affluent parts of the world, the developscape consists of images and categorization of the "developing world." Development organization along with public and policy discourses promote certain ideas, which then serve to divide the world into countries that are developed and those that need "development." The relationships maintained between countries are informed but also constrained by such ideas and by the praxis of development. The suffering of the African body has long been popularized through the media, where the care of strangers traveling to distant lands is given a leading role (Bornstein and Redfield 2010). Here again, mobility of experts from the Global North is seen as natural and self-evident, while those in the "developing" countries are portrayed as waiting to be acted on by the generosity of those in the Global North. The more recent mobility of this population "into" Europe contributes to the images of the developscape in the Global North, i.e., that migration from the African continent to Europe is in some way unnatural and new, constituting a "flood" of people.

The developscape thus underlies and informs the global nature of development and the movement of people and their desires, influencing local settings which are then appropriated and modified in these localities. Simultaneously, the physical and emotional presence of development also shows the interconnection between different parts of the world. Thus, while various aid workers that I talked to during my research in the late 1990s emphasized Niger's isolation and lack of development, the opposite seemed true to me. I was also struck by the sheer numbers—perhaps even excessive—of people working in the developscape, and by the collective blindness of many to how they unthinkingly reproduced colonial power structures through their daily praxis in Niger (see discussion in Loftsdóttir 2009).

Toward Increased Militarization and Restricted Mobility

People in precarious situations are not necessarily interested in speaking about their difficulties and lives to strangers. As an Italian colleague pointed out to me, refugees and asylum seekers in Italy grew tired of speaking to journalists as nothing seemed to change as a result of them speaking out. When people decided to talk to me for my research there were two main reasons that explained their willingness to speak to me. In fact, I believe these two aspects were, in most cases, the reasons that most people were willing to talk to me at all. First, and perhaps most crucially, was that I had once lived in Niger with marginalized people, even though a very long time ago. When my Nigerien friends approached others to ask them if they were willing to talk to me, I saw how the interest changed from non-existent to more positive, once they learned I had lived in Niger.[3] People seemed to feel that as I had lived in Niger in difficult conditions, I should therefore be able to recognize the poverty that dominated their lives in Niger. At the same time, they assumed that as I had lived with local people and shared their lives, I must also have been able to understand the joys of life in Niger and that in spite of it all, Niger is a good place with good people. The possibility that I was familiar with the pleasures of life in Niger seemed to be the second key reason people were willing to talk to me.

My interlocutors told me that things are even more difficult now than when I lived in Niger, as is well documented in recent scholarship relating to Niger. During the last two decades, difficulties have intensified greatly, particularly with regard to increased insecurities connected to the global War on Terror and the strategic importance of Niger for the West in that context (Elischer and Mueller 2018: 1), as well as an emphasis of the EU to externalize migration controls (Majcher et al. 2020; Tinti and Westcott 2016).

After the September 11 attacks on the United States in 2001, Niger was pulled into the global war on terrorism, and was labelled as one of the "frontline states" which implied that the country might possibly be a terrorist breeding ground (Göpfert 2012: 58). In 2003, Niger joined the Pan-Sahel Initiative, funded by the US State Department, and was tasked with training Sahelian military units to fight against terrorism in the area. In 2007, Niger also became a member of the Trans-Saharan Counterterrorism Initiative, also initiated by US agencies to address perceived increased terrorist risks in the Sahel. After 2011, the EU then became active in the Sahel area, citing strong security concerns (Elischer and Mueller 2018; Idrissa 2019). Further increased militarization of the region is reflected in the recent building of US drone bases in Niamey and Agadez (Ajala 2018), which have used armed drones since 2018 (Schmitt 2018).

Niger has become one of the largest recipients of aid from the EU Trust Fund for Africa, established in 2015, which was largely aimed at migration control (Majcher et al. 2020: 462). Majcher et al. describe the Fund as an "important current tool" to externalize EU migration controls (2020: 462; see also van Dessel 2019). As indicated by Idrissa, this means that Niger became "Europe's immigration officer" (2019: 30). In 2016, Niger became "the focus of EU financed migration-related projects," with the combined value of these projects being nearly 200 million EUR (Majcher et al. 2020: 462). This effort has been criticized strongly, particularly regarding "questionable voluntary return" (463). Niger's role here started with EU's emphasis on Niger as a partner in security measures; in 2012 the EU set up EUCAP Sahel Niger whose role was to "reinforce the capacities of Nigerien security forces" (Idrissa 2019: 30) as well as pressuring the country with massive funding to adopt legislation in 2015, in which migrant transport was criminalized (31). Rahmane Idrissa points out that between 2016 and early 2018, military personnel in Niger's desert bases grew from 200 to 450, benefiting from EU funding of various military related equipment and trainings (Idrissa 2019: 31). A Frontex liaison office was then opened in Niger by the EU in 2017 to further strengthen the border control with Libya (Idrissa 2019: 31). As Idrissa (2019) describes it, this recent militarization and security focus on Niger by the EU is due to the increased importance of Niger in regard to migration to Europe. At the beginning of a new millennium most migrants from West Africa went through Mali, while most of those going through Niger ended in Libya (Idrissa 2019: 30). As discussed earlier, with the fall of Gaddafi's regime and the civil war, migrants there had to decide either to return, stay, or take the sea route to Europe. Political unrest in Mali—which was also affected by Gaddafi's death—compelled more people to take the road through Niger and especially Agadez for migration to Europe (Idrissa 2019: 30). Niger has thus become a transit hub for migrants seeking to cross the Sahara en route to Europe (Schapendonk 2011: 120); according to Peter Tinti and Tom Westcott, half of the migrants that came to Lampedusa in 2014 had transited through Agadez in Niger (2016: 9). Consequently, the EU started paying interest to the migrant transport industries in Niger, which had developed earlier for migrants going to Libya but were then not of any interest to the EU as these migrants did not end up in Europe (Idrissa 2019: 30). These transport industries, notably, do not necessarily revolve around travel to Europe, with locations such as Agadez being historically important for mobilities across different parts of West and North Africa (Xchange 2019).

Conflicts in North and West Africa, along with persistent poverty, have in general intensified migration to and from Niger. Its geopolitical location, situated between sub-Saharan Africa and the Maghreb, have made Niger a

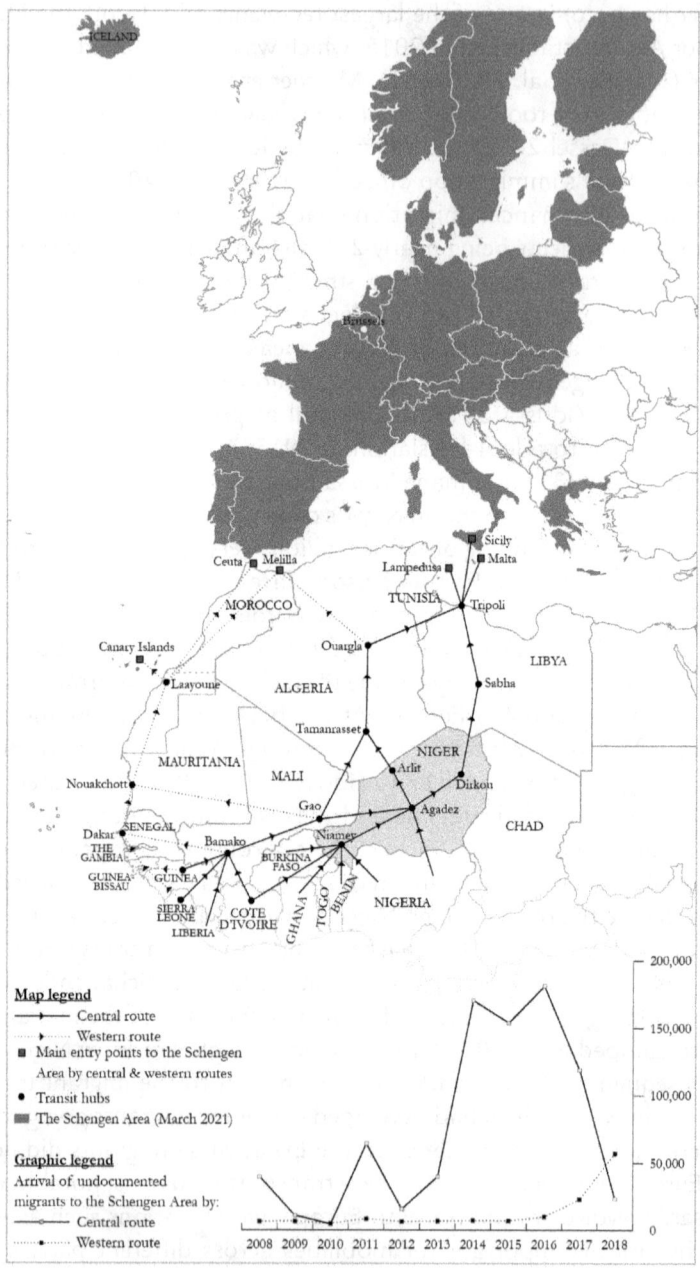

Map 6.1. Map of the main African central and western migration routes to the European Schengen Area, used by undocumented migrants between 2008 and 2018. Source of data: Frontex and IOM. © Kristín Loftsdóttir, Ignacio Fradejas-García, and Jana Ohanesyan.

major transit zone in recent years for migrants either on their way to Europe or returning home from Libya and Algeria or other conflict zones (Koser 2011: 3; Youngstedt 2012). While some are displaced people of various nationalities escaping the conflicts in the north (Koser 2011: 3), and en route back to their countries of origin (Veronese et al. 2019), others are going through the Sahara in hope of ending up in Europe (Schapendonk 2008: 130). Again, migration to Niger is not explained by better conditions there, but, as indicated, is mainly due to increased conflicts in the neighboring countries (Youngstedt 2012: 4), and the continued stress of European leaders to externalize Europe's borders (Majcher et al. 2020; Idrissa 2019). Civil war in Côte d'Ivoire in 2002 to 2004, and then again in 2011, led to many Nigeriens living there fleeing back to Niger, with some landing in refugee camps. Malien refugees fled to Niger after conflicts in Mali in 2012 that involved Tuareg uprisings in the country. In addition, the terrorism of the Boko Haram Islamist movements in the northern part of Nigeria led both Nigerians and Nigeriens working there to seek shelter in Niger (Youngstedt 2012: 5-6; see also discussion in Adeniran 2020: 43-49). Contemporary alarmist narratives in Europe and the United States of the migration of desperate people escaping war and conflict seem to forget the fact that it is actually countries outside of Europe that bear the major brunt of refugees and asylum seekers (Koser 2011).

Julien Brachet's (2016) discussion of policies concerning the International Organization for Migration (IOM) illustrates the intensity of this control of mobility as well as its multiple ramifications. He stresses—as has been indicated in different chapters here—that control of mobility no longer centers just on the borders of the Schengen area, but is externalized to the coastline in north and western Africa, which have become a buffer zone, with various actions taken to slow down migrants. The third frontier, Brachet points out, is the Sahara itself which, as we can see from Idrissa's discussion above, has also become Europe's border (2016: 276). Brachet (2016) stresses that the wealthiest and most powerful governments are especially active in management of migration and employ to that end international organizations as well as supranational organizations and agencies such as the EU and Frontex. IOM is the most important organization worldwide in terms of managing migration and depends, for example, for the most part on donations from individual states that are used to implement special projects, so as phrased by Brachet "project put into practice correspond to the expectations of their sponsors" (2016: 275; see also discussion in van Dessel 2019).

Idrissa's interviews with officials in Niger reveals that, in addition to the humanitarian factors, Niger accepted to cooperate with the EU to combat against migration largely because of the funding provided. Here the difficult and violent circumstances in the neighboring countries are important, along with the extensive number of refugees that Niger hosts (2019: 31). As Idrissa points out, in his analysis of these changes it is really alarming how "Niger's security personnel have internalized the notion that a migrant—and not just the so-called human trafficker—is a criminal" (2019: 34). This means that even those who are migrating in West Africa with no intention of continuing to Europe are also intercepted (Idrissa 2019: 34; Xchange 2019). Thus, as reported by Brachet: "Europe attempts not only to control entries in its territory but also movements within the African continent" (2016: 276). This is done both by these direct interventions, i.e., military assistance to police the borders, but also through making all migration suspicious.[4] The IOM along with various NGOs have thus embarked on campaigns that try to discourage migration to the north and try to advocate "voluntary" return (Brachet 2016; see also Rodriguez 2019). Through these various initiatives, all mobility across the Sahara is reduced to a potential transcontinental migration (Brachet 2016: 276). Here again, it has to be stressed that mobility has been a key survival strategy in the north of Niger with various relations with the neighboring states, and a long history of communities in the north assisting with mobility of goods and people (Tinti and Westcott 2016; Adeniran 2020; Xchange 2019). Thus, considering especially the role of various forms of mobility, historically for Niger and for those living in the Sahel area and the Sahara, this is a radical intervention into people's lives in this part of the world.

Also, Idrissa points out in his 2019 report that the benefits of all this massive EU funding is not visible to the general public in the country. What is visible is new infrastructure, such as hotels, a thermal power plant, and a third bridge over the river that runs through the capital. Officials at the Ministry of Interior claimed in the interviews that was because the EU had not provided funding for the social sector, which as, Idrissa claims, is impossible to verify. The government has, however, during this time imposed new taxes and raised electricity and water rates, which according to Idrissa, is so that they are "barely affordable to the country's small middle class, let alone the underprivileged majority" (2019: 34). There have also been delays in meeting payrolls, with those protesting jailed and any critical media being harassed or shut down (Idrissa 2019: 35). As Idrissa concludes, for the majority in the country, Niger's collaboration with European leaders in this regard is seen as a loss of the country's independence (2019: 35).

EU officials have claimed that the Migration Partnership Framework is already working, citing IOM data showing that human transit through Niger to Libya has lessened. Peter Tinti (2017) suggests that this could just as well be due to smugglers changing routes to avoid detection, with usually low-level operatives being targeted in such efforts. Tinti stresses that these are not "meaningful measures to offer alternatives to irregular migration" (2017) but rather increased border patrol and law enforcements regulations forces migrants into paying more to smugglers and taking more risks.

The systematic poverty that sparks migration from Niger has thus accelerated in the present. Also, the groups making up that migration come not only from those traditionally based on pastoralism but also other groups such as the Hausa (Youngstedt 2012). Destination countries for these migrants include the Côte d'Ivoire, Burkina Faso, and Nigeria (Afifi 2011: 105), along with countries farther afield. Nigeriens have formed expat communities in different European cities, as well as in, for example, New York (Stoller and McConatha 2001; Reynolds and Youngstedt 2004; Youngstedt 2004b). In southern Niger, poverty and food insecurity have stimulated migration from rural areas to cities. For many, as earlier mentioned, an important coping strategy seasonally and during periods of droughts is temporary household migration (Afifi 2011).

Part of Niger's militarization has also revolved around the country's most valuable resource—uranium. Niger is one of the world's largest uranium producers (Elischer 2013). The mines are in areas where Tuareg have been in great majority, where poverty is extreme in spite of the wealth generated there (Flynn and de Clercq 2014). A report by Greenpeace on the Arlit area of the Sahara, conducted in collaboration with other organizations, indicates a complete disregard for local health in the process of extracting uranium from these mines, including water contamination, draining of aquifers, as well as hints of exposure to radioactive dust (Dixon et al. 2010). According to the report, only a few studies exist on the consequences of this on human health and the environment, while it is clear that radioactivity levels are unacceptable (Dixon et al. 2010). For many years, the French company Arveva monopolized production of uranium in Niger, but today more companies have been permitted by the Nigerien state to come to the table, including in 2007 the Chinese company Somina (Grégoire 2011).

Recently, rebellion movements have protested the deplorable conditions the operators of the uranium mines have created (McGregor 2007). The group *Le Movement des Nigeriens pour la Justice* (MNJ), led by Tuaregs, has forcefully protested the marginalization of the local population in the mine operations, as well as the environmental degradation it has produced. Instability in the area has prompted France to deploy soldiers to protect the mines, which created militarized zones in the northern part of the country (Elischer 2013). While Niger's president tried to suppress news coming from the area, the rebels actively utilized new communication technologies to promote their cause (McGregor 2007: 8). As indicated earlier, Tuaregs have for long felt economically marginalized and discriminated against by the Niger state, and they are increasingly perceived as a security threat by the state, partly due to fear of rebellion in the north (Elischer 2013).

Uranium mining in Niger is exceptionally lucrative: in 2010 alone, the export value of the country's uranium was 348 million euros (Larsen and Mamosso 2013). Larsen and Mamosso (2013) point out that this export value is more than twice the total financial development assistance Niger received during the same year. They also claim that the benefits brought by the uranium mining industry has primarily been externalized, with most of the uranium being exported to the EU, mainly to France. In fact, according to Elischer (2013), Niger's uranium provides France with about three-quarters of its energy. In recent years, Larsen and Mamosso (2013) argue, uranium revenues received by the state of Niger correspond to only around twenty percent of the export value, and the revenues have "not yet responded to the increase in sales prices" (2013: 18).

Seeing little financial benefit from the mining activities in Niger, the local population has suffered increased poverty and pollution (see discussion in Larsen and Mamosso 2013). Larsen and Mamosso set these human rights violations in the context of activities conducted by the various international development organizations operating in Niger, claiming that they focus on the economic aspects of the uranium sector in Niger with little regard to the cost to local people in terms of their environment and health. They state:

> In the joint evaluation of the 2000–2008 cooperation with the European Commission, Belgium, France, Denmark and Luxembourg ... attention is paid to the economic potential of the uranium mining sector and concerns are raised regarding transparent and democratic revenue distribution. However, no reference is made to environmental impacts or risks associated with uranium mining. (Larsen and Mamosso 2013: 22)

Uranium in Niger was invoked in the West during the US's Bush-era invasion of Iraq to overthrow Saddam Hussein, which included false claims that Iraq was buying uranium from Niger (Wilson and Wilson 2013). In addition to global attention to its uranium deposits, interest in Niger has accelerated in the Western media in the last few years, as Sebastian Elischer and Lisa Mueller (2018) have pointed out. A great deal of that interest, they say, has focused on attacks by extremist groups and Islamic fundamentalists, in addition to reports on the kidnapping of Westerners in Niger (Elischer and Mueller 2018: 8–9). As they show in their analysis of armed conflicts, most attacks are on the state, not on foreigners, and the attacks affect the government more than civilians. The attacks in which civilians have died have usually been targeted at the state (2018: 9).

The end of Gaddafi's regime in Libya meant that small arms and weapons became far more accessible in the Sahel and Sahara region. While some of these weapons had allegedly been provided by the United States and Europe to those protesting in Libya, they are now used by those seen as rebels and terrorists (Danjibo 2013: 17–19).

In addition, corruption has been a persistent problem. Ousseina Alidou claims that international foreign aid allocated to Sahel has been misappropriated by various regimes in Niger and that "revenues generated by uranium and coal mines benefited mainly the ruling political leaders" (2005: 174). Olivier de Sardan's (2011) analysis of the provision of public goods in Niger, indicates a sense of prevailing corruption, which takes place at most levels of the government (see also Keough and Youngstedt 2019: 47).

The people I spoke with in Europe recognized these problems, seeing them as symbols of the continued corruption of the ruling elite in the country and the continued interests of more powerful European countries and the United States in the affairs of Niger to promote their own political and economic interests. It was striking how uniform the accounts of this situation from different individuals were both in northern Italy and Belgium. For example, in Milan, Karim explains to me that the "Americans" come "into our countries, Niger, Mali, and they put militaries there. We [the nationals of these countries] don't have problems, we are living our lives in peace. We don't have problems, but why do they bring arms? We have also an army. Our own army can defend us; why are they bringing their own?" When I speak over the phone to one of my old friends in Niger and ask him how things are in the present, he tells me things have changed a great deal since I was there. "Now there are always big airplanes flying over from different foreign armies." After a moment of silence, he adds: "People are afraid."

My research for this project did not initially focus on Niger. In my early interviews, I did not ask much about Niger directly. However, as I read through the transcripts and my notes, I was struck by how the conversations constantly revolved around the country or went back to it. Many of these men had been away for several years, but they kept in contact with their families and friends through various information technologies. They kept up on events happening there on an everyday basis, demonstrating how much of their lives are engaged with Niger. It was Niger, not Europe, that was the focus of their attention even though most of their lives were unfolding in Europe. And while they were extremely critical of their life in Niger, and my first-hand knowledge of the poverty there was important to them, equally vital was my acknowledgment and understanding that Niger was a good place. That Niger was, in spite of all this, a place with kind people, strong family and ethics, and that it should be recognized as such.

Figure 6.2. The author celebrating with young WoDaaBe girls in the pastoral area in Niger in 1998. © Kristín Loftsdóttir.

It is easy to recall this aspect of Niger, which I encountered every day when I lived there. In Niamey, the street and public areas are vibrant and sociable with the most common jobs taking place outdoors. People usually know their neighbors and engage generally in intensive but pleasant social interaction on an everyday basis (Keough and Youngstedt 2019: 48–49). I also remember the strong bonds and support for one's family, respect for elderly people regardless of if they were related to you or not or from the same ethnic group, generosity toward those who were poor, even among those who were poor themselves. I saw people's respect and kindness in mundane interactions, not only toward me as a foreigner but in interactions with others. Casual, pleasant conversations happened when taking transport in Niamey or just shopping at the market. But also, people were willing to assist, for example, when I, along with two WoDaaBe friends, had to move from the camp where I was staying in the bush to the closest town due to political unrest in the area. We had to ask total strangers if we could stay overnight as it was getting dark and the town was still too far away. At every level of my research in Niger, all kinds of people would be willing to assist with various things without getting compensation. When I often uttered surprise at how strangers could be so helpful and caring, my Nigerien friends would explain that they do it for God, as a way of stressing the natural decency and common humanity. Scott Youngstedt's (2012) narrative about his travel with Hausa friends in a taxi-bus captures well this smoothness of everyday interactions, where it is seen as natural to most Nigeriens to receive help with their luggage and children from people they don't know. Youngstedt (2012) stresses that he is not diminishing the harsh economic conditions and structural violence that characterizes the lives of most people in Niger, but that people not only seek to survive but to "survive with dignity" (2012: 5–6).

In this brief historical contextualization of Niger, I have highlighted colonialization, international development, and militarization not only because they have been significant in shaping the present but also because these histories speak against the notion of Niger referred to above—as isolated and plagued by ahistorical poverty. Placing Niger in the context of Stoler's (2008) concept of "ruination" captures the shared histories of Niger with countries in Europe and the United States, with increased militarization, destruction of the natural environment, and controlling people's mobility and aspirations for mobility that have been important strategies of survival, identity, and well-being for centuries.

A risk of the emphasis that I select here is, however, that it can reduce Niger to nothing more than an object of colonialism or neocolonialism and cast its people as passive agents or victims. Clapperton C. Mavhunga, Jeroen Cuvelier, and Katrien Pype (2016) have, for example, stressed the need to reject Eurocentric perspectives of mobility, where people in Africa are often only seen as acted upon from outside. The emphasis on African people as passive and acted on by outside forces follows a longstanding racist tradition of seeing Black and African people as docile subjects, unable to act or govern themselves. However, for the wider story that I tell, the context of colonialization and neocolonialization is essential, and so is it for the individual stories that I hear, as they too emphasize the history of colonialization and neocolonialization as the key drivers that have led them away from home.

We sometimes learn lessons the hard way. After the financial crash in Iceland that basically bankrupted the country, people started reevaluating the self-evident truth of corruption being the realm of Africa (Loftsdóttir 2019). In April 2016, Ali and I are walking back to my hotel. It is cold and I feel tired. "How is the situation in Iceland?" he asks me as he often does when we have not met for a while. I tell him sadly that actually things are not so good, as there were recently revelations that some prominent Icelandic politicians were using tax havens. Once again, I see him look at me with pity mixed with patience, probably because he feels that as a privileged Westerner, I could not understand the real world. He explains that *of course* it is like that in Iceland. He had seen a news report on this recently concerning the Panama files. "Everywhere it is the same thing" he explains to me. "Corrupted leaders taking big things for themselves. Why should it be any different in Iceland?" I laugh bitterly and explain that actually we thought until recently that it was different in Iceland, speaking of corrupted African leaders that had to learn the rules of democracy from us Europeans. Manifesting just one of the ways in which within Europe, Europe and Africa are so often seen as separate entities, inhabited by people that are somehow intrinsically different.

NOTES

1. The Human Development Index ranks countries according to various social and economic indicators.
2. Within Niger there are also different versions of hierchies of darker and lighter, which engage with more recent colonial racist classifications (on WoDaaBe see for example Loftsdóttir 2002b; on Tuareg, Rasmussen 1992: 356; Alidou 2005: 176-77).
3. When I was present, my friends asked usually in Nigerian languages to make it easier for the person to refuse, but I could roughly understand the conversation from the context.
4. Ignacio Fradejas-García and Linda M. Mülli (2019) point out that ironically the United Nations promotes the mobility of its own employees while restricting the mobility of others, thus taking part in reproducing the inequalities of the current mobility regime.

CHAPTER
7

Nostalgic Colonialism
Different Kinds of Otherness

I am walking down a side street in Brussels with two of my Nigerien friends. I am also accompanied by Eloise, who was introduced to me a few days earlier by one of them. Eloise has lived in Brussels for a few years but comes from another part of Belgium. She lives alone, and I have seen indications of a precarious life of economic hardship. Despite this, she ligated her Nigerien friends' visa applications and is also helping them to sell distinctively marked Tuareg and WoDaaBe jewelry, such a silver rings and leather necklaces. Our Nigerien friends walk in front of us, deep in conversation. Both are wearing clothing that is distinctively Tuareg: a long and bright one-color West African robe and a large turban that covers the upper part of their head and is wrapped under the chin. It is practical in the desert and has complex social meanings as well. The men are tall and thin and walk down the street with authority. Eloise turns her head toward me, leans her body in my direction, as if we are close friends or share an intimate bond, and whispers: "Aren't they exotic! Don't you see, everyone is observing *us*?"

She may have been right, but then this was in the early 2000s. Today, these same Nigerien friends tell me that, especially after the 2016 terrorist attacks in Brussels, a turban like this is looked at with suspicion. Before that, they say, the turban was more a sign of something exciting and curious. Renato Rosaldo points out in his classic 1989 work *Culture and Truth* that the Other can be seen as composed of two different bodies, i.e., the exotic other, purified of forces of mobility, and those seen as impure, dangerous and threatening. The concept "Indigenous" signals attachment to this purity, but it has had a problematic and static connection to ideas of unchanging traditions.

In this chapter, I reflect on Europe's problematic relationship with its historically constituted "others" by focusing on Nigerien men, who occupy the slot of the exotic in European thought. WoDaaBe and Tuaregs have historically been identified as "exotic others" by Europeans and, as such, they have continued to be objects of excitement and curiosity. The discussion shows how the idea of the "exotic" constitutes one of Europe's "imperial ruins" (Stoler 2008) and exists apart from the figure of the Muslim migrant, the potent marker of dangerous "others" today. Furthermore, I ask what kinds of subjects are recognized as cosmopolitan in the European landscape and what kinds of "strangers" or "others" are welcomed into the space of Europe.

Tuaregs started traveling to Europe and the United States to sell jewelry well before 2000, and in the new millennium WoDaaBe started doing the same. Both attempted to create new opportunities for survival, which incidentally coincided to some extent with growing identifications of Muslims as dangerous others (Rehman 2007; Abu-Lughod 2002). As long as these men marked themselves as "exotic others," as idealized in past colonial imagination, they were not placed in the "threatening migrant" slot. Rather they were seen as a part of European cosmopolitan experiences. I start this discussion by contextualizing it with a brief discussion about Tuareg's and WoDaaBe's historical positions in Niger, and then move toward their circular migration to and from Europe. I show how it rests on a particular conceptualization of the "Indigenous" while related to historical conceptions of WoDaaBe in Europe that separated them from spaces of Islam and Blackness (Loftsdóttir 2007, 2008), paying attention to what it tells about the way in which mobility and differences are conceptualized in Europe.

Exotic People

Tuaregs and WoDaaBe are quite different ethnic groups with different languages, as well as being internally different. Tuaregs in Niger are a part of Kel Tamashek, that is, those who speak Tamashek and have historically occupied the northern Sahel part of West Africa and the Sahara Desert, an area that now is divided into several nation states, including Mali, Niger, Algeria, and Libya. WoDaaBe are a part of the Fulani (Fulbe, Peuhl) ethnicity, which traditionally occupied the Savanna part of the Sahel and are found in many West African countries. Tuaregs, being more numerous in the north, have traditionally been associated with camel herding, while WoDaaBe, concentrated historically more in the southern part of the Sahel where there is more rain, are more associated with cattle. While Tuaregs were brutally repressed by the French colonial authorities, WoDaaBe had, for the most part, peaceful relations with the colonial authorities, even though they, like the Tuaregs, suffered from policies that reduced their land and civil rights (Loftsdóttir 2008). Imposition of taxes and attempts to regulate the caravan trade caused irreversible disruption in Tuareg society, coupled by increased marginalization of pastoral groups within the state of Niger (Rasmussen 2005).

Tuaregs and WoDaaBe have histories of relations with Europeans in which they have been exoticized and seen as superior to other ethnic groups in Niger. These romantic visions of pastoral people have long been held in the Global North. Tuaregs were characterized by the French colonial powers as superior to their Black neighbors, that is, "whiter" and thus better (Alzouma 2009). Similarly, prior European accounts of WoDaaBe characterize them as less "Black" than the surrounding populations and as more noble and graceful (Loftsdóttir 2007, see e.g., Alexander 1908; Vieillard 1932). As nomadism was glorified in popular European depictions, intersecting environmental and political factors made nomadism as a way of life increasingly difficult in Niger (Rain 1999: 50). A strong emphasis on groundnut as a cash crop, both by the colonial government and independent Niger state, helped, along with population growth, to push herders further and further north where their livelihood was riskier (Rain 1999: 50). Extreme droughts in 1974 and 1984 had drastic consequences for them, as they had moved further and further into the Sahel and Sahara where rainfall is less predictable and thus the risk of drought higher.

When I did my ethnographic fieldwork in Niger in the late 1990s, many young WoDaaBe men and women had migrated to Niamey. Some of them engaged in artisanry work directed at tourists and expatriates (Loftsdóttir 2008). In this, WoDaaBe benefitted from the much longer artisanal tradition of Tuaregs, who are well known as skillful silver craftsmen. Tuareg involvement started in the 1960s, in the northern part of Niger when tourists from the Global North and aid workers started having more presence there. This market grew, but when the Tuareg rebellion movements in the early 1990s made the northern part of Niger unsafe for aid workers and tourists, many Tuareg artisans migrated to the capital (Davis 1999: 488). Traditionally, Tuareg blacksmiths crafted the jewelry, household tools, and weapons for the—now impoverished—noble part of the segregated Tuareg society, as well as providing musical entertainment and serving as intermediators in various *rites de passage* (Rasmussen 1995: 592). Tuaregs' long history of artisanry is intertwined with the history of colonialization in Niger (Rasmussen 1995; Davis 1999), and the old notion of Tuaregs as more "interesting" than their neighbors became refashioned in the tourist sector and expatriate industry in Niger (Alzouma 2009; Grégoire and Scholze 2012).

While jewelry making has not been as important historically among WoDaaBe, their ability to enter into this market—producing and selling leather products marketed as authentic WoDaaBe products—rests on a European fascination with WoDaaBe as more culturally pure than other populations in Niger (Loftsdóttir 2008), which mirrors the fascination with Tuaregs. As Davis (1999) discusses and as I witnessed in Niger, the only people buying the silver objects and other artisanal items were Westerners or other Nigeriens intending to sell them in Europe or the United States. Susan J. Rasmussen (2005) has pointed out that when Westerners became buyers of Tuareg jewelry, instead of Tuaregs nobles as in the past, the relationship between the buyer and seller of these products continued to be organized as patron-client relationship (see also Rasmussen 1995).

At the time of my research, both WoDaaBe and Tuaregs felt strongly marginalized both politically and economically within the Nigerien state. This grew intensively after 1990 and 1991 when militia attacked civilians in Niger and Mali, leading to rebellion movements among Tuaregs (Rasmussen 2005: 799; see also Diallo 2018 on Tuaregs in Mali). The rebellion movement became a part of the fascination with Tuaregs at the beginning of the new millennium, with interest in their artisanal production growing, alongside interest in their musical traditions, history, and culture (Rasmussen 2005; Lunaček 2013). The romantic vision of the Tuaregs is captured by a discussion of a traveling tour of Tuareg artifacts and culture in the United States, where it was said that Tuaregs "ability to master the harsh and forbidding desert environment and to repel, control, or withstand outsiders, colonial powers, and modern governments has engendered an almost mythical quality in the Tuareg" (Seligman 2006: 59; Grégoire and Scholze 2012). As critically phrased by another scholar, Sarah Lunaček, "The Tuareg image so popular in Europe [is]: les hommes bleus, Saharan warriors, noble, beautiful, like middle age knights, the carriers of values that are about to disappear . . ." (2013: 170).

WoDaaBe became more securely embedded in the slot of the "Indigenous" for expatriates and tourists in the early 1990s, when they were featured in several coffee table books that became extremely popular in the Western commercial mass media including appearing on the cover of *National Geographic Magazine*. These works had a strong focus on a particular ceremony, Gerewol, which is ideally held annually, bringing together different WoDaaBe linages. Most if not all discussions framed Gerewol as an exotic and traditional ritual, distancing it from political and historical conditions of WoDaaBe in the present, downplaying any temporality (Loftsdóttir 2008; see also Lutz and Collins 1993: 91).

During my fieldwork in Niger, I analyzed the engagement of WoDaaBe migrant workers with these stereotypical representations for Western tour-

Figure 7.1. Gerewol dance. While the photo was taken by the author in Niger during 1997, it reflects a popular representation of WoDaaBe in the European imagination. © Kristín Loftsdóttir.

ists and expatriates, and how WoDaaBe created new subsistence possibilities for themselves in a changing world by playing on Westerners' notion of their culture as authentic and unchanged. As I noted then:

> This growing interest, which arises at a time when the WoDaaBe are becoming more and more marginalized, takes the form mostly of discourses that reflect them as peaceful and beautiful people, existing outside history, preoccupied with exotic performances, with a particular focus on dance performances taking place during the rainy season. (Loftsdóttir 2002a)

The interest of people from the Global North in buying from WoDaaBe and Tuaregs can be seen as resting on their role as Indigenous authentic subjects (see also Loftsdóttir 2008; Lunaček 2013). Renato Rosaldo spoke a long time ago about "imperial nostalgia" which both revolves around innocent yearning for the past and dismissal of one's complicity in the brutality of that past (1989b: 108).

Renée Sylvain (2002) has maintained that, with globalization, it is not necessarily Western culture that has taken hold elsewhere, but also the idea of "what culture is," i.e., that culture is fixed in time and place, and is authentic and pure. This means that culture does not only become a marker for something threatening and dangerous as we see in stereotypes about "Muslim culture" but also that ethnicity has become increasingly commercialized in a globalized neoliberal world (Comaroff and Comaroff 2009: 28). The commercialization of ethnic identities has also revolved around the idea of the "African." Thus, Paul Stoller's (2010) classic study on the ethnic reification of West African street vendors in New York where they creatively adapt to the interest of their consumers, by selling something perceived as generic "African," surrounding themselves with signs that affirm the "Africanity" of the product.

As several scholars have shown, Indigenous people often homogenize their cultural identities, in accordance with historical Western stereotypes to gain rights as "Indigenous" people (Hodgson 2011: 5). The growing interest in rights of Indigenous people in the last few decades by the Global North has not replaced persistent cultural stereotypes of Indigenous people as exotic and different (Sylvain 2002). Within this wider commercialization of ethnicity and culture, the past racist and colonial association with the "exotic" become a resource that can be manipulated by the people in question. Some scholars have used the concept "ethnosexuality" in this context—referring to ethnic identities that are racialized and sexualized—to capture this process of commercialization and consumption, and also to capture how these representations are acted on in different ways, where "representation of ethnosexuality shape collective belonging" (Meiu 2016: 217).

Overall, this draws attention to how communities, such as the WoDaaBe and Tuaregs, can in the present manipulate particular ideas of culture and the exotic, derived from older colonial and racist imaginaries as tools to secure or facilitate particular economic and political resources (on the San Indigenous people, see also Sylvain 2002).

Tuaregs and WoDaaBe in Europe

In the late 1990s Tuaregs and WoDaaBe extended their mobility by traveling on commercial trips to Europe. A group of Tuareg musicians, Tartit, gave their first European performance in Belgium in 1995 but this group was originally formed by people meeting in refugee camps in Burkina Faso and eastern Mauritania (Rasmussen 2005: 800). Groups of professional Tuareg musicians have traveled in Europe and the United States to promote Tuareg culture and their cultural survival (Rasmussen 2005).[1] In that context, as Rasmussen has shown, Tuaregs have continued being racialized, enforcing the distinction between "lighter" and "darker" Africa, coupled with attempts to distance them from other African Muslims (2005: 806).

This helps "to totalize and essentialize the culture and religion, and to mask internal variations within Tuareg culture and society" as phrased by Rasmussen (2005: 807).

In 1998, when I was about to leave Niger, some of my WoDaaBe friends were invited on a tour to Belgium for a dance performance, capitalizing on the interest in the Gerewol dance and festival. There was great excitement among the group, with Europe being the long-held focus of their subsistence strategy (making and selling jewelry), even though none had traveled there. They were, however, anxious about offending the European managers of the trip by making too many demands or asking too many questions regarding practical issues, which vividly indicates the discrepancy of power. I also saw then and during other trips at the same time, that people were collecting all kind of artifacts, swords, clothing, beadwork in the hope of selling them while abroad, explaining to me that the trips did not pay much, rather the possibilities to profit were by selling items during these performances (Loftsdóttir 2002a).

Since then, many Tuaregs and WoDaaBe including some of those who were my interlocutors in this research in Belgium, have migrated to Europe to conduct performances but also to sell jewelry and artisanal items. The networks of European friends established in Niger earlier is crucial in this context (Lunaček 2013). The encounters with European tourists and expatriates in Niger created for Tuaregs and WoDaaBe the financial basis to be able to travel to Europe, where they made use of these networks to have a place to stay, to assist with gaining visas, and to help with various accommodation issues. As each trip can take a few months, it can be economically beneficial to avoid hotels, and extensive networks allow even for a movement between different accommodations, utilizing different contact persons and increasing prospects for more market opportunities. The exceptions are musical performance groups that stay in hotels, but their travel is usually organized and subsidized (Lunaček 2013). People also travel to visit friends, and thus naturally they like to stay with friends when possible or someone they know instead of in an impersonal hotel (Lunaček 2013). This reflects the intersecting motivations where trips to Europe can be economically significant while also providing new experiences and possibilities of maintaining and enhancing friendship ties. Additionally, these encounters take place within a postcolonial space where the identities of Tuaregs and WoDaaBe have long been imagined in particular racial and essentializing way. Tuaregs and WoDaaBe often travel to various European countries, including Belgium of course, but also often to France, Germany, Italy, and Switzerland. The jewelry is sold at music festivals or other public events or at private gatherings in the homes of European friends. Some also sell jewelry at local bars, an arrangement also facilitated by their European friends.

In some cases, NGOs have nurtured relationships between these mobile Tuaregs and WoDaaBe and their European friends, aiming to enhance the quality of life back home in Niger. Both Tuareg men and women have traveled to Europe for such various commercial purposes (Rasmussen 2005; Lunaček 2013), but, in my experience, WoDaaBe women are, for the most part, absent from these migrations to Europe.[2]

When I started the research in Belgium in 2005, it was clear that both WoDaaBe and Tuaregs were in high demand at various festivals, as Eloise's reaction reflected. They were perceived as exotic and exciting, wearing turbans that were not strongly associated with Taliban and Islamic terror as would be the case in the years to come. As one of my WoDaaBe friends explained to me in 2017, after the Brussels terrorist attacks in 2016 he stopped using his turban during annual visits there or he would place it more as a scarf over the head. During my visits in the 2000s, avoiding the use of clothing that appeared "different" was mainly to be free from too much "positive" attention. One WoDaaBe told me that he actually only used his regular Nigerien clothing and turban when trying to sell something. And I did see it when either going with them to different sites where they sell artifacts or during walks around town for other purposes. Probably the most extreme were women who did not know the men, trying to hug, touch, and flirt with them, but also people taking photos without permission. As Susan Rassmussen reports (2005) regarding a tour to the United States by a famous Tuareg band, the media tried to distance them from their Muslim identity, given the negative image of Muslims in the United States at the time. This is in spite of the fact that a majority of WoDaaBe and Tuaregs are Muslims.

During my first trip to Antwerp, I was accompanied by my two-year-old son and my sister Ásta who was helping me with him so I would have more research time. We both felt shocked at the experience of being openly stared at, as we walked with my WoDaaBe friend, Bermo, especially when he held my son in his arms. The stares were friendly and more curious than anything else, but simultaneously rude and objectifying. When the three of us took my son to the Antwerp Zoo, Ásta commented to me in Icelandic: "I have never experienced this before; while we were looking at the caged animals, the people in the zoo were looking at us."

This objectifying is certainly used and manipulated by Tuaregs and WoDaaBe to their advantage. When I asked Mohammed—the Tuareg man who felt trapped in Brussels but who has also sold some artisanry items—if it is actually easier for WoDaaBe and Tuaregs to sell those things than it is for other Nigeriens, he proclaimed smiling: "It is easier!" Ali, who is with Mohammed and me, feels the need to add to and strengthen this point of how ethnicity matters: "Those who sell the jewelry, they will always claim that they are Tuaregs, even if they are not." Mohammed nods and explains to me: "Because it is more authentic. Those who buy the jewelry already know the value of things so when they know that you are Tuareg or WoDaaBe, they know that you are a nomad, so it gives more value." I was with a small group of WoDaaBe at a festival in a town outside Brussels, when they asked me to be of service by confirming to potential buyers that they were "real" WoDaaBe and nomads, from the pastoral part of Niger. Thus, the value of the items being sold is integrated with the presumed identity of the seller.

A similar point was emphasized by two Tuareg men that I met. They were staying in Brussels for short time with bags packed with silver jewelry. One of them told me that it was important for them to dress in clothing that was distinguished as Tuareg to help sales. "You knew that I was a Tuareg," he asks me, "due to the clothing that I am wearing, right?" I nod and he explains, "this clothing associated with Tuaregs allows people to recognize me as such." He smiles to himself as if remembering something and continues: "I was once at the airport in the USA on my way back here and this man stops next to me and says in Tamashek, 'the trousers of my country.' He was a Tuareg too, and we talked, and it was all thanks to the trousers." However, as explained by a WoDaaBe friend, when putting aside the turban

Figure 7.2. Selling jewelry at a music festival in Brussels in 2014. © Kristín Loftsdóttir.

and the colorful gown he could put his exotic identity aside and would then become just like any other African person in Brussels, blending in with the crowds and becoming invisible to most of the population.

When dressed in similar clothing as Tuaregs, and selling similar artifacts, WoDaaBe would often be confused with Tuaregs, who are a larger ethnic group with wider representation historically in Europe. During my fieldwork in Niger in late 1990s, the WoDaaBe who were selling artisanal items felt the need to emphasize to their customers that even though they were partly selling Tuareg items, they were a different ethnic group. I observed the same thing during my first trip to Belgium in 2004, where WoDaaBe there were generally selling a mixture of Tuareg and WoDaaBe artisanal items, such as leather jewelry and embroidery. Ten years later, in 2014, I was surprised to see that the silver jewelry made by Tuaregs had almost completely replaced the WoDaaBe artifacts; if WoDaaBe artifacts were present at all they were displayed on the least desirable part of the selling table. This does not have to be seen as an erosion of ethnic identity, but instead acknowledgement that within this space one ethnic label can easily be exchanged for another for commercial purposes, to a label more familiar to the clients, replacing one "exotic Indigenous" identity for another.

Complicated Relationships

With those I spoke to and as is also reflected in Lunaček (2013) research among Tuaregs, their business model rests on networks of European friends, who are not only crucial in providing lodging but also in helping with visa and other formalities and to arrange the selling of artifacts or performances. It is difficult to know whether WoDaaBe and Tuaregs systematically enlarge their networks in Niger with future prospects in mind (Lunaček 2013), but these friendships can be precious while simultaneously deeply practical. As Lunaček (2013) also notices, for both Tuaregs and WoDaaBe, mobility and networking have historically been important and flexible strategies in constantly having to deal with new environmental circumstances. This circular mobility to Europe can thus in a sense be categorized as a continuation of a traditional livelihood strategy.

Even though these friendships can be deep, they are still fraught with ambiguity especially when positioned within a historical context of the racialized exoticization of WoDaaBe and Tuaregs in Europe. The issue revolves not only around past depictions of WoDaaBe and Tuareg identity but a discourse that continues to circulate globally. Also, Tuaregs' and WoDaaBe's dependency on their hosts can create an unequal power-relationship on top of the economic disparities that are usually involved. One man that I knew that had gone back and forth a few times between Belgium and Niger had a falling out with his closest friend in Belgium, who then no longer wanted to help him with his visa application. This means that the man was unable to visit Europe because for him to obtain the visa, he needed someone to send him an invitation to the Schengen area. Also, I knew of Belgian men who convinced some of their Nigerien migrant friends to bring them small antique items. Another friend, a Belgian woman, told me that these men did this knowingly, that the Nigerien men did not realize that they were committing a crime. The display of power can go both ways, where several of the Belgian women also told me of their disappointment with the men they had helped, including providing a place to stay, food from quite scarce resources, and other help; all of which they felt not having received much acknowledgement for from these men who had benefitted from their assistance. Regardless, these relationships should not be reduced to only power dynamics or racialized encounters; they are complex and diverse, with people staying friends for many years.

Muhammad Ali, a WoDaaBe man who has been traveling back and forth between Niger and Belgium for several years, links together the tourism in Niger with his mobility to Europe and the importance for WoDaaBe to navigate through many types of occupations to survive: "We [in Niger] have had tourists. We are nomadic; we have never been in school. If we cannot even farm, then how we will live? Thanks to the people who come to us, the tourists, we had to change. We engage in some trading, but not much."

As other WoDaaBe men have told me, Muhammad Ali says that he has to seek out buyers in Europe for his products, and that he is tired of the traveling and work that brings in very little income. Here again the question is not whether this mobility revolves around drudgery or pleasure. I noted when I lived in Niger in the 1990s that younger WoDaaBe men held ambivalent feelings regarding migrating between the pastoral area and the city where they sold jewelry. They felt trapped in a life of poverty, in the city far away from their families in the bush, even as they emphasized and took pride in learning multiple skills for the present (Loftsdóttir 2008). This is similar to what Rasmussen has shown in relation to Tuaregs' involvement with migrant work (2005: 795). Work in cities in other countries selling artisanry items is approached with a similar kind of ambivalence: it provides some sort of pleasures and new experiences, but is also, in the end still constitutes a part of a life of poverty.

When conducting research in the late 2000s and early 2010s, I was struck by the more varied options that these WoDaaBe and Tuareg men had compared to many of the other precarious migrants that came to Belgium. This was seen even more intensively when Nigeriens came from Libya after 2011, entering the country through risky means, while WoDaaBe and

Tuareg artisanal item-makers and artists could enter legally, stay for few months, and then return. Lo Sardo stresses this as well when pointing out that Hausa migrants in Brussels tend to develop very little or no relationship with Europeans in the city (2010: 39).

There were certainly Tuaregs and probably some WoDaaBe who also became part of the precarious migrant population in Brussels, especially after the interest in these groups as innocent others did seem to diminish in the early 2010s. The economic crisis, WoDaaBe and Tuareg artisanry sellers told me, was clearly felt; one suggested that there was less interest in these artifacts due to saturation of the market. Additionally, Tuaregs became, as Lunaček notes in 2013 increasingly associated with terror in the Sahara, due to the Tuareg rebellion movement, interlinked with increased general insecurity in the area due to the Libya crisis leaving their image somewhat "tarnished" (2013: 171).

In the 2000s and when I was in Belgium in the early 2010s, the environment was, however, one of excitement. WoDaaBe and Tuareg identification as exotic seemed to neutralize them as any kind of threat to Belgian identity. My interlocutors from these two ethnic groups that stayed in Brussels for a short time trying to sell artisanal artifacts, or longer, also said that during the 2010s, the economic precarity of a part of Europe's population continued to be felt, and in addition to that their objects were no longer seen as fashionable. The market works that way, one WoDaaBe man explained to me: "Things go out of fashion."

Cosmopolitan Subjects on the Move

The NH Hotel chain's idea of the "global citizen," discussed earlier, captures how some people's mobility is rendered natural and positive while others are criminalized. WoDaaBe and Tuareg mobility generally falls into the positive category due to their historical placement as one of Europe's "exotic others." This has in some sense resulted in new ties with the Niger state, as seen for example in that the homepage of the Nigerien embassy in Brussels features an image of WoDaaBe in dance clothing—while these exotic representations are also drawn on by some members of these ethnicities to create new strategies of survival. Thus, while these representations are positioned in a racialized and colonial history and continue to be recreated in the present, this imagination also allows the WoDaaBe to have access to a broader range of possibilities that are closed to individuals belonging to other ethnic groups in Niger. These include being generously assisted by "white" European friends who help them get visas to come to Brussels, give them a place to stay, and better access to spaces to sell. When keeping in mind the restrictions that European powers are imposing on the mobility of Nigeriens in Niger, the wider historical context of this exoticization becomes even more disturbing and more of a disjunction that hides larger trends of power disparities and racism.

Different discourses celebrating cosmopolitanism and tourism or condemning migrants send as well a message about the compatibility of particular people and bodies within the space of Europe. Just as a nation becomes "more real" by patrolling its borders, Europe can be seen as becoming solidified as a project through discourses about which bodies belong within its space and which bodies do not.

NOTES

1. The internationally recognized band Tinariwen gave their first European performance in Denmark in 2001 (Concert Archives 2021a) and Bombino in the Netherlands in 2011 (Concert Archives 2021b).
2. As the ethnic label Tuareg refers to a highly diversified and stratified society, this mobility is not necessarily available to all who identify as Tuaregs, but depends on various variables. As Souleymane Diallo argues in his dissertation on two groups of Malian Tuareg refugees in Niger, clan structures have become less relevant while the separation between those who used to be slaves and masters continues to be salient, while simultaneously negotiated by different actors (2018: 17, 123-24).

CHAPTER
8

Spaces of Innocence
Belgium's Colonial History and Beyond

Ardo shows up early one morning in my rental flat, announcing firmly: "I want to show you something different." Research projects are supposed to adhere to specific rules, including a coherent topic and well-defined group of people to interview. Anthropology has always resisted this to some extent, possibly due to a methodology that embraces larger contextualization as well as tackling a quite complex reality through its ethnographic field methods. I have tried to explain to Ardo many times how my research is defined, what it focuses on, and what people I am interested in interviewing. He does not say much about it, but simply shows me what he feels I should do. He ignores the distinction between refugee, asylum seeker, and economic migrant; I learn early on that he is right. He also to some extent ignores that the research is about people from Niger, as he feels I should also talk to people from other West African countries, because after all their experiences echo his own. Ardo, along with others that I engage with, shape not only my ideas and results but also the path that the research takes.

I have for several days been telling him about some European history museums that I want to visit. But this morning he decided that it is better for me to see a small piece of Belgian history that is not locked inside a museum or an exhibition area. Matonge is a corner of the crowded Ixelle commune of Brussels, which is strongly influenced by the Congolese diasporic cultures. The route there leads us through some of the city's most exclusive shopping districts. There is something astonishing about moving swiftly through the street with grand buildings and expensive brand names to this small area; in my notebook I write that I felt almost like I entered a "wormhole" when I move between the somewhat sterile Avenue Louis to lively Matonge.

Matonge is commercialized with African hair salons, clothing stores, and, during the evening, lively nightlife (Demart 2008). However, not only is the neighborhood vibrant and colorful, but it is also a salient reminder of Belgium's tortuous colonial aspirations, realized in one of Europe's most horrible colonies, the Congo. Ardo thus draws my attention once again to interlinked spaces and entangled histories of Europeans and people living in Africa.

This chapter goes back in time for a look at Belgium's imperial and colonial history, continuing to present day. There, I draw attention to Belgium's similarities to the part of the Europe which I am from, in terms of both having strongly emphasized innocence from Europe's colonial histories.

Agents of Horror

In the history of colonialism, Belgium is probably best known for its association with Congo, where some of the most intense brutality and horrors of nineteenth-century colonial rule took place. Rule over this territory gave Belgium enhanced status among the other European countries, and a wider international recognition (Buettner 2016: 168; Demart 2013: 3). As phrased by Buettner, "ruling of Congo transformed Belgium into *la plus grande Belgique*, not at least in the national imaginary" (2016: 16).

From 1885 until 1908, Congo was the private property of the Belgian king, Leopold II, whose ownership of the massive territory was ratified at the 1884-85 Berlin conference, where the main European powers formalized and organized their colonialization of the African continent and exploitation of the abundant resources found there. One justification for the establishment of the colony then was that it freed the inhabitants from "Arab" slave traders on Africa's eastern coast (Buettner 2016: 166; Ewans 2003), thus engaging with the self-perception of Europeans as a civilizing force, and humanitarian actors.

As a property of the king, the Free State of Congo (as it was ironically called), was tasked to produce vast quantities of ivory and rubber, with severe punishment for those failing to fulfill quotas (Buettner 2016: 165). A few companies were allowed to use whatever means they felt were necessary to maximize the production of rubber (Ewans 2003). Whipping was practiced extensively, using whips made from hippopotamus hide, called *chicotte* (Ewans 2003: 169). Failure to reach the quota resulted also in kidnapping, massacres, mutilations (mainly amputation of limbs), in addition to whole villages being burned (Weisbord 2003: 36; Roes 2010). Some have surmised that between 1880 and 1920, Congo's population was reduced by half. This was due to starvation, new diseases which people had difficulties resisting because of their horrible conditions, massive infant mortality, lower fertility, and people fleeing (Gewald 2006; Roes 2010). The extent of deaths is so enormous that the word genocide has been applied (Weisbord 2003; Licata and Klein 2010).

Historians and others have debated extensively over the number of people who died; some claim ten million, while others have estimated a lower number. Gewald argues: "In the end it has to be borne in mind that it is not so much the number of people killed, either directly or indirectly, that is of greatest importance; instead it must be recognized that a crime of tremendous proportion was committed" (2006: 486).

At the turn of the century, British humanitarian advocates, followed by those in the United States, started to criticize the extensive horrors in Congo. The Belgian state took over and the Belgian Congo was created in 1908. Leopold II was heavily compensated, which, as phrased by Buettner, "added to the vast profit already earned from his territory" (2016: 166). Leopold destroyed a great deal of records when giving up Congo, and important remaining sources were kept closed to researchers and state officials for most of the twentieth century (Ewans 2003: 170). Buettner points out that while some of the worst practices were outlawed in Belgian Congo, forced labor continued along with *chicotte* punishments and a complete absence of political rights for the Congolese people. This was contrary to what was happening in other European colonies at this time as people were gaining various rights and degrees of self-government (2016: 167). Before Leopold transferred the territory to the Belgian government, he created various companies with partners from other European countries and the United States, which ensured his continued control over various enterprises and their revenues (Ewans 2003: 171). Private companies were the basis of the economy, with Congolese people kept away from governance and from higher education (Goddeeris 2015a). Forced labor was important in maximizing these profits, or as viewed by Martin Ewans: "It was in the interests of these and similar companies that the Belgian Congo was essentially run" (2003: 171). Congo was subsequently under Belgian state control until 1960. Belgium also gained a trusteeship over Rwanda and Burundi after World War I (Demart 2013: 2), thus having various engagements with colonial and postcolonial Africa.

Internally, the Congo colony, alongside the monarchy, was used to create a stronger sense of Belgian national unity (Buettner 2016: 168), where the Belgian nation was portrayed as idealistic, paternalistic, and as "only" wanting to protect and civilize the Congolese natives (Buettner 2016: 170). The story of Belgium's relationship with Congo becomes thus a metanarra-

Figure 8.1. The leopard man (Aniota) at the AfricaMuseum at Tervuren (photo taken in 2019), with iron claws and spotted-skin costume. The statue iconized the savagery of Congo for Europeans, and inspired Hergé in his making of Tintin in Congo. © Kristín Loftsdóttir.

tive of civilization and modernization; the relationship between these two often conceptualized as similar to that between a parent and a child (Licata and Klein 2010).

Early migration from Congo to Belgium was exceptionally low, when compared to other colonial situations (Demart 2013; Schoumaker et al. 2018: 218). After World War II, for example, eighteen hundred Africans were estimated as living in Belgium, of which only ten were from the Congo (Demart 2013: 3). Significant migration to Belgium from Congo started only in the 1970s and 80s, due to difficult conditions there and in neighboring countries (Demart 2013: 4–5; see also Bragard 2011). The scattered groups of people coming from Congo to Belgium prior to this had been students or invited guests at the numerous colonial exhibitions held in Belgium (Demart 2013: 4). Demart argues that, prior to the late 1980s, diplomats, civil servants, and students started arriving in Brussels from Congo, constituting a mobile upper class which went back and forth, and who saw Europe as a "fashionable destination" (2013: 4).

The key reasons that so few Congolese were migrating to Belgium earlier were racism and discrimination. During colonial times, Belgium saw it as economically more fruitful to use laborers in Congo. In fact, people from Congo were prohibited from coming to Belgium, except with the "explicit permission from Colonial General" (Ceuppens 2014; Bragard 2011: 97). Groups of Congolese people could visit to take part in various displays and performances for the enjoyment of the Belgian and European public such as to the 1930 World exhibition, where Congolese people performed (Demart 2013). Like WoDaaBe and Tuaregs in the early 2000s, they could travel to Europe to stay for a short time, belonging to the "savage" slot, as exotic and exciting.

After the 1980s, an increasing number of Congolese applied for political asylum in Belgium (Bragard 2011: 98; Schoumaker et al. 2018: 219). While the Congolese constitute a minority in Belgium compared to other migrant groups (Eurostat n.d.), they are still the largest group of sub-Saharan immigrants in the country. About half of Belgium's Congolese population lives in the Brussels capital area, and a great majority are Francophone like Belgium's historical elite (Schoumaker et al. 2018: 219). Despite being the migrant group with the highest level of education, they also have the highest unemployment rate (Bragard 2011: 98; see also Schoumaker et al. 2018).

Ghosts, Legacies, and Ruins

To many the fifty-year anniversary in 2010 of Congo's independence was symbolic of the way in which Belgium's colonial past has been forgotten and suppressed, as well as reflecting the lack of interest in the Congolese diaspora in wider Belgium (Bragard 2011; see also Demart 2013; Mielants 2006: 319). Since the turn of the millennium, growing demands for reevaluation of Belgium's colonial past have been stimulated by the publications of new research on Congo's and Belgium's past, as well as critical artist interventions, which have included those belonging to the Congolese diaspora and migrants (Ewans 2003; Goddeeris 2015a, 2015b; Arnaut 2019; Silverman 2015). While not the first to criticize the dominant historical view of Belgium's relationship with Congo, Adam Hochschild's book *King Leopold's Ghost: A Story of Greed, Terror and Heroism in Colonial Africa* published in 1998 was extremely important in drawing attention to the horrors and abuses taking place in the Free State of Congo; the book's publication also led to vigorous debates on how bad colonialism had actually been (Licata and Klein 2010). The image of Leopold II and the representation of Belgium's colonial past, thus "oscillates between shame and genius" (Bragard 2011:

94), remaining an "unresolved issue," despite new, emerging critical voices (Silverman 2015: 631).

Addressing this dismissal of Belgium's colonial past, Bambi Ceuppens (2014) suggests the term "cloistered remembering" regarding Leopold II's Congo, instead of amnesia. The term "cloistered remembering" was coined by Benjamin Stora to capture how memories often do not simply disappear but are skewed and fragmented into different legends and stereotypes (discussed in Ceuppens 2014: 86). As Ceuppens argues, this means that:

> the violence that went on in the Congo Free State has never been forgotten but that memories of it have long been dominated by narrow, simplified, mythologized forms of cloistered memory, associated with ex-colonials for whom Leopold II remains to this day the founding father of Belgium's colonial history, the visionary genius who "gave" little Belgium an enormous colony. (2014: 86)

Leopold II's memory continues thus to be celebrated by scholars and the public alike, in different ways. One aspect of this is the numerous public monuments that honor Leopold II, as well as great many streets named after him and others associated with colonialism (Goddeeris 2015a). Goddeeris points out that:

> while there are no monuments to Congolese in Belgium, Leopold II remains the sole king with an equestrian memorial in the shadow of the royal palace. The king also has statues in Ixelles, Ostend, Arlon, Mons and Antwerp, and busts in Forest, Oudergem, Tervuren, Halle, Ghent, Hasselt and Ostend. (Goddeeris 2015b: 449)

Some of these statues have over the years been subject to strategic vandalism, including incidents where red paint has been splattered over them, often by artists, to draw attention to the abuses that were part of the Free State of Congo and the amnesia in present-day Belgium (Stanard 2011). Included in what these activists called "artistic mutilations" was a hand getting sawn off one statue of a Congolese subject, as it "corresponds better to historical reality," i.e., a reminder of the inhuman punishment inflicted on the Congolese people (Goddeeris 2015b; Licata and Klein 2010; Silverman 2015: 630). In 2020, the monuments to Leopold II became crucial sites to protest racism in Belgium (Rannard 2020; Wynne 2020), which possibly will create a lasting reassessment of Belgium's colonial heritage.

Belgium is, of course, far from being alone in forgetting or pushing aside its colonial past. Other European countries have done so as well, using various ways to render the colonial past as insignificant or irrelevant. Concepts such as post-racism used in the early 2000s in relation to the United States and United Kingdom (discussed in Chapter 2) reflect one way of pushing

Figure 8.2. Protest of Belgium's colonial heritage included strategic vandalism of King Leopold II's statues. © Jean-Marc Pierard / Alamy Stock Photo.

this past away. Those countries that did not have colonial possessions have often seen themselves as not belonging to the colonial past. Referring to these countries, Barbara Lüthi, Francesca Falk, and Patricia Purtschert use the phrase "blank spaces in colonial history" (2016: 1). They mention Switzerland as an example, where an important feature of national identity in Switzerland has been its presumed distance from the history of colonialism (Lüthi et al. 2016). Alongside an emphasis of bringing to the front the colonial histories of different nation states, it is important to analyze the entanglement of these histories with one another, where there was not only competition between different empires but also engagement and collaboration between them (Schär 2019a; see also Stanard 2011). Bernhard C. Schär's discussion of the Dutch East Indies documents that 40 percent of the soldiers in the Dutch colonial service were from other European countries, and that the effects of Dutch imperialism were felt throughout Europe (2019a: 9). Scientific "knowledge" gained via colonialism, such as in the field of race science, was exchanged and co-produced across national boundaries and empires (Schär 2019b).

Similarly, in the part of the world where I come from, both external and internal narratives of the Nordic countries have ignored or dismissed their own involvement in colonialism (Keskinen et al. 2009; Loftsdóttir and Jensen 2012). When colonialism is acknowledged, it is often seen as having been gentler and more humane than the colonial projects of other countries (Naum and Nordin 2013; Loftsdóttir and Jensen 2012). The Nordic countries had a different relationship with the colonial project where some, such as Denmark, were colonial empires participating in the slave trade and operating plantations in the Caribbean built on slave labor (Naum and Nordin 2013; Green-Pedersen 1975), while others like Iceland were under Danish rule trying to gain independence in late nineteenth century (Loftsdóttir 2019). The Nordic countries have still largely been seen as excepted from colonialism, which has been filtered in various ways in the present, so that they are seen as exceptionally peaceful, tolerant, equal, non-racist, and well suited for peacekeeping (Loftsdóttir and Jensen 2016).

In Iceland, the engagement with colonialism and imperialism was thus certainly different from Belgium due largely to their different geopolitical positions within Europe and political status. It did, however, certainly exist. Icelanders participated in setter colonialism to South and North America and thus benefitted from the extensive violence taking place against those native people (Brydon 2001; Eyford 2006; Bertram 2018; Eyþórsdóttir and Loftsdóttir 2016). They also took part in producing a racist imaginary of colonized people that closely engaged with other European writings and discourses (Loftsdóttir 2009). Since Iceland was trying to gain independence from Denmark (gained fully in 1944), this racism took on particular forms where in the late-nineteenth and early-twentieth centuries it became important to stress that Iceland was not like other colonized people that were dominated by the Danish. Thus, through racist depictions and texts the Icelandic people asserted that they were not like the colonized people in the African continent and elsewhere (Loftsdóttir 2019).

Contemporary discussions about racism in Iceland make similar claims to innocence toward colonialism and racism (Loftsdóttir 2014, 2013), as scholars have discussed in relation to Dutch identity (Wekker 2016). In both cases, this "innocence" works as a shield against claims that particular actions or words are racist. In Belgium, the forgetting of colonialism exists in both its erasure and when acknowledged, it is on the premise that it did not really involve that many people killed, or that colonialism was also beneficial for the people of Congo (Licata and Klein 2010).

In Iceland, there are no monuments celebrating powerful figures in the history of colonialism, as there are in Brussels, nor are there squares, palaces, or other grand structures that were built with the wealth of colonial or imperial profit as so widely in other parts of Europe. Iceland's story of colonialism has revolved around Icelanders as the victims; of a nation resisting colonial rule and then bravely acquiring independence. This makes perhaps the experience of innocence simultaneously more intense and hidden in Iceland. The privileges of being Icelandic rest not only in the "white" skin of most of the population, but also in being part of larger global power structures that were built through imperialism and colonialism. The privilege of being Icelandic, then, is to be "untainted," in multiple senses, by a world created by colonialism (Loftsdóttir 2019). However, as the Dutch experience shows us, the presence of physical structures, buildings, and monuments does not really prevent a sense of being untainted or innocent of colonial violence.

During one of my first visits to Belgium, I walk with Ardo to downtown Brussels, because he thinks I must be interested in the popular tourist sites. He takes me first to the Grand Place, where we are surrounded by a herd of tourists. There he asks, "Beautiful, yes?" I nod, looking at the buildings around me, forced to tilt my head upward because they are so tall, with graceful statues and decorations placed high up. The gold-plated structures glitter in the sun. "This is all due to Congo," Ardo explains. He repeats firmly, as to himself, "All this is Congo." What he means is that the colonial wealth extracted from Congo made this opulence possible. Babouli, another precarious migrant who I meet a few times, also mentions the Grand Place to me when we are talking about Europe and the disparities of wealth between Europe and Africa. "Look at Belgium. This is one tiny country. What does it have? Nothing! The Grand Place, for example. Congo. Congo made the Grand Place."

Grand Place, the lavish central square of Brussels, predates Belgian involvement in Congo (World Heritage Convention, UNESCO n.d.),[1] with its oldest structures dating from the twelfth century. The square was restored after 1695, and again at later dates, overlapping with Belgium's colonial acquisitions and dealings, including the Congo, and therefore leading to massive wealth flowing into parts of the city like this. For centuries, ships brought enormous fortune to the Dutch countries from colonized populations, including sugar, spice, and slaves, while bringing immense suffering to its colonies. As scholars have pointed out regarding colonialism in the not-so-remote Nordic countries, there are no spaces in Europe untouched by colonialism (Horning 2013: 297).

NOTE

1. Grand Place is a UNESCO world heritage site. In the brief synopsis of its "outstanding universal values," UNESCO says: "The Grand-Place testifies in particular to the success of Brussels, mercantile city of northern Europe that, at the height of its prosperity, rose from the terrible bombardment inflicted by the troops of Louis XIV in 1695." Nowhere on the UNESCO site is there any mention of where this wealth came from (World Heritage Convention, UNESCO n.d.).

PART III

Europe's Past and Future

CHAPTER
9

The Heart of Darkness
EUrope as a Concept

As I navigate through this space that is Brussels, usually by myself with my Nigerien friends but occasionally with my children, I struggle to reconcile different narratives around me. How do these different voices and positionalities play into larger narratives of mobility, national identities, and colonial histories? Essentially, in regard to who is welcome into the space of Europe and to whom does the concept Europe belong? Trying to dig a little deeper below the surface of Europe as imagination and a project, this chapter presents fragments that aim to give insights into what constitutes Europe. What kind of coherence does this concept, Europe, have and for whom? What is associated with this concept and how can we understand its meaning through the eyes of precarious migrants, as well as through those who consider themselves as belonging to its space?

I anchor the discussion around two displays of Europe in Brussels: Mini-Europe in Bruparck and the House of European History in the Eastman building in Leopold Park. These sites serve here as a way of thinking about boundaries and subject positions of those who navigate the city, as well as constructing meaning in regard to the idea of Europe. Along with monuments, museums can be seen as giving the narrative of Europe a particular form and coherence (Perchoc 2017; De Cesari 2017). Some of the most prestigious museums in the Global North historically were established through massive looting of various artifacts during the colonial and imperial era—something that Belgium also took part in (Silverman 2015: 622-23). The origin of museums in Europe is strongly intertwined with nineteenth-century nationalism entangled with colonialism (Errington 1998: 18-19), while today many are often trying to recontextualize this heritage and their collections (Apor 2015: 52).

Museums in general and other permanent displays constitute an important part of Brussels' front stage—museums are often promoted as one of the key things to "do" in Belgium for more privileged mobile populations such as tourists and Eurocrats (Jansen-Verbeke et al. 2005: 114), with Belgium being known for its strong nationalizing of particular artists (Poulot 2015: 99). Various sites and museums in Brussels also celebrate and promote the EU and unavoidably affirm the idea of Brussels as the "heart" of the EU; but an emphasis on the transnational and supranational does not necessarily replace the emphasis on the nation (De Cesari 2017: 18). We can rephrase Gabriella Elgenius's insight with regards to national museums (2015: 146) and claim that EU museums and displays probably authenticate, just as the national ones, boundaries against others, as well as identifying the origin of those within its boundaries and their characteristics.

While quite different, both sites of display that I focus on here claim the label European and are funded by the EU. To me both raise questions of belonging within Europe on a complex scale of European North-South, European West-East, EU/Europe, and of Global North-South. I juxtapose these sites' representations of Europe with my interlocutors' negotiation of this term and European humanitarianism.

A Small Version of Europe

I try to convince Ardo to come with me and my children to Mini-Europe park, but without success. He has no interest and makes up some excuse, while expressing positively that the park is really good for children. Commissioned by the Belgian government, the Mini-Europe park was opened in 1989 by Belgium's Prince Philip (Brussels.info. n.d.a). The Brussels Atomium that stands next to it was built in conjunction with the 1958 World Exhibition. Today it symbolizes Brussels, as well as being a landmark of the advance of science. On this site in 1958, Belgium and other European nations justified their "civilizing" colonial project, where colonized people were on display. Belgium continued as it had done in previous decades to display a Congo section, promoting Belgian colonialism as well as aiming to generate pride in Belgium's "accomplishments" in Central Africa (Stanard 2005). The World Exhibitions that started in 1851 reinforced a sense of Europeanness as posed against colonized others, simultaneously as enforcing nationalism and regionalism (see for example, Storm and Vandevoorde 2012). King Leopold II decided to move a part of what was on display in another earlier exposition, that is, Brussel's International Exposition of 1897, to his palace in Tervuren, which became the site of a new museum, *The Royal Museum of Central Africa*, displaying geographic specimens, stuffed animals, and cultural artifacts from Congo (AfricaMuseum 2020). For a hundred years, as phrased by Silverman, the museum stood as a "petrified forest of imperial triumphalism" (2015: 627). The current museum's website, of the renovated museum that has been renamed AfricaMuseum, stresses that Leopold II saw the museum "as a propaganda tool for his colonial project, aimed at attracting investors and winning over the Belgian population" (see AfricaMuseum 2020).

In the light of this history, the Mini-Europe park certainly looks small and modest. After entering the park, visitors move along a narrow path where they are expected to stop at designated places representing a building or heritage site associated with a particular country in the EU. The miniatures are twenty-five times smaller than the monuments represented, and are most often easily recognizable, like Big Ben and the Arc de Triomphe. Each country's display area is clearly marked with the country's name, capital, size, population, currency, and date when it became a part of the EU. At some of the displays, features have been added such as small train tracks, airplanes, human figurines, and buttons that can be pushed to get mini-vehicles or other items moving around. Occasionally, playful cut-out boards are found along the path, intended for children to put their head through and have their photo taken, which echoes how the park is presented on the website as particularly appealing for children (Mini-Europe 2019; Brussels.info. n.d.a). As a whole, Mini-Europe represents a well-organized and bounded space that can be navigated through easily.

In his insightful analysis of Mini-Europe, Tuuli Lähdesmäki (2012) observes how the display of clearly defined countries are supplemented by emphasis on Europe, which in the park seems to mean the EU:

> The tour in the park starts with models from "Europe." Even though all the other models represent some particular state, the first two buildings are introduced with the title of Europe. These buildings are the Berlaymont (the main seat of the European Commission in Brussels) and an old farm house close to Paris in which "Jean Monnet and some close colleagues penned the Robert Schuman declaration, heralding the birth of the European Union." (Lähdesmäki 2012: 32–33)

An emphasis on Europe and the EU can be seen in the brochure distributed to the guests, where Europe and the EU serve a key role. While the EU began in the late 1950s with the coordination of economic marketplaces and alliances between independent states, it was only in the late 1980s that the focus shifted toward a perceived need to foster an attachment to the EU itself (Eriksen 2002: 74). Shore claims that this shift was not necessarily aimed at generating support for the EU, rather the goal was to invent a sense of a wider "European public" (2004: 31). To accomplish this, symbols of shared European-ness were strategically created, symbols that are usually associated with different nation states, such as a logo, flag, and anthem (Shore 2004). The discrepancy between the text of the brochure and the rigid separation of each nation state that the park visually displays, reflects how the park both emphasizes clearly delineated countries and Europe as one whole. At first, I found the emphasis on separate nation states *and* a joint Europe or EU to be a contradiction, but when I started thinking about the park in relation to the late nineteenth to early twentieth-century World Exhibitions, I remembered how they sought simultaneously to display the distinctive different European nation states *and* Europe as a singular space, progressive and as the site of civilization. This was not unique but throughout that period, various discourses sought to construct the sense of separate, culturally distinctive nation states alongside an emphasis on the idea of Europe or Europe-derived populations as intrinsically different from other populations. In my earlier analysis for example on nation-making in Iceland, I demonstrated, how it took place by claiming Iceland's distinctiveness within Europe, while also claiming Iceland belonged with Europe as it tried to find its place within racist and imperialistic European histories (Loftsdóttir 2009, 2019).

When the Mini-Europe park is introduced in the brochure by emphasizing Europe's common roots (Mini-Europe 2019), the way in which Europe has sought its identity from its colonial history is nowhere to be seen. Or as it is phrased there:

> From the origins of democracy to the enterprising spirit, from our Greek, Roman or Viking heritage to the political transformations of the 21st century, you will find commentary at every stage of the journey in the free catalogue. (Mini-Europe 2019: 6)

The brochure also moves effortlessly between "Europe" and the "EU" in sentences such as: "During your visit, you will discover our European roots, the Member States of the European Union, and the European Union and its implementation in Brussels" (see brochure Mini-Europe n.d.). During inaugurations of new buildings various representatives from the EU are invited, which in itself shows clearly the park as a project of the EU (Lähdesmäki 2012).

The frequent slip between the "EU" and "Europe" was not lost on my children, who were somewhat offended by the fact that the park had nothing on Iceland. When I reminded them that Iceland is not a member of the European Union, they replied that if that were the case, then Mini-Europe should change its name to "Mini-European Union." Indeed, the association between the EU and Mini-Europe is made evident immediately at the front gate, where guests see an image of Europe where EU countries are

Figure 9.1. Visiting Mini-Europe Park in Bruparck, 2017. The author's son and the miniatures display. © Kristín Loftsdóttir.

colored in dark grey, while non-EU countries are in a lighter shade. The map also displays segments of Europe that are geographically in other parts of the world, such as the Canary Islands, reminding us that the EU includes thirty-four overseas areas of six European member states that are a direct consequence of their colonial and imperial histories (Boatcă 2018). These overseas territories, enclaves, and dependencies are neatly inserted into the image of Europe with the use of frames where these areas have been cut out of their actual geographical locations and pasted next to Europe on the map. It makes them appear almost as if they exist physically in the same geographical space as the countries they belong to. What does that mean in regard to where we "find" Europe? Where is Europe then geographically speaking?

Furthermore, there is a difference among those EU countries that are displayed at Mini-Europe. The older member states are usually presented with larger buildings or several models, as well as located in the center of the park. As Lähdesmäki points out, this can be explained by practical factors, but regardless "visually marks the cultural core of Europe" (2012: 32). On the way out of the park there is a small exhibition, entitled the "Spirit of Europe" where the visitors can learn more about the history of the EU and what the EU does for "its citizens" as it is phrased on Mini-Europe's website (Mini-Europe.brussels n.d.).

Connecting more broadly this visual representation of Europe's cultural core and the slip back and forth between Europe and the EU, with some European countries' existing longstanding and current anxieties regarding securing one's country's position within the European community (Loftsdóttir et al. 2018: 16), this begs the question: what kind of Europe is being displayed and for whom?

As I walk around the park and its well-organized display, I think of some of my interlocutors' struggle with the concept of Europe, including their recognition of Europe as not a singular space but a hierarchical one. Similar to people in Iceland, many people from the Eastern part of Europe do not feel to be fully acknowledged as a part of Europe, often aspiring like Icelanders are to be acknowledged as proper European subjects (Dzenovska 2018). Especially after the extension of the EU to the east when new member states, for example Poland and Lithuania, were able to access the wider European labor market, and those seeking occupation in the western part of Europe were often racialized and discriminated against (Loftsdóttir 2017; Lapiņa and Vertelytė 2020). Chapter 4 hinted at the internal differentiation and hierarchies that exist even within the privileged expat community of the EU (Rozanska 2011; Lewicki 2016), which here can be seen as reproduced in this miniature display of different buildings where the "cultural core" of

Europe becomes marked (Lähdesmäki 2012). What other European nationalities or communities within Europe feel excluded in navigating this space?

My interlocutors refer more often to the differences between North and South when talking about Europe, rather than East and West as is understandable from their own mobility and travels from the Global South to Europe's South and from there either moving to the northern parts of Europe or trying to access them. Those precarious migrants I spoke to in Italy desire to go further north, almost as if not considering Italy as part of Europe, and similarly those few I spoke to who had arrived through Spain, seemed to see Spain more as an in-between space of Europe and Africa. Their experience of being "stuck" in Italy, unable to go further north, reflects that Europe's multiple borders do not end at Schengen's delimitation of Europe. Within Europe, including Belgium, asylum seekers or people without travel documents risk being put in detention or deported (Majcher et al. 2020: 365). In trains and public transport inside Europe, border guards check for those without proper documentation (Schwarz 2016). When Ali and I had, for example, planned to meet in Paris in 2016, Ali called me on short notice and told me that he could unfortunately not risk traveling there from Brussels as he was afraid of being apprehended by the French police due to intensive security measures at the time in trains and buses. Also, as this discussion has already hinted at, racism and various structural racialized discrimination creates various borders for racialized populations—not only migrants but also citizens—in the western part of Europe. Inga Schwarz (2016) stresses how these checks often involve racial profiling that effects racialized people regardless of their citizen status, as well as making them appear suspicious as a potential security threat.

Most of those I spoke to for this research did not know very much about Iceland, but the idea of Iceland as an exception has perhaps bled into some of their conceptions just as it had for others living in Europe. I am often somewhat eagerly asked by my interlocutors how it is in Iceland: how are migrants doing there; are they welcomed; how has Iceland welcomed asylum seekers and refugees? While Iceland has for long time been on the margins of Europe in a wide pan-European sense (Loftsdóttir 2019), Iceland has certainly eagerly tried to comply with actions of other European countries that are located here at the center of the Mini-Europe park. Icelandic people not only actively reproduced racist texts and images in the past—but today the Icelandic government actively deports a majority of those who seek humanitarian shelter within the country's boundaries (Tryggvadóttir and Loftsdóttir 2020).

More importantly, my interlocutors try to reconcile notions of what Europe "should be" with their actual experiences. As indicated earlier some emphasize Europe as a site of modernity as well as a site of exploitation of West Africa, but some of my interlocutors strongly seem to identify Europe as a site of human rights and equality. Accounts of what constitutes Europe were contradictory in these men's narratives about the "refugee crisis" in Europe. Some, when discussing the refugee situation, position Europe as a place of modernity in the sense that they associate human rights with Europe. By presenting modernity as emanating from Europe, they echo a hegemonic Eurocentric understanding of Europe as not only the starting point of history but as disseminating modernity and progress to the rest of the world (Bhambra 2011).

Idrissa explains to me that for him Belgium and Europe are places of "solidarity, unity where people's human rights are respected." Idrissa has earlier stressed rather strongly that there is no racism in Belgium, but then later he connects racism and the situation of undocumented workers in Belgium, even though I did not ask him about this specifically. Even though he also critically discusses what he sees as France's continued muddling in Niger's affairs, his strong association of Europe with human rights and justice seems to go unchallenged.

Idrissa explains, going slightly back and forth in his notion that there is no racism in Belgium, which seems to have been contested recently due to the treatment of asylum seekers: "But if you have papers, then there is equality here. Equality, justice and human rights (*droits de l'homme*). Because this exists, we cannot talk about racism. If you don't have papers, the police will probably arrest you but then set you free. They will probably not send you back to Niger. Thus, we cannot really say that there is racism here." The first sentence seems to imply that these human rights are only reserved for those who are legally in the country or citizens, while the latter sentences seem to conclude that due to a lack of harassment from the police, justice and equality can be assumed to exist in Belgium. His accounts, stressing humanitarianism, challenges in crucial ways the reification of precarious migrants as only seeking economic benefits in media generated depiction of Europe in relation to this crisis.

The sense of Europe as symbolic for modernity and human rights was probably most strongly evoked in my interview with Muhammed, the Tuareg man who had recently moved to Brussels in hopes of gaining an income to send back home to his elderly parents, wife, and children. He tells me directly that Europe is a place of humanitarianism. Like Idrissa, Muhammed earlier emphasized rather strongly that there is no racism in Belgium, but it is clear he is having difficulties reconciling it with Europe's treatment of asylum seekers. The reaction to the migrant crisis of 2016 is particularly puzzling to him and he seems unable to reconcile the current reality with his earlier conceptions of Europe in this regard. He explains that he understands that Europe cannot accommodate everyone, saying softly: "If the population [of Europe] increases suddenly, it might just destabilize the country and its economy. But I think a sense of humanity must be above some economic calculations." There is a moment of silence and then he continues, almost as if pleading for my understanding of their predicament: "For many people in the world, Europe symbolizes humanitarianism, and people think that if they come to Europe, even without papers, they will be protected against war, against hunger, against all the problems they fled." My feeling is that he is not passing judgment; it is more as if he hopes that I can provide an explanation for this that will restore his faith in Europe as a symbol of humanitarianism. He speaks rhetorically, as if he is having a conversation with someone who demonizes refugees' attempts to come to Europe, asking why they did not attempt to go somewhere else. Replying to his own question, he explains that the fact that they try to come to Europe must be because Europe has a particular meaning to them as shelter and site of human rights.

Muhammed points to himself, saying that he did not come to Europe because he wanted to. Rather he left, "Because I am like a lot of the immigrants you see here. Either they are chased by wars, or they are chased by stories, otherwise no one wants to leave home." He continues gently, "So I think it is true, it is difficult to welcome a lot of immigrants to Europe, but Europeans must know that those who come here do not want to come. Rather, they are obliged. So, you have to have a little bit of a human spirit and acknowledge that the immigrants have not come to disturb Europeans, no. If you look at the situations that pushed them to come, you will know that there was a reason that they come here. So, this is the message I want to send to Europeans: Show some humanity, that's it." Obviously even though not stating so explicitly Muhammed is engaging with the larger mediascape where refugees are seen as a problem for Europe as discussed in Chapter 2 and possibly he feels the need to present Europe to me in a positive light. However, his gentle questions and the disappointment with Europe that they convey should still be taken seriously.

In Milan at the bench where I am talking to one of the homeless asylum seekers from Niger, he is also struggling with the idea of human rights and his lived reality. He states: "You know in Africa, it is not like here in Europe where people are equal." He repeats, "In Europe everyone is equal. Regardless of if we are white, Black, Arabic, we are equal here. But in Africa it is not like that, that's our problem. This is something that I liked about Europe; because of the freedom; you can do what you want, there is no problem. That is what I liked about Europe. But actually, in reality it is not like that. Europe is shit for me. I am sorry, here I am. Me and my bag. I am sleeping on the street."

Others, I spoke with, critically stress Niger's postcoloniality in this context and the differences in power between "Europe" and the refugees. For example, Babouli remarks somewhat humorously, when addressing the current refuge situation, that when people come from Africa to Europe, they are only offered the floor of the train station to sleep on and nothing to eat, but when Europeans come to Niger they are greeted with hospitality. They are offered a place to stay and food to eat, treated with dignity and respect. When I listen to this, I nod because I know this, I have experienced it in the pastoral area in Niger, in the small towns, and in the capital.

In the Mini-Europe brochure, the guests are reminded of Europe as the domain of equality. Under the heading "The European Union has enjoyed many great successes" sentences like this one can be found: "Peace: the longest period of peace for the past 1000 years" and "Democracy: which is reinforced little by little, every day." Also, "The EU encourages Equality between men and women." These concepts are strongly associated with the idea of Europe as the cradle of democracy and equality, simultaneously as it equates EU to Europe.

It would be interesting to know what Ardo and my other Nigerien interlocutors would think of another item of this list of Europe's self-declared success as presented the Mini-Europe brochure. That success is related to mobility and says: "Freedom of Movement of persons: every citizen can travel and work where s/he wishes." At times when there is urgent fortification of this space—"Europe"—this text looks odd somehow and misplaced. How can this be a part of Europe's success when there have been such active restrictions in place for the last few decades to restrict mobility of areas that have been part of Europe in the past or that have intimate connections to Europe?

Mobility in the context of Europe's imperial and colonial history is briefly referred to in the brochure—but as a game where children are supposed to fill in a blank in a few places in the text, marked with numbers. The second line with one of the missing words in the brochure says:

> The spirit of _____ #2 also characterizes all Europeans. They explored every land and sea since the Vikings up until Christopher Columbus and even went into space. (Mini-Europe n.d.)

The missing word number two that one is supposed to insert is "adventure," which reduces the complexities of these brutal periods in Europe's history to something intrinsic to "all Europeans," simultaneously as turning the explorations into something fun and innocent.

Colonialism as a part of Europe's history is much more evident at Brussel's new museum House of European History that opened in 2017. As I peak through the polished glass of one of the exhibits with my son, I see for the first time the signed Berlin convention from 1885. A sheet of paper with elaborate signatures that I cannot read, and a red wax stamp. Earlier the same morning, I was reading with him about colonialism in his history textbook—the chapter that he was to learn this week for his school in Iceland—and the text briefly talked about the importance of the Berlin convention in the slicing up of the African continent. These signatures not only legitimated King Leopold II's possession of a particular area and of people far away but also justified the rule of other European countries over distant territories. And here on display is this document that affected the lives of so many people and linked together even more strongly the fate of people living in the African continent with those living in Europe.

The aim of the House of European History is to give a sense of the shared history of Europe, the interconnection of different European countries and its relationship with the rest of the world. This approach mirrors the ideals that were put forth on the website of the European parliament, which was responsible for establishing the museum. There it states:

> It takes a transnational approach to the origins and evolution of Europe and the diverse legacies, traditions and interpretations of its history. While learning about Europe's place in the world, visitors are encouraged to think critically about its past in order to engage in its future and present-day issues. (European Parliament n.d.)

The critical engagement with the past that the museum invites guests to think about includes colonialism, but also the conflicts between different European nation states. "Memory" as collective remembering is key here, as the museum's website makes clear when stating that one of the goals of the House of European History is to be a "permanent source for the interpretation of Europe's past—a reservoir of European memory" (House of European History n.d.). Despite the museum's emphasis on colonialism as part of Europe's history, Buettner (2018) remarks that the museum does not say much about what happened after the empires ended formally, that is, the efforts of European states to retain neocolonial influence over their former colonies. Buettner (2018) remarks how the museum is, for example, silent for the most part about Congo after the end of Leopold II's reign, and of Belgium's neocolonial influence in the area. Similarly, as with Mini-Europe, the museum does not address the colonial histories associated with the overseas territories that are a part of the EU. Also made invisible in the museum are Europe's Muslim heritage and intercontinental migration as an integral part of Europe and its population (Buettner 2018).

The museum's emphasis on memory seems to be embedded with the project of the European Union that often is defused with Europe as is reflected in this sentence: "Visitors are encouraged to think about the Europe of today, the status and position of the European Union, and the part that everyone can play in shaping Europe's future" (European Parliament Visiting n.d.). As I write this, I am reminded of the early 2000s when there was an emphasis on enhancing Brussels' attractiveness as a tourist destination by branding it as having a "European theme," where European museums "should become a symbolic, functional and social focus for the European Community in Brussels" (Jansen-Verbeke et al. 2005: 120). As in the Mini-Europe display, I ask myself who are the Europeans that the museum is appealing to with this common history?

Armed with their experience at Mini-Europe, my children noted that the iPads with which visitors navigate the exhibitions at the House of European History, did not offer any explanations in Icelandic, only, as one of the museum staff explains to my son, in the "official languages of the EU." Echoing his question at Mini-Europe, my son asked the staff why the museum was called the House of *European* History. He is, however, upset not only because our small country is not represented here but also because the whole project of Europe is starting to sound rather suspicious to him. This is due to the fact that Ardo is not with us here. For my son, his friendship with Ardo has opened his eyes even more to the fact that not everyone is welcome to the physical space of Europe nor this symbolic representation of it.

Ardo, who was uninterested in visiting Mini-Europe, was in fact excited to join us at the House of European History. When I asked Ardo if he wanted to come with us to the museum, he said excitedly that it would probably be quite beneficial for him to learn something about the history of Europe. We had decided to walk together to the museum the next day, meeting up at my place. However, as I was searching the museum's website for the best way to get there, a few moments before my appointment with Ardo, I noticed that the museum required personal identification to enter the museum.[1] I knew instantly that this meant that Ardo was unlikely join us. He showed up wearing a white shirt and business jacket, obviously dressing up for our trip. Hesitantly, I told him about the identification requirement, explaining that we might be able to get in if we tell the guards that we did not know about the requirement in advance. Ardo overstayed his visa, and his passport is not valid anymore. Most important, he does not want to draw attention to himself. "I cannot go" he told me. "It is too much of a risk." His anxieties in regard to risking being noticed, draws attention to how many precarious migrants always feel as if they have to be invisible in the larger communities in which they live. There are, however, cases of undocumented migrants and others using the physical structure of the museum as a site of resistance: Shoah Memorial in Milan, a Holocaust memorial, transformed some of its space into a shelter for migrants in July 2015 (Levin 2017: 3-4);

undocumented migrants in Paris occupied the French National Museum of Immigration in 2010–11, to draw attention to the inequalities that they had to endure (Ostow 2017).

Here I still recall Chiara De Cesari's comments that museums can be seen as "bordering practices," where they participate in reproducing "spatial imaginaries of containment," that help to justify and naturalize the hard borders of Europe, executed by Frontex and other interlinked institutionalized practices (2017: 18). In this case, however, the borders are not symbolic but also are manifested physically.

Ardo still walks with us to Leopold Park, where the museum is located, stopping at a safe distance from the museum and directing us to it. As I stand there with him, looking at this House of European History from the distance that he feels is safe for him, I cannot help but feel that the museum's very existence makes a powerful statement. It is not only about who is included or excluded from that history, or who is welcome and who is not within the doors of the museum itself. But also who is entitled to explore the history of Europe. The fact that we stand in a park carrying the name of King Leopold brings it even closer to home.

And who is welcome and who is not? With the terrorist attacks in 2016, Brussels became emblematic of Europe's dystopian future seen as characterized by insecurity and threat by dangerous Muslim "others." My interlocutor's clearly felt the fear in the air. Youssouf explained to me: "People are too afraid because of the ISIS problem. It is afraid of Muslim because they say that Muslims have done this." He adds sadly, referring to others in the same position as him. "You are not staying here because of something like this. You just want to make a life here like the others that live in this city."

Less than three weeks after the March 2016 terrorist attacks at the international airport and the Maalbeck metro station, my partner and I had arrived in Brussels. The streets downtown were empty; almost no cars and only a few people walking around. Parked next to the subway entrances stood large military trucks with soldiers. Also desolate was the Place de la Bourse—the gathering point for people after the attacks to commemorate and pay tribute to those killed and injured. Back in Iceland I had seen images in the media of people gathering there in respect for the victims and to gain support from the presence of one another. Decaying flower bouquets still covered a large part of the ground, as well as wet banners, flags, and different personal objects. They had been placed there by someone remembering their loved ones, reflecting the lives lost and the shattering pain of those left behind.

It rained softly while we stood there. It felt like we had entered a space where things had already passed and are somehow fading slowly from view,

Figure 9.2. Place de la Bourse in March 2016. After the attacks this was a gathering place to commemorate and pay tribute to those killed and injured. © Kristín Loftsdóttir.

while their impression on the present still lingered. The Brussels international airport also felt strikingly altered as well, but in different ways. We passed through passport control into an area where everything was in a state of confusion, and we then became a part of an irregular stream of people heading to the dark bottom level of the building, a garage which had been transformed into a transportation hub. There were no available trains or taxis, only buses. It was a space of complete chaos, where we were surrounded by other equally tired and confused passengers, trying to find out which transport we could take. Some of them had certainly been traveling a much longer way than we had, with lots of luggage and holding the hand of their small children. We were all under the gaze of men in full military outfit. The expression of these men was not hostile but blank, as they stood in pairs with large machine guns and heavy military clothing. I come from a country without soldiers. I am not used to seeing them or walking past them. To me, they seemed ready for anything, not a sign of security or peace but of violence and fear.

When I meet Ali and have tea with him and his Zarma friend Issa later, I ask about recent events, he shakes his head in disbelief. "These men are not Muslims," he tells me referring to the terrorists, "because such actions are not the actions of Muslims." He adds, "They are Belgians, not refugees or migrants." Addressing the increased hostility and racism, Issa stressed that the violence affects everyone and adds, "A bomb is unable to ask you if you are white, or if you are European or Indian . . . A bomb does not ask you before it explodes."

This feeling of everyday life having broken down becomes even more salient several days later when my partner and I leave Brussels. Again, military men everywhere with big guns; their faces do not show any expression. We have to wait in several long lines with other passengers, both inside and outside temporary tents, as well as present our identification materials during several stages, again in the presence of soldiers. I find myself checking frequently for my passport and travel documents as if fearing that they will vanish somehow. All of this is new to us; the waiting in endless lines, showing the same identification again and again; the sense of being reduced to both a faceless crowd and an object of surveillance. These are the things that have become a part of the daily experience for my interlocutors in this research along with many others in the world today. Those who have been marked as different racially or culturally have always been potential suspects, which has only intensified. I ask myself if this is a new Europe, or just the same Europe with its suspicions and fears revealing themselves to larger parts of its population? Have particular layers been stripped away, momentarily exposing to the more privileged parts of the population what is a part of the everyday for many others?

But the issue is not only one of securitization but also one of creating categories where some people and some parts become, consciously or not, associated with danger and criminality, creating boxes and lines between Us and Them. I come back later during the fall of the same year. When Ardo comes over to my apartment, he tells me that we have to go somewhere. When I ask where we are going, he does not want to tell me but smiles somewhat secretively. I ask him if I can take my son who is also accompanying me on this trip. I think it would be good for him to go out a little bit. "It is even better if he comes too," Ardo proclaims, clearly seeing it as adding value to the trip. My son does not speak French, so it is not always easy for them to communicate but they still manage pretty well with limited vocabulary and body language. We leave the house and go directly to the train station. Only when we have boarded the train, can I convince Ardo to tell me where we are going.

"Yesterday" he tells me obviously very pleased with himself, "you asked me how Yakubu was doing and said that you really wanted to see him again." I nod, remembering this. I had done an interview with Yakubu when I first met him a few years earlier, and then we had met each other few times more during that same trip. He had lived in Belgium for a few years, without any legal documentation, and was at the time enduring hardship, trying to look for work.

"So, I did not want to tell you, but he actually got married," Ardo proclaims, "and the woman is from Belgium, so he is doing really well. She is an African like him but moved here as a young girl. You will see her. She is more like a Belgian person than African actually." I am really pleased, knowing that this has probably turned his life around.

It is only when I hear where we are going that I feel startled: Yakabu is waiting for us at Molenbeek, where he lives now. Molenbeek has been all over the news as the neighborhood where those committing the terrorist act conducted in Brussels came from. I don't say anything to Ardo but I feel all kinds of thoughts swirling around in my head. What am I doing taking my son there? I had certainly been several times before in this neighborhood, but I feel all of a sudden, a sense of helplessness and fear. At the same time, I try to struggle with this feeling, hating myself for it, it pops up again and again and again in my mind like something that has its own life.

The train stops and Ardo tells us to go out. We leave with two other people and other two enter the train. It is cold and somewhat gloomy outside, a woman in a black jacket, with a black hijab carries her grocery bags and another woman holds the hand of her small child. A young teenager and an elderly man sit at the stop waiting for the next train. They look at me without any interest. I think about the power the media has in creating demons, building on long history of racism that I, as others, have breathed, in the space we call Europe.

NOTE

1. On the museum's website in 2018 it states: "All visitors and bags may be subject to airport-style security checks before entry. Firearms, explosive or inflammable substances, pepper sprays, sharp items and other objects that could be considered weapons are prohibited. In accordance with Belgian national legislation, certain prohibited items may be handed over to the police. A valid identity document (an ID card, passport or driving license) may be requested in order to access the House of European History" (European Parliament Visiting n.d.).

CONCLUSION

Welcome to the Future
Dismaland and Anxieties in Europe

Babouli tells me that "this is all Congo," while pointing at the Grand Place in the midst of Brussels. He continues by proclaiming that now "Europe is finished." By asserting this, he is referring to Europe's cultural and political hegemony over the world. He has seen that the economic crisis hit many Europeans hard and his delusions of Europe as a place where everything is good, where everyone lives in prosperity and safety, and as a place that will help Niger and other countries out of their poverty are long gone. For some reason, I think about his words when looking at images of the theme park Dismaland, created in 2015.

I have never been to Dismaland itself. As a phenomenon, Dismaland—created by the artist and activist Banksy in 2015—can probably be better described as an intervention rather than an actual park. Open for only one month, Dismaland was composed as a theme park, with several artists making the different "attractions," such as the security station made out of cardboard when entering the park, fairy castle, and selfie hole. With purposefully distorted and shabby park attractions, Dismaland can to some extent be understood as the dark version of Gardaland, which promised fun, adventure, and excitement. It does, however, not only unravel the obsession with "fun" and leisure as have been so important to the idea of modernity, but also exposes a sense of modernity in crisis.

Alongside their references to actual moments or monuments of the past, parks often project imagined future technologies. The name Dismaland is clearly engaging with Walt Disney's Disneyland—the first such park opening in California in 1955—which was revolutionary in how connected the theme park was with such a projection of the future, with modernity-as-promise-of-magical-future. Technology was the key to prosperity, freedom, and well-being.¹ Maria-Lydia Spinelli points out that Disney's use of the term "Imagineering"—a combination of imagination and engineering—refers to the "the process of translating cultural concepts into concrete reality," which then "validates Disneyland's slogan and prime message that 'dreams come true'" (1995: 3).

Recalling Babouli's words that Europe is finished, Banksy's Dismaland raises questions about a lingering sense of crisis and the links of crisis-talk to visions of the future and the past, interlinked with racialization of our current security and mobility regime (Loftsdóttir et al. 2018). When I was working on this research, crises of different kinds seemed to arise all around me from the beginning of the research to its end. It was not only the talk of the crisis of multiculturalism or "the refugee crisis," but also crisis talk of other kinds—of the EU, of the financial crisis, and of diverse sets of austerity measures that hit me as hard as everyone else in Iceland. Added to this can be a crisis of representation that many museums have experienced in presenting "Europe" and its heritage (De Cesari 2017).

As I was writing this book, these different crises converged through COVID-19, intensifying the economic precarity of those already in difficult positions in addition to exposing the various structural racisms that have led to Black people being over-represented in mortality statistics. While my fieldwork did not take place during the COVID-19 pandemic in Belgium and in Italy, the crises were all part of the environment in which the research took place and which shaped my experiences and the experiences of those who were at the center of my research. The Nigeriens spoke with sympathy of the economic difficulties being endured by those with whom they shared geographical space—the Belgian people. The Nigeriens reacted indirectly and directly to popular depictions of migration that are, after all, also part of this space where they live—depictions of people as potential terrorists, fake asylum seekers, or as the ultimate threat to Europe's future.

In this final chapter, I want to tease out this joint sense of crisis that creates a shared existence for my interlocutors and others living in this space we call Europe and how it links with mobility and racialization. As Babouli seems to believe, these narratives often jointly project a sense of Europe's end. His reference to Europe as "finished" struck me because, even though articulated differently, it echoes the persistent current discourse in Europe and the Global North as living in a state of crisis, of a particular era or imaginings of a future as "finished" in some sense.

In Iceland, what ended with the economic crash was not only a sense of economic security for the future but also a particular type of innocence, where future aspirations used to be deeply nationalistic, of being somehow not burdened by the history of imperialism and colonialism, with all of their evils. As well, what disappeared during the crash was a possible future that would automatically be progressive and prosperous for people living in Iceland as a whole (Loftsdóttir 2019; Heffernan and Pawlak 2020). Crisis has—simply speaking—not only appeared as a description of a particular historical period, but as a frame for thinking about our present, where "crisis talk" of different kinds attempts to capture present events (Loftsdóttir et al. 2018; Dines, Montagna, and Vacchelli 2018).

Past, Present, and Future in Crisis Moments

The words of many of my interlocutors linger with me when they indicate that they came to Europe to have the possibility of a future. Mobility of these men to Europe can thus be seen as a part of their future orientations—a way of claiming agency, of trying to create a tangible future and livable present for those who remain in their countries of origin. As I have indicated throughout the book, mobility is nothing new, neither for West Africans nor Europeans, but a part of being and acting in the world that we inhabit. Babouli's words about wealth being taken from Niger and his decision to follow it captures indirectly how a key reason for Nigerien mobility to Europe can be perceived as a future that has been taken away from people. The continued "ruination" of countries like Niger in no way exists separately from Europe but is rather a shared history where mobility (of people, wealth, technologies, and ideas) has always played a key role. As Chapter 6 on Niger reflects, European powers today directly try to control and render suspicious the mobility of people, even those who are far from the space of Europe.

While mobility has become important in defining the future of more elite Europeans through cosmopolitan ideas, mobility as a part of what made Europe and Africa into what they are today has too often been written out of European history. Discussions surrounding the crisis of multiculturalism and the refugee crisis concentrate on people from the Global South "flowing" over Europe. Such discussions exist separately from any historical acknowledgement of the long interrelationship of Europe with other parts of the world—interrelationship characterized by intense brutality, racism, and wealth extraction from one continent to another (Loftsdóttir 2020). Current engagements of the EU in Niger remain completely invisible, shaping the country as part of an externalization of migration control. This colonial amnesia or "cluster remembering" can be linked to what Hakki Taş (2020) has stressed, that is populist leaders aiming to create a comprehensive narrative with a clear past, present, and future as well as clear subjects that have places within this narrative. Part of this, Taş says, is a desire for a particular past of which people living today were never a part and which in fact never existed, but that is seen as having to be reclaimed and created in the present. Anxieties for the future therefore rest on a particular vision of the past. Across Europe, colonial relationships of the past have been hidden, neglected, or rendered irrelevant.

In relation to colonialism, selective memory is a characteristic of museums which are important for displaying and shaping European history and reputation. Regarding museums that display European history, Chiara De Cesari (2017) argues that they seek to produce a new master narrative of European history which becomes essentially a teleological story of success. According to De Cesari, in this type of story, remembering the past and learning from it (while only relaying very selective parts) is narrated as an important or true European value (2017: 19). The activism directed at Belgian monuments of Leopold II tries to redress the falseness of the past that such monuments project when glorifying his persona. Through red paint or removal of the statue's hands, these acts assert reminders of the brutality and inhumanity that was part of Leopold II's reign and the world that it created.

In some sense traditional theme parks can be thought of as versions of museums that have developed in different directions. As with museums, theme parks project the past through small patches of experience such as the Ancient Egypt ride or the Wild West ride, mixing such patches of past with imaginary worlds of the lost city of Atlantis or alien existence. Historically, museum displays of different cultures and histories have conversed and intermingled with the colonial expositions of rides and theme-park displays of colonial and marginalized subjects. Like museums, large theme parks are spaces of privileged mobile subjects—often overtly white as evident in Gardaland when I visited. Some African people such as the WoDaaBe and the Tuaregs are welcome as a part of "imperial nostalgia" (Rosaldo 1989b) or as curiosity, just as the Congolese were in the early twentieth century in the context of world exhibitions.

Meanwhile, the current regime of mobility criminalizes the mobility of other West Africans, framed as a crisis facing European countries (Lüthi 2017). Scholarly discussions within the migration paradigm often simplify West African mobility as resulting from migrants' desire for settlement in Europe. This is extrapolated from simplistic models where migration is seen as movement between two points in space, separated by borders rather than as part of multi-fold mobilities (see Schapendonk et al. 2020: 12). For West African migrants, Europe is not necessarily an object of desire.

Again, I feel drawn to Dismaland as it revolves around symbols from our past and the present, juxtaposing seemingly innocent theme-park attractions against more brutal manifestations of the present. Instead of ducks or boats that can be moved around a pond, for example, the viewer witnesses overcrowded boats teeming with refugees trying to cross "safely" to a shore which, in fact, is nowhere to be seen. To capture a past gone "mad" and possibly the loss of hope for a fairytale with a happy ending, the death of Princess Diana is used. She is depicted as Cinderella in her Pumpkin carriage, frozen in time at the moment of the accident that took her life, with the paparazzi's disturbing camera flashes going on and on, which thus objectify her endlessly.

To me, many of the images that Dismaland offers capture that, for many in the Global North, precarity has become an important condition of life. Instead of things moving forward as modernization appeared to promise several decades ago—then into more prosperity, wealth, and security—many feel as if the promise of modernity has been broken. Several scholars have noted how neoliberal policies have changed conditions in the lives of many in the Global North through risky employment status, welfare, and education—conditions shared by many migrants. However, migrant populations have to deal additionally with insecure legal status and obligations across borders. This shows how "different forms of precarity are intersecting and mutually reinforcing" (Paret and Gleeson 2016: 287). I ask myself if the promise of modernity is also seen as broken in countries like Belgium, with Brussels being the heart of Europe characterized by great disparities in wealth and power. The segregated neighborhoods of people with mi-

Figure 10.1. Dismaland's Cinderella: the dream of a happy ending in a disarray.
© Guy Corbishley / Alamy Stock Photo.

grant backgrounds, as well as those who see themselves as not belonging within that category (even though many surely do), are reflected all over Europe. Brussels is divided not only on the lines of precarious migrants and affluent residents but also in regard to affluent EU migrants and precarious residents. This draws attention to how precarity has become a condition shared by great numbers of people regardless of their origin, while it also has to be acknowledged that the position of migrants intensifies this precarity as earlier stated.

Recent films and science fiction novels demonstrate this sense of a bleak future that characterizes the present as a promise of a "future that never was" (Coleman and Tutton 2017). Instead, the future appears now as an "unavoidable catastrophe" that we are unable to escape (Coleman and Tutton 2017: 442). It draws attention to how the present is often shown as a constant grief over a future that has not yet happened, but one that is imagined as taking place in crises.

For the last decade in the Global North, the future has been seen as at stake in the various discussions of migration. In my own part of Europe and in the United Kingdom, these anxieties have taken the form of discussions of the welfare state as under siege (J. Andersson 2009; Norocel 2013; Elgenius and Rydgren 2019). Anti-migration populism engages with this affective sense of a future cancelled for citizens through the construction of clear narratives that Taş (2020) indicates is characteristic of populist rhetoric in the present. This means that the exclusion of certain populations from livable futures and humanitarian spaces is perceived as reinstating the future that the modernity paradigm promised.

I want to stress that it is not only populist leaders who push this idea; an effort of several governments has been to create agreements with countries bordering Europe, which essentially works to block people from seeking refuge. We have subsequently seen a drastic reduction of people coming to Europe to seek international protection, since they are simply unable. There was a surge in use and creation of detention in regard to migrant populations after the "refugee crisis" while, as Majcher, Flynn, and Grange (2020) point out, this trend was facilitated with changes in the EU legal framework and policy that had been made previously. This increase in detention continued after border crossings in 2018 reached its lowest count in five years, with the EU consequently contributing to the "trivialization and normalization of the use of detention" (Majcher et al. 2020: 2, 452).

While children were not part of my research, research has shown that children have constituted a large number of asylum seekers and the migrant population—one-fourth in 2018 (Majcher et al. 2020: 451). According to the UN, children constitute 40 percent of those who are displaced worldwide (UNHCR 2020). A review by Majcher, Flynn, and Grange (2020) of different practices in the EU shows that children seeking asylum are detained in many European countries along with other migrant populations, often in prison-like facilities or in actual prisons. Here, again, it can be stressed that these are not populist trends of different parties or leaders, but practices found all over Europe.

Another part of the general trend has been the outsourcing of Europe's borders, again indicating how Europe's borders are constantly on the move with the EU and its member states having funded migration controls beyond Europe. As Ruben Andersson points out, the measures of outsourcing the borders draws attention to how this makes the borders fluid with a large buffer zone rather than as a fortress (2014b: 121). Border politics have now expanded from the coast of North and West Africa into the Sahel. In reality, Europe's borders are also everywhere inside the Schengen area for those who are racialized, with citizens and non-citizens captured and detained in "border" facilities inside and outside of Europe.

The Global Detention Project has shown that European leaders have for long stressed externalization of migration controls. These leaders have as well recently actively promoted and financed such efforts in countries including Ukraine, Turkey, and Libya (Majcher et al. 2020: 460; see also Pinelli 2018). The EU member states initiated a series of measures to stop people coming from Libya to Europe, regardless of the conditions from which they came and regardless of the conditions awaiting those who could not leave or were sent back to Libya (see Majcher et al. 2020: 460–63). Luiza Bialasiewicz (2012) points out that, following these agreements, some people intercepted by the Italian Coast Guards were sent directly to Tripoli without any consideration as to whether they needed international protection. Such agreements between the Libyan government and the European governments have persisted since the beginning of the war in Libya, in spite of a series of horrific human right abuses. As described by Amnesty International, "refugees and migrants in Libya are exposed to horrendous human rights violations in a country where institutions have been weakened by years of conflict and political division" (2017a: 7). These agreements have surely led to a reduction of refugees in Italy by 67 percent between July and November 2017 (Amnesty International 2017a: 7). But at what cost? Already in 2017, Amnesty International (2017a) stressed that these horrible human right abuses against migrants in refugee camps in Libya were well known by European leaders, who continue to make agreements to keep away people seeking international protection.

EU member states finance and assist with the establishment of detention centers as well as the interception of migrants by Libyan Coast Guards. Migrants are returned to Libya where they encounter various Libyan local authorities and armed groups "to encourage them to stop the smuggling of people and to increase border controls in the south of the country" (Amnesty International 2017a: 9). As stated by Amnesty International, this collaboration takes place in spite of it being well known that Libya has not ratified the 1951 Refugee Convention (2017a: 7; for overview of this collaboration, see for example Torresi 2013). The press release for Amnesty International's report bluntly states: "European governments have not just been fully aware of these abuses, they are complicit in them" (2017b).

Several years ago, I saw the future-orientated film *Children of Men*. The film's story seems even more relevant now than when first shown in 2006—or, as phrased by one film analyst in 2016, the film's "version of the future is now disturbingly familiar" (Barber 2016). The film depicts a future United Kingdom, where a crisis situation is met by extreme security measures centering around migrants' bodies. It becomes acceptable to cancel the human rights of some people by "activating traditional forms of racism" (Chaudhuri 2011: 194). As Chaudhuri's analysis of the film suggests, this is made acceptable due to the view that only racialized others will be affected. In fact, no one is safe. Rather, people—those seen as migrants and those seen as not—live under circumstances of shared vulnerability (2011: 201).

Research has revealed that those who voted for Donald Trump in the 2016 US election and for Brexit are not only worse off but also people who could be defined as middle-class (Bhambra 2017; Bangstad, Bertelsen, and Henkel 2019). Increased precarity or vulnerability can still be seen as characterizing these lives with increased neoliberalism in the Global North, even among those who are middle-class. Dace Dzenovska (2018) points out that Eastern Europe—often negatively depicted as lagging behind Western Europe—forecasted the future of increased precarity for Europe as a whole. The "transition" from socialism to capitalism in Eastern Europe was characterized by practices and developments increasingly experienced in Western Europe that involve various abuses of labor and diminishing social welfare programs (Dzenovska 2018: 24-25). Similarly, Structural Adjustment Programs imposed by the World Bank and the International Monetary Fund in places such as Niger and other countries in the Global South in the 1980s forecasted privatization policies and austerity measures later to be imposed in the Global North (Powers and Rakopoulos 2019; Pfeiffer 2019).

Not everyone in the Global North is convinced of the future that the populists are claiming to secure. Rather, for others the question revolves around what it means for our society if we cancel the humanity of others. Some who believe the fundamental values on which the European project was based, similar to some of my interlocutors, express deep concern with the direction that European leaders are taking. Majcher, Flynn, and Grange point out how the development of EU law regarding migration has shaped Europe's response to the humanitarian crisis. This response, they stress, has undermined the core of what the European project should be about—"respect for human dignity and human rights; freedom; democracy; equality; and the rule of law" (2020: 11). The growth of detention centers alone should, as they argue, be a warning sign for the future that Europe is creating.

Thus, in addition to the intense suffering of those excluded from seeking humanitarian assistance or escaping intolerable circumstances, we may ask what such inhumane actions do to the future that we are entering and to the kind of humanity which we ourselves embody. Again, I want to refer to science fiction to demonstrate this. The book *Do Androids Dream of Electronic Sheep?* was published in the late 1960s in the context of the Vietnam War and was later used as a steppingstone for the movie *Blade Runner*. It depicts a future crisis where androids who look, act, and feel as humans have escaped from their spatial designation to dwell alongside "real" humans. While the androids may even think that they are human beings, they are not and, thus, need to be exposed and exterminated.[2] Testing is seen as necessary to determine who is a real human and who is not, even when it means that innocent humans will be sacrificed as well. The emphasis on testing reminds me of the "categorical fetishism" (a term from Apostolova 2015, quoted in Crawley and Skleparis 2018) that I discussed in Chapter 2, where it is seen as crucial to categorize who is a migrant, asylum seeker, or refugee and to give rights accordingly—as if these are clear categories within which real individuals can be put. Even more alarming is the increased and growing use of evolving digital technologies such as biometric data in border patrolling, which Ioana Vrăbiescu (2020) explains as "any foreigner becomes a potential over-stayer, criminal or illegal immigrant." This creates new possibilities for testing the bodies of certain racialized people to see if they are right-bearing citizens or something else.

The key point of *Do Androids Dream of Electronic Sheep?* is, in my view, to draw attention to the consequences of right-to-life refusal to those who look and act like humans, even though they are in some sense not. How does it impact those who are the "real" humans? How does their humanity become disputable as well, in the sense of how acts of extreme violence rob people potentially of their own humanity? What kind of society makes everyone a potential threat, a potential suspect?

Tucson is far away from Niger, far from Brussels and Iceland. I still want to take this story back there because, in a larger perspective where we scale back, all of these stories are interrelated. When visiting Tucson in 2018, I am on sabbatical and so is my partner. Strangely, this town seems not to have changed since we lived there several decades ago. While it is clear that the lives of many are characterized by poverty, it was also clear before. It is, however, different being there as a visitor rather than as a student; we are somehow less sheltered from the "real" world, especially since our children are with us, creating a different kind of link to the diverse communities that live in this city. What has changed in Tucson, people tell me, is the more open hostility to people who again are not necessarily migrants, but Spanish-speaking citizens of the United States.

When my girls start in a regular neighborhood school, I see their blond heads move in an ocean of mostly dark-haired children, as they run to their class. Many of the youngsters in this school do not seem very privileged, as I can see when my daughters don't want to dress in expensive brand names for school, and when they are warned by school personnel never to show if they have any kind of money on them. Their Icelandic nationality is a cause of excitement, but most surprising to their classmates is the fact that we decided to come to Tucson of all places. Why would we want to go to Tucson when we have the option of going and staying anywhere we want? "Why did you come to Tucson? Why not New York or somewhere up north?" the kids ask my girls, not as a question but more to bring forward the point that we should have gone somewhere else where there are much better economic opportunities. They seem to be asking, why does someone who is privileged enough to be able to go away come here? Puzzled, my girls tell us that the biggest desire of their classmates and their parents is to go away—to escape their lives here—in the hope that somewhere else holds a more prosperous future. My girls are shocked as well to discover their own privileges in terms of mobility and the desires of their friends to escape from their underprivileged and precarious circumstances. They don't connect this to mobility or to Ardo and Ali whom they have come to know.

As I am writing this book, it is hard not to think about this in context of each other. Contrary to what surfaces in many of the media narratives on migration and in the rhetoric of the populist parties, mobility—in search of something hopefully better—has been and is a part of being human. Ardo and all the others with whom I speak, spending years away from their families back home, are precisely trying to create a new future for themselves and their families, actively using the means at their disposal to do so, their own mobility.

NOTES

1. Often the imagination of the future in the original Disneyland and other such parks was fused with static presentations of pure, authentic folk communities and the exotic pasts of other people.

2. For the author, Philip K. Dick, the androids were not the metaphor for those who were discriminated against but those who were "physiologically human but behaving in a non-human way" and thus "cruel," "without-empathy," and "less-than-human entities" (Sammon 2007: 244, 262). According to Dick, the Vietnam War context made him feel that that the androids personally were so lethal that it was justified to kill them. Regardless of whether it was justfied to kill the androids or not, the dilemma would be "Could we not become like the androids in our very effort to wipe them out?" (2007: 244).

References

"2000: World Celebrates New Millennium." 2000. *BBC*, 1 January. Retrieved 29 October 2020 from http://news.bbc.co.uk/onthisday/hi/dates/stories/january/1/newsid_2478000/2478173.stm.

Abram, Simone, Bela Feldman Bianco, Shahram Khosravi, Noel Salazar, and Nicholas de Genova. 2016. "The Free Movement of People Around the World Would Be Utopian: IUAES World Congress 2013: Evolving Humanity, Emerging Worlds, 5-10 August 2013." *Identities* 24(2): 123-55. https://doi.org/10.1080/1070289X.2016.1142879.

Abu El-Haj, Thea Renda. 2002. "Contesting the Politics of Culture, Rewriting the Boundaries of Inclusion: Working for Social Justice with Muslim and Arab Communities." *Anthropology & Education Quarterly* 33(3): 308-16.

Abu-Lughod, Lila. 2002. "Do Muslim Women Really Need Saving? Anthropological Reflections on Cultural Relativism and Its Others." *American Anthropologist* 104(3): 783-90.

Adeniran, Adebusuyi Isaac. 2020. *Migration Crises in 21st Century Africa: Patterns, Processes and Projections*. New York: Palgrave Macmillan, Springer Nature.

Afifi, Tamer. 2011. "Economic or Environmental Migration? The Push Factors in Niger." *International Migration* 49: e95-e124.

AfricaMuseum. 2020. "Museum history." Retrieved 23 March 2020 from https://www.africamuseum.be/en/discover/history.

Agamben, Giorgio. 1995. "We Refugees." *Symposium: A Quarterly Journal in Modern Literatures* 49(2): 114-19.

Aguilera, Jasmine. 2019. "Here's What to Know about the Status of Family Separation at the US Border, Which Isn't Nearly over." *Time*, 25 October. Retrieved 25 June 2020 from https://time.com/5678313/trump-administration-family-separation-lawsuits/.

Ajala, Olayinka. 2018. "US Drone Base in Agadez." *The RUSI Journal* 163(5): 20-27. https://doi.org/10.1080/03071847.2018.1552452.

Alexander, Boyd. 1908. *From the Niger to the Nile*. Vol. I. London: Edward Arnold.

Alidou, Ousseina D. 2005. *Engaging Modernity: Muslim Women and the Politics of Agency in Postcolonial Niger*. Madison: The University of Wisconsin Press.

Alzouma, Gado. 2009. "The State and the Rebel: Online Nationalisms in Niger." *Journal of Contemporary African Studies* 27(4): 483-500.

Amnesty International. 2017a. "Libya's Dark Web of Collusion: Abuses Against Europe-Bound Refugees and Migrants." London: Amnesty International. Retrieved 29 October 2020 from https://www.amnesty.org/download/Documents/MDE1975 612017ENGLISH.PDF.

Amnesty International. 2017b. "Libya: European Governments Complicit in Horrific Abuse of Refugees and Migrants." Amnesty.org, 12 December. Retrieved 29 October 2020 from https://www.amnesty.org/en/latest/news/2017/12/libya-europe an-governments-complicit-in-horrific-abuse-of-refugees-and-migrants/.

Ámundadóttir, Aðalheiður. 2018. "Segir þvingunarúrræði lögreglu ómannúðleg og niðurlægjandi." Vísir, 29 (August). Retrieved 25 June 2020 from http://www.visir.is/g/2018180828831.

Andersson, Jenny. 2009. "Nordic Nostalgia and Nordic Light: The Swedish Model as Utopia 1930–2007." *Scandinavian Journal of History* 34(3): 229–45.

Andersson, Ruben. 2012. "A Game of Risk: Boat Migration and the Business of Bordering Europe." *Anthropology Today* 28(6): 7–11.

———. 2014a. *Illegality, Inc.: Clandestine Migration and the Business of Bordering Europe*. Oakland: University of California Press.

———. 2014b. "Hunter and Prey: Patrolling Clandestine Migration in the Euro-African Borderlands." *Anthropological Quarterly* 87(1): 119–49.

———. 2016. *Why Europe's Border Security Approach Has Failed—and How to Replace It*. Paper commissioned by the Human Security Study Group, SiT/WP/08/16, Friedrich Ebert Stiftung.

Anthias, Floya, and Nira Yuval-Davis. 1983. "Contextualizing Feminism—Gender, Ethnic and Class Divisions." *Feminist Review* 15(1): 62–75.

Apor, Péter. 2015. "Museums of Civilization, Museums of State, Museums of Identity: National Museums in Europe, 1918–2000." In *National Museums and Nation-Building in Europe 1750–2010: Mobilization and Legitimacy, Continuity and Change*, ed. Peter Aronsson and Gabriella Elgenius, 33–65. Oxon: Routledge.

Appadurai, Arjun. 1996. *Modernity at Large: Cultural Dimensions of Globalization*. Minneapolis: University of Minnesota Press.

Arnaut, Karel. 2019. "African Diaspora between Editorial Challenges and Planetary Futures: Interview with Hélène Neveu Kringelbach." *African Diaspora* 11(1–2): 10–12.

Baban, Freyzi. 2013. "Cosmopolitan Europe: Border Crossings and Transnationalism in Europe." *Global Society* 27(2): 217–35. https://doi.org/10.1080/13600826.2012.762344.

Baker, Mona, and Bolette B. Blaagaard. 2016. *Citizen Media and Public Spaces: Diverse Expression of Citizenship and Dissent*. Abingdon: Routledge.

Bakewell, Oliver, and Hein de Haas. 2007. "African Migrations: Continuities, Discontinuities and Recent Transformations." In *African Alternatives*, ed. Patrick Chabal, Ulf Engel, and Leo de Haan, 95–118. Leiden: Brill.

Balibar, Etienne. 1991. "Is There a 'Neo-Racism'?" In *Race, Nation, Class: Ambiguous Identities*, ed. Immanuel Wallerstein, 17–28. London: Verso.

Balibar, Etienne, and Frank Collins. 2003. "Europe, an 'Unimagined' Frontier of Democracy." *Diacritics* 33(3): 36–44.

Bangstad, Sindre. 2014. *Anders Breivik and the Rise of Islamphobia*. London: Zed Books.
———. 2018. "The New Nationalism and Its Relationship to Islam." In *Diversity and Contestations over Nationalism in Europe and Canada*, ed. J. E. Fossum, R. Kastoryano, and B. Siim, 285–311. London: Palgrave Macmillan.
Bangstad, S., B. E. Bertelsen, and H. Henkel. 2019. "The Politics of Affect: Perspectives on the Rise of the Far-Right and Right-Wing Populism in the West." *Focaal* 83: 98–113.
Bank, Roland. 2000. "Reception Conditions for Asylum Seekers in Europe: An Analysis of Provisions in Austria, Belgium, France, Germany and the United Kingdom." *Nordic Journal of International Law* 69(3): 257–88.
Barát, Erzsébet, and Ebru Sungun. 2012. "The French Ban on Headscarves: Rendering Racism Respectable." In *Teaching "Race" with a Gendered Edge*, ed. Brigitte Hipfl and Kristín Loftsdóttir, 111–26. Budapest: Central European Press.
Barber, Nicholas. 2016. "Why *Children of Men* Has Never Been as Shocking as It Is Now." *BBC Culture*, 15 December. Retrieved 25 July 2020 from https://www.bbc.com/culture/article/20161215-why-children-of-men-has-never-been-as-shocking-as-it-is-now.
Basok, Tanya, Danièle Bélanger, Martha Luz Rojas Wiesner, and Guillermo Candiz. 2015. *Rethinking Transit Migration: Precarity, Mobility, and Self-Making in Mexico*. New York: Palgrave Macmillan.
Baumann, Gerd. 1999. *The Multicultural Riddle: Rethinking National, Ethnic, and Religious Identities*. New York: Routledge.
Beauvilain, Alain. 1977. "Les Peul du Dallol Bosso et la Secheresse 1969–1973, Niger." In *Strategies Pastorales et Agricoles des Sahaliens durant la Sécheresse 1969–1974*, ed. Jean Gallais, 169–98. Paris: Centre d'Etudes de Géographie Tropical.
Beck, Ulrich. 2012. "Redefining the Sociological Project: the Cosmopolitan Challenge." *Sociology* 46(1): 7–12.
Benli, Ali Emre. 2017. "Refugee Crisis in Europe: The March to Claim Rights." *20 Consiglio Nazionale delle Ricerche—Istituto di Ricerche sulla Popolazione e le Politiche Sociali. (IRPPS), Working Paper* 97: 1–20.
Berlin, Ira. 2010. *The Making of African America: The Four Great Migrations*. New York: Viking.
Bertram, L. K. 2018. "'Eskimo' Immigrants and Colonial Soldiers: Icelandic Immigrants and the North-West Resistance, 1885." *Canadian Historical Review* 99(1): 63–97.
Bhambra, Gurminder K. 2011. "Historical Sociology, Modernity, and Postcolonial Critique." *The American Historical Review* 116(3): 653–62.
———. 2017. "Brexit, Trump, and 'Methodological Whiteness': On the Misrecognition of Race and Class." *British Journal of Sociology* 68(S1): S214–S232.
Bhambra, Gurminder K., and John Narayan. 2017. "Introduction: Colonial Histories and the Postcolonial Present of European Cosmopolitanism." In *European Cosmopolitanism: Colonial Histories, and Postcolonial Societies*, ed. Gurminder K. Bhambra and John Narayan, 1–14. Abingdon: Routledge.
Bhui, Hindpal Singh. 2016. "The Place of 'Race' in Understanding Immigration Control and the Detention of Foreign Nationals." *Criminology and Criminal Justice* 16(3): 267–85. https://doi.org/10.1177 percent2F1748895816646613.

Bialasiewicz, Luzia. 2012. "Off-Shoring and Out-Sourcing the Borders of Europe: Libya and EU Border Work in the Mediterranean." *Geopolitics* 17(4): 843–66.

Blainey, Marc G. 2016. "Groundwork for the Anthropology of Belgium: An Overlooked Microcosm of Europe." *Ethnos* 81(3): 478–507.

Blommaert, Jan. 2001. "Investigating Narrative Inequality: African Asylum Seekers' Stories in Belgium." *Discourse & Society* 12(4): 413–49.

Boatcă, M. 2018. "Caribbean Europe: Out of Sight, Out of Mind?" In *Constructing the Pluriverse: The Geopolitics of Knowledge*, ed. Bernd Reiter, 197–218. Durham, NC: Duke University Press.

Bornstein, E., and P. Redfield. 2010. "An Introduction to the Anthropology of Humanism." In *Forces of Compassion: Humanitarianism between Ethics and Politics*, ed. E. Bornstein and P. Redfield, 3–30. Santa Fe: School for Advanced Research Press.

Boulila, Stefanie C., and Christiane Carri. 2017. "On Cologne: Gender, Migration and Unacknowledged Racisms in Germany." *European Journal of Women's Studies* 24(3): 286–93.

Bowden, Charles. 2007. "Our Wall." *National Geographic Magazine*, May 2007. Retrieved 20 June 2020 from http://soulproject.synthasite.com/resources/border/our%20wall%20(national%20geographic),%20charles%20bowden.pdf.

Boyce, Geoffrey, and Jill Williams. 2012. "Intervention—Homeland Security and the Precarity of Life in the Borderlands." *Antipode Foundation*, 10 December. Retrieved 3 March 2021 from https://antipodefoundation.org/2012/12/10/intervention-homeland-security-and-the-precarity-of-life-in-the-borderlands/.

Brachet, Julien. 2016. "Policing the Desert: The IOM in Libya beyond War and Peace." *Antipode* 48(2): 272–92.

Bragard, Véronique. 2011. "'Indépendance!': The Belgo-Congolese Dispute in the Tervuren Museum." *Human Architecture: Journal of the Sociology of Self-Knowledge* 9(4): 93–104.

Brancato, Giovanni, Alessandro Ricci, and Melissa Stolfi. 2016. "From Home Safety to International Terrorism: How Italian Talk Shows Framed Migration after the Paris Attacks." *Journal of Liberty and International Affairs* 1(1): 16–25. https://nbn-resolving.org/urn:nbn:de:0168-ssoar-46882-1.

Brussels.info. n.d.a. "Mini-Europe Brussels Belgium." Retrieved 25 June 2020 from https://www.brussels.info/mini-europe/.

———. n.d.b. "Welcome to Brussels Belgium." Retrieved 25 June 2020 from http://www.brussels.info.

Brydon, Anne. 2001. "Dreams and Claims: Icelandic-Aboriginal Interactions in the Manitoba Interlake." *Journal of Canadian Studies* 36(2): 164–90.

Buettner, Elizabeth. 2016. *Europe After Empire: Decolonization, Society, and Culture*. Cambridge, UK: Cambridge University Press.

———. 2018. "What–and Who–Is 'European' in the Postcolonial EU? Inclusions and Exclusions in the European Parliament's House of European History." *BMGN-Low Countries Historical Review* 133(4): 132–48.

Bunzl, Matti. 2005. "Between Anti-Semitism and Islamophobia: Some Thoughts on the New Europe." *American Ethnologist* 32(4): 499–508.

Caestecker, Frank. 2000. *Alien Policy in Belgium, 1840–1940: The Creation of Guest Workers, Refugees and Illegal Aliens*. New York: Berghahn Books.

Carter, Chelsey. 2018. "'The Personal is Political': Reflection, Critique, and Steps Forward in the Era of Donald Trump." *American Ethnological Society*, 19 February 2018. Retrieved 25 June 2020 from https://americanethnologist.org/features/reflections/the-personal-is-political.

Castagnone, Eleonora, Tiziana Nazio, Laura Bartolini, and Bruno Schoumaker. 2014. "Understanding Transnational Labour Market Trajectories of African-European Migrants: Evidence from the MAFE Survey." *International Migration Review* 49(1): 200-31.

Ceuppens, Bambi. 2006. "Allochthons, Colonizers, and Scroungers: Exclusionary Populism in Belgium." *African Studies Review* 49(2): 147–86.

———. 2014. "From Colonial Subjects/Objects to Citizens: The Royal Museum for Central Africa as a Contact-Zone." In *Advancing Museum Practices*, ed. Francesca Lanz and Elena Montanari, 83–99. Turin: Umberto Allemandi & Co.

Chaudhuri, Shohini. 2011. "Unpeople: Postcolonial Reflections on Terror, Torture and Detention in *Children of Men*." In *Postcolonial Cinema Studies*, ed. Sandra Ponzanesi and Marguerite Waller, 191–204. Abingdon: Routledge.

Coleman, Rebecca, and Richard Tutton. 2017. "Futures in Question: Theories, Methodologies, Practices." *Sociological Review* 65(3): 440–47.

Comaroff, John, and Jean Comaroff. 2009. *Ethnicity, Inc.* Chicago: University of Chicago Press.

Concert Archives. 2021a. "Tinariwen's Concert History." Retrieved 23 February 2021 from https://www.concertarchives.org/bands/tinariwen?page=3#concert-table.

———. 2021b. "Bombino's Concert History." Retrieved 23 February 2021 from https://www.concertarchives.org/bands/bombino?page=3#concert-table.

Crawley, Heaven, and Dimitris Skleparis. 2018. "Refugees, Migrants, Neither, Both: Categorical Fetishism and the Politics of Bounding in Europe's 'Migration Crisis.'" *Journal of Ethnic and Migration Studies* 44(1): 48–64.

Daniszewski, John. 2020. "Why We Will Lowercase 'white.'" *AP (Associated Press)* blog post, 20 July 2020. Retrieved 15 July 2021 from https://blog.ap.org/announcements/why-we-will-lowercase-white.

Danjibo, Nathaniel. 2013. "The Aftermath of the Arab Spring and Its Implication for Peace and Development in the Sahel and Sub-Saharan Africa." *Strategic Review for Southern Africa* 35(2): 16–34.

Darby, P., G. Akindes, and M. Kirwin. 2007. "Football Academies and the Migration of African Football Labor to Europe." *Journal of Sport and Social Issues* 31(2): 143–61.

Davis, Elizabeth A. 1999. "Metamorphosis in the Culture Market of Niger." *American Anthropologists* 101(3): 485–501.

Deboosere, Patrick, Thierry Eggerickx, Etienne Van Hecke, and Benjamin Wayens. 2009. "The Population of Brussels: A Demographic Overview." *Brussels Studies* [Online], *Synopses, CFB* 3. https://doi.org/10.4000/brussels.891.

De Bruijn, Mirjam. 2014. "Connecting in Mobile Communities: An African Case Study." *Media, Culture & Society* 36(3): 319–35.

De Cesari, Chiara. 2017. "Museums of Europe: Tangles of Memory, Borders, and Race." *Museum Anthropology* 40(1): 18-35.

De Cleen, Benjamin, Jan Zienkowski, Kevin Smets, Afra Dekie, and Robin Vandevoordt. 2017. "Constructing the 'Refugee Crisis' in Flanders: Continuities and Adaptations of Discourses on Asylum and Migration." In *The Migrant Crisis: European Perspectives and National Discourses*, ed. M. Barlai, B. Fähnrich, C. Griessler, and M. Rhomberg, 59-78. Berlin: LIT.

de Haas, Hein, and Nando Sigona. 2012. "Migration and Revolution." *Forced Migration Review* 39: 4-5.

Demart, Sarah. 2008. "De la distinction au stigmate, Matonge, un quartier congolais dans Bruxelles." *Cahiers de la Fonderie* 38: 58-62.

———. 2013. "Congolese Migration to Belgium and Postcolonial Perspectives." *African Diaspora* 6(1): 1-20.

Deshingkar, Priya. 2019. "The Making and Unmaking of Precarious, Ideal Subjects—Migration Brokerage in the Global South." *Journal of Ethnic and Migration Studies* 45(14): 2638-54. https://doi.org/10.1080/1369183X.2018.1528094.

Deycard, Frédéric. 2012. "Political Cultures and Tuareg Mobilizations: Rebels of Niger, from Kaocen to the Mouvement Des Nigériens Pour La Justice." In *Understanding Collective Political Violence*, ed. Yvan Guichaoua, 46-64. London: Palgrave Macmillan.

Diallo, Souleymane. 2018. *"The Truth about the Desert": Exile, Memory, and the Making of Communities among Malian Tuareg Refugees in Niger*. Cologne: Modern Academic Publishing. https://library.oapen.org/bitstream/handle/20.500.12657/30608/645078.pdf?sequence=1.

Dickerson, Caitlin. 2020. "Parents of 545 Children Separated at the Border Cannot Be Found." *The New York Times*, 21 October. Retrieved 12 April 2021 from https://www.nytimes.com/2020/10/21/us/migrant-children-separated.html.

Dines, Nick, Nicola Montagna, and Elena Vacchelli. 2018. "Beyond Crisis Talk: Interrogating Migration and Crises in Europe." *Sociology* 52(3): 439-47.

Dirk, Jacobs, and Andrea Rea. 2007. "Brussels Youth: Between Diversity and Adversity." *Brussels Studies* [Online] 8. http://brussels.revues.org/437.

Dixon, Andrea A., Romain Chabrol, Bruno Chareyron, Alexandra Dawe, Nina Schulz, Rianne Teule, and Aslihan Tumer. 2010. "Left in the Dust. AREVA's Radioactive Legacy in the Desert Towns of Niger." *Greenpeace*. Retrieved 21 October 2020 from https://www.sortirdunucleaire.org/IMG/pdf/greenpeace-2010-left_in_the_dust-areva_s_radioactive_legacy_in_the_desert_towns_of_niger.pdf.

Dzenovska, Dace. 2013. "Historical Agency and the Coloniality of Power in Post-Socialist Europe." *Anthropological Theory* 13(4): 394-416.

———. 2018. "Emptiness and Its Futures: Staying and Leaving as Tactics of Life in Latvia." *Focaal* 80: 16-29.

Edmunds, June. 2013. "Human Rights, Islam and the Failure of Cosmopolitanism." *Ethnicities* 13(6): 671-88. https://doi.org/10.1177 percent2F1468796812470796.

Eide, E., R. Kunelius, and A. Phillips, eds. 2008. *Transnational Media Events: The Mohammed Cartoons and the Imagined Clash of Civilizations*. Gothenburg: Nordiskt Informationscenter.

Ekman, Mattias. 2018. "Anti-Refugee Mobilization in Social Media: the Case of Soldiers of Odin." *Social Media + Society* 4(1).

Elgenius, Gabriella. 2015. "National Museums as National Symbols." In *National Museums and Nation-Building in Europe 1750–2010*, ed. Peter Aronsson and Gabriella Elgenius, 145–66. London: Routledge. https://doi.org/10.4324/9781315737133.

Elgenius, Gabriella, and Jens Rydgren. 2019. "Frames of Nostalgia and Belonging: The Resurgence of Ethno-Nationalism in Sweden." *European Societies* 21(4): 583–602. https://doi.org/10.1080/14616696.2018.1494297.

Elischer, Sebastian. 2013. "After Mali Comes Niger." *Foreign Affairs* 12. https://sahelresearch.africa.ufl.edu/files/Elischer_Foreign_Affairs_2013.pdf.

Elischer, Sebastian, and Lisa Mueller. 2018. "Niger Falls Back off Track." *African Affairs* 118(471): 392–406.

Englund, Harri, and J. Leach. 2000. "Ethnography and the Meta-Narratives of Modernity." *Current Anthropology* 41(2): 225–48.

Eriksen, T. H. 2002. *Ethnicity and Nationalism: Anthropological Perspectives*. London: Pluto Press.

Errington, Shelly. 1998. *The Death of Authentic Primitive Art: And Other Tales of Progress*. Oakland: University of California Press.

Esson, James. 2015. "Better off at Home? Rethinking Responses to Trafficked West African Footballers in Europe." *Journal of Ethnic and Migration Studies* 41(3): 512–30.

European Parliament. n.d. "House of European History." Retrieved 20 October 2020 from https://op.europa.eu/en/publication-detail/-/publication/546c1520-c848-11e8-9424-01aa75ed71a1/language-en/format-PDF.

European Parliament Visiting. n.d. "House of European History." Retrieved 25 June 2020 from http://www.europarl.europa.eu/visiting/en/brussels/house-of-european-history.

Eurostat. n.d. "Database. Population (Demography, Migration and Projections)." Retrieved 25 June 2020 from https://ec.europa.eu/eurostat/web/population-demography-migration-projections/data/database.

———. 2020. "Migration and Migrant Population Statistics: Statistics Explained." Retrieved 30 June 2020 from https://ec.europa.eu/eurostat/statistics-explained/pdfscache/1275.pdf.

Ewans, Martin. 2003. "Belgium and the Colonial Experience." *Journal of Contemporary European Studies* 11(2): 167–80. https://doi.org/10.1080/1460846032000164609.

Eyford, Ryan. 2006. "Quarantined Within a New Colonial Order: The 1876–1877 Lake Winnipeg Smallpox Epidemic." *Journal of the Canadian Historical Association* 17(1): 55–78.

Eyþórsdóttir, Eyrún, and Kristín Loftsdóttir. 2016. "Vikings in Brazil: The Iceland Brazil Association Shaping Icelandic Heritage." *International Journal of Heritage Studies* 22(7): 543–53.

Fadil, Nadia. 2009. "Managing Affects and Sensibilities: The Case of Not-Handshaking and Not-Fasting." *Social Anthropology* 17(4): 439–54.

———. 2011. "Not-/Unveiling as an Ethical Practice." *Feminist Review* 98(1): 83–109.

———. 2014. "Asserting State Sovereignty: The Face-Veil Ban in Belgium." In *The Experiences of Face Veil Wearers in Europe and the Law*, ed. Eva Brems, 251–62. Cambridge, UK: Cambridge University Press.

Fassin, Didier. 2011. "Policing Borders, Producing Boundaries. the Governmentality of Immigration in Dark Times." *Annual Review of Anthropology* 40: 213–26.

Fekete, Liz. 2009. *A Suitable Enemy: Racism, Migration and Islamphobia in Europe*. London: Pluto Press.

———. 2018. *Europe's Fault Lines: Racism and the Rise of the Right*. London: Verso Books.

Flynn, Daniel, and Geert de Clercq. 2014. "Special Report: Areva and Niger's Uranium Fight." *Reuters Business News*, 5 February. Retrieved 30 June 2020 from https://www.reuters.com/article/us-niger-areva-specialreport-idUSBREA140AA20140205.

Flynn, Michael. 2014. "How and Why Immigration Detention Crossed the Globe." *Global Detention Project*, Working Paper No. 8 April 2014. http://archivio.lasciatecientrare.it/attachments/article/82/Flynn_diffusion_WorkingPaper_v2.pdf.

Fontanari, Elena. 2017a. "It's My Life. The Temporalities of Refugees and Asylum-Seekers within the European Border Regime." *Etnografia e ricerca qualitativa* 10(1): 25–54.

———. 2017b. "Looking for Neverland. The Experience of the Group 'Lampedusa in Berlin' and the Refugee Protest of Oranienplatz." In *Witnessing the Transition: Moments in the Long Summer of Migration*, ed. Regina Römhild, Anja Schwanhäußer, Birgit zur Nieden, and Gökce Yurdakul, 15–33. Berlin: BIM.

Fortier, Anne-Marie. 2006. "The Politics of Scaling, Timing and Embodying: Rethinking the 'New Europe.'" *Mobilities* 1(3): 313–31.

———. 2007. "Too Close for Comfort: Loving Thy Neighbour and the Management of Multicultural Intimacies." *Environment and Planning D: Society and Space* 25: 104–19.

Fox, Jon E., Laura Moraşanu, and Eszter Szilassy. 2012. "The Racialization of the New European Migration to the UK." *Sociology* 46(4): 680–95.

Fradejas-García, Ignacio, and Linda M. Mülli. 2019. "(Im)Mobile Workers: Entangled Regimes of (Im)Mobility Within the United Nations System." *Mobilities* 14(6): 906–22. https://doi.org/10.1080/17450101.2019.1669914.

Franke, Richard W., and Barbara H. Chasin. 1980. *Seeds of Famine: Ecological Destruction and the Development Dilemma in the West African Sahel*. New Jersey: Rowman & Allanheld Publishers.

Frye, Reilly. 2020. "Family Separation under the Trump Administration: Applying an International Criminal Law Framework." *The Journal of Criminal Law and Criminology* 110(2): 349–77.

Garner, Steve. 2007. "The European Union and the Racialization of Immigration, 1985–2006." *Race/Ethnicity: Multidisciplinary Global Contexts* 1(1): 61–87.

———. 2009. *Racisms: An Introduction*. London: Sage Publication.

Gatti, Emanuele. 2009. "Defining the Expat: The Case of High-Skilled Migrants in Brussels." *Brussels Studies. The e-Journal for Academic Research on Brussels* 28. https://doi.org/10.4000/brussels.681.

Gewald, J. B. 2006. "More than Red Rubber and Figures Alone: A Critical Appraisal of the Memory of the Congo Exhibition at the Royal Museum for Central Africa, Tervuren, Belgium." *The International Journal of African Historical Studies* 39(3): 471–86.

Gibson, Sarah. 2006. "'The Hotel Business is About Strangers': Border Politics and Hospitable Spaces in Stephen Frears's *Dirty Pretty Things*." *Third Text* 20(6): 693–701.

Giudici, Daniela. 2013. "From 'Irregular Migrants' to Refugees and Back: Asylum Seekers' Struggle for Recognition in Contemporary Italy." *Journal of Mediterranean Studies* 22(1): 61–85.

Glick Schiller, Nina, and Noel B. Salazar. 2013. "Regimes of Mobility across the Globe." *Journal of Ethnic and Migration Studies* 39(2): 183–200. https://doi.org/10.1080/1369183X.2013.723253.

Glorius, B., and J. Domínguez-Mujica, eds. 2017. *European Mobility in Times of Crisis: The New Context of European South-North Migration*. Bielefeld: Transcript Verlag.

Goddeeris, Idesbald. 2015a. "Colonial Streets and Statues: Postcolonial Belgium in the Public Space." *Postcolonial Studies* 18(4): 397–409. https://doi.org/10.1080/13688790.2015.1191986.

———. 2015b. "Postcolonial Belgium: The Memory of the Congo." *Interventions* 17(3): 434–51.

Goffman, Erving. 1959. *The Presentation of Self in Everyday Life*. New York: Doubleday.

Goodman, Simon, and Susan A. Spear. 2007. "Category Use in the Construction of Asylum Seekers." *Critical Discourse Studies* 4(2): 165–85.

Göpfert, Mirco. 2012. "Security in Niamey: An Anthropological Perspective on Policing and an Act of Terrorism in Niger." *The Journal of Modern African Studies* 50(1): 53–74.

Green-Pedersen, Svend E. 1975. "The History of the Danish Negro Slave Trade, 1733–1807. An Interim Survey Relating in Particular to Its Volume, Structure, Profitability and Abolition." *Revue française d'histoire d'outre-mer* 62(226–227): 196–220. https://doi.org/10.3406/outre.1975.1826.

Grégoire, Emmanuel. 2011. "Niger: Un État à forte teneur en uranium." *Hérodote* 3(142): 206–25.

Grégoire, Emmanuel, and Marko Scholze. 2012. "Identity, Imaginary and Tourism in the Tuareg Region, in Niger." *Via* 2: 1–14. https://doi.org/10.4000/viatourism.1108.

Grosfoguel, Ramon. 2011. "Decolonizing Post-Colonial Studies and Paradigms of Political-Economy: Transmodernity, Decolonial Thinking, and Global Coloniality." *Transmodernity: Journal of Peripheral Cultural Production of the Luso-Hispanic World* 1(1): 1–37.

———. 2012. "The Multiple Faces of Islamophobia." *Islamophobia Studies Journal (ISJ)* 1(1): 9–33.

Grosfoguel, Ramon, Laura Oso, and Anastasia Christou. 2015. "'Racism': Intersectionality and Migration Studies: Framing Some Theoretical Reflections." *Identities: Global Studies in Culture and Power* 22(6): 635–52.

Guðjónsdóttir, Guðbjört, and Kristín Loftsdóttir. 2016. "Being a Desirable Migrant: Perception and Racialisation of Icelandic Migrants in Norway." *Journal of Ethnic and Migration Studies* 43(5): 791–808.

Günel, Gökçe, Saiba Varma, and Chika Watanabe. 2020. "A Manifesto for Patchwork Ethnography." Member Voices, *Fieldsights*, 9 June. Retrieved 11 April 2021 from https://culanth.org/fieldsights/a-manifesto-for-patchwork-ethnography.

Hage, Ghassan. 2016. "État de Siège: A Dying Domesticating Colonialism?" *American Ethnologist* 43(1): 38–49.
Hagopian, A., A. Ofosu, A. Fatusi, R. Biritwum, A. Essel, L. G. Hart, and C. Watts. 2005. "The Flight of Physicians from West Africa: Views of African Physicians and Implications for Policy." *Social Science & Medicine* 61(8): 1750–60.
Hall, Alexandra. 2012. *Border Watch: Cultures of Immigration, Detention and Control*. London: Pluto Press.
Hamani, Djibo. 1977. "Pasteurs Nomades et Agricultures Sédentaires dans l'Histoire du Soudan Central." University of Khartoum. Institute of African and Asian Studies. *Third International Conference on the Central Bilad Al-Sudan: Tradition and Adaptation*. Archival documents at the l'Institute de Recherches en Science Humaines, Niamey, Niger.
Hebberecht, Patrick. 1997. "Minorities, Crime and Criminal Justice in Belgium." In *Minorities, Migrants and Crime: Diversity and Similarities Across Europe*, ed. Ineke Haen Marshall, 151–74. Thousand Oaks: Sage Publications.
Heffernan, Timothy, and Marek Pawlak. 2020. "Crisis Futures: The Affects and Temporalities of Economic Collapse in Iceland." *History and Anthropology* 31(3): 314–30.
Herzfeld, Michael. 1989. *Anthropology through the Looking-Glass: Critical Ethnography in the Margins of Europe*. Cambridge, UK: Cambridge University Press.
———. 2016. *Cultural Intimacy: Social Poetics in the Nation-State*. New York: Routledge.
Hipfl, Brigitte, and Daniela Gronold. 2011. "Asylum Seekers as Austria's Other: The Re-Emergence of Austria's Colonial Past in a State-of-Exception." *Social Identities* 17: 27–40.
Hochschild, Adam. 1998. *King Leopold's Ghost: A Story of Greed, Terror and Heroism in Colonial Africa*. Boston: Houghton Mifflin.
Hodgson, Dorothy Louise. 2011. *Being Maasai, Becoming Indigenous: Postcolonial Politics in a Neoliberal World*. Bloomington: Indiana University Press.
Horning, Audrey. 2013. "Insinuations: Framing a New Understanding of Colonialism." In *Scandinavian Colonialism and the Rise of Modernity: Small Time Agents in a Global Arena*, ed. Magdalena Naum and Jona M. Nordin, 297–305. New York: Springer.
House of European History. n.d. "Mission and Vision." Retrieved 25 June 2020 from https://historia-europa.ep.eu/en/mission-vision.
Human Rights Watch. 2012. "Unacknowledged Deaths: Civilian Casualties in NATO's Air Campaign in Libya." Retrieved 6 August 2017 from https://www.hrw.org/report/2012/05/13/unacknowledged-deaths/civilian-casualties-natos-air-campaign-libya.
Humblet, Perrine, Gaëlle Amerijckx, Stéphane Aujean, Murielle Deguerry, Michel Vandenbroeck, and Benjamin Wayens. 2015. "Young Children in Brussels: From an Institutional Approach to a Systemic View. BSI Synopsis." *Brussels Studies. The e-journal for academic research on Brussels*. https://journals.openedition.org/brussels/1306.
Idrissa, Rahmane. 2019. *Dialogue in Divergence: The Impact of EU Migration Policy on West African Integration: The Cases of Nigeria, Mali, and Niger*. Report published by Friedrich Ebert Stiftung, Leiden University. http://hdl.handle.net/1887/72355.

Ingvars, Árdís K. 2019. "The Social Butterfly: Hunted Subjectivity and Emergent Masculinities among Refugees." *NORMA* 14(4): 239–54.

Ísleifsson, Atli. 2017. "Sækir um hæli á Íslandi eftir sautján ár í Noregi." *Vísir*, 31 October. Retrieved 15 June 2020 from https://www.visir.is/g/2017171039842.

Jansen-Verbeke, Myriam, and Robert Govers. 2009. "Brussels: A Multilayered Capital City." In *City Tourism: National Capital Perspectives*, ed. Robert Maitland and Brent W. Ritchie, 142–58. Wallingford: CABI.

Jansen-Verbeke, Myriam, Sylvia Vandenbroucke, and Sofie Tielen. 2005. "Tourism in Brussels, Capital of the 'New Europe.'" *International Journal of Tourism Research* 7(2): 109–22.

Jervis, Rick, and Alan Gomez. 2019. "Trump Administration Has Separated Hundreds of Children from their Migrant Families since 2018." *USA Today*, 17 December. Retrieved 12 April 2021 from https://eu.usatoday.com/story/news/nation/2019/05/02/border-family-separations-trump-administration-border-patrol/3563990002/.

Jezierska, K., and A. Towns. 2018. "Taming Feminism? The Place of Gender Equality in the 'Progressive Sweden' Brand." *Place Branding and Public Diplomacy* 14(1): 55–63.

Jiwani, Yasmin. 2008. "Sports as a Civilizing Mission: Zinedine Zidane and the Infamous Head-Butt." *TOPIA: Canadian Journal of Cultural Studies* 19: 11–33.

Kagné, B., and M. Martiniello. 2001. "L'immigration subsaharienne en Belgique." *Courrier hebdomadaire du CRISP* 1721(16): 5–49. https://doi.org/10.3917/cris.1721.0005.

Kasparek, Bernd. 2016. "Complementing Schengen: The Dublin System and the European Border and Migration Regime." In *Migration Policy and Practice*, ed. Harald Bauder and Christian Matheis, 59–78. New York: Palgrave Macmillan.

Keough, S. B., and S. M. Youngstedt. 2019. *Water, Life, and Profit: Fluid Economies and Cultures of Niamey, Niger*. New York: Berghahn Books.

Keskinen, Suvi, Salla Tuori, Sara Irni, and Diana Mulinari. 2009. *Complying with Colonialism: Gender, Race and Ethnicity in the Nordic Region*. Farnham: Ashgate.

Klein, Adam. 2012. "Slipping Racism into the Mainstream: A Theory of Information Laundering." *Communication Theory* 22(4): 427–48.

Knight, Daniel, and Charles Stewart. 2016. "Ethnographies of Austerity: Temporality, Crisis, and Affect in Southern Europe." *History and Anthropology* 27(1): 1–18. https://doi.org/10.1080/02757206.2015.1114480.

Koca, Burcu Togral. 2016. "New Social Movements: 'Refugees Welcome UK.'" *European Scientific Journal* 12(2): 96–108.

Kohl, Ines. 2002. "The Lure of the Sahara: Implications of Libya's Desert Tourism." *The Journal of Libyan Studies* 3(2): 56–68.

Koser, Khalid. 2011. "Responding to Migration from Complex Humanitarian Emergencies: Lessons Learned from Libya." Briefing Paper. London: Chatham House.

Kunz, S. 2020. "Expatriate, Migrant? The Social Life of Migration Categories and the Polyvalent Mobility of Race." *Journal of Ethnic and Migration Studies* 46(11): 2145–62.

Lähdesmäki, Tuuli. 2012. "Politics of Cultural Marking in Mini-Europe: Anchoring European Cultural Identity in a Theme Park." *Journal of Contemporary European Studies* 20(1): 29–40.

Lapiņa, Linda, and Mantė Vertelytė. 2020. "'Eastern European,' Yes, But How? Autoethnographic Accounts of Differentiated Whiteness." *NORA—Nordic Journal of Feminist and Gender Research*. https://doi.org/10.1080/08038740.2020.1762731.

Larémont, R. R., M. O. Attir, and M. Mahamadou. 2020. "European Union and Italian Migration Policy and the Probable Destabilization of Southern Libya and Northern Niger." *The Journal of the Middle East and Africa* 11(4): 359-80.

Larkin, B. 1997. "Indian Films and Nigerian Lovers: Media and the Creation of Parallel Modernities." *Africa* 67(3): 406-40.

Larsen, Rasmus Kløcker, and Christiane Alzouma Mamosso. 2013. *Environmental Governance of Uranium in Niger: A Blind Spot for Development Cooperation?* No. 2013: 02. Copenhagen: DIIS Working Paper.

Leinonen, Johanna. 2012. "Invisible Immigrants, Visible Expats? Americans in Finnish Discourses on Immigration and Internationalization." *Nordic Journal of Migration Research* 2(3): 213-23. http://doi.org/10.2478/v10202-011-0043-8.

Leman, Johan. 1997. "Undocumented Migrants in Brussels: Diversity and the Anthropology of Illegality." *Journal of Ethnic and Migration Studies* 23(1): 25–41. https://doi.org/10.1080/1369183X.1997.9976573.

Lenshie, Nsemba Edward, and Fef Ayokhai. 2013. "Rethinking Pre-Colonial State Formation and Ethno-Religious Identity Transformation in Hausaland under the Sokoto Caliphate." *Global Journal of Human Social Science Political Science* 13(4): 1–10.

Lentin, Alana, and Gavan Titley. 2011. *The Crises of Multiculturalism. Racism in a Neoliberal Age*. London: Zed Books Ltd.

———. 2012. "The Crisis of 'Multiculturalism' in Europe: Mediated Minarets, Intolerable Subjects." *European Journal of Cultural Studies* 15(2): 123-38.

Levin, Amy K. 2017. "Introduction: Global Mobilities." In *Global Mobilities: Refugees, Exiles and Immigrants in Museums and Archives*, ed. Amy K. Levin, 1–26. London: Routledge.

Lewicki, Paweł. 2016. "European Bodies?: Class and Gender Dynamics among EU Civil Servants in Brussels." *Anthropological Journal of European Cultures* 25(2): 116-38. https://doi.org/10.3167/ajec.2016.250206.

———. 2020. "Polishness and Eurostyle in Brussels: Struggles over Europe in Bodily Performances among Polish EU Civil Servants." *Ethnologia Europaea* 50(1): 128-44.

Lewis, Hannah, Peter Dwyer, Stuart Hodkinson, and Louise Waite. 2015. "Hyper-Precarious Lives: Migrants, Work and Forced Labour in the Global North." *Progress in Human Geography* 39(5): 580-600.

Licata, Laurent, and Olivier Klein. 2010. "Holocaust or Benevolent Paternalism? Intergenerational Comparisons on Collective Memories and Emotions about Belgium's Colonial Past." *International Journal of Conflict and Violence (IJCV)* 4(1): 45-57.

Loftsdóttir, Kristín. 2002a. "Knowing What to Do in the City: WoDaaBe Nomads and Migrant Workers in Niger." *Anthropology Today* 18(1): 9–13.

———. 2002b. "Never Forgetting? Gender and Racial-Ethnic Identity during Fieldwork." *Social Anthropology* 10(3): 303–17.

———. 2007. "Bounded and Multiple Identities: Ethnic Identities of WoDaaBe and FulBe." *Cahiers d'Études africaines* XLVII 185(1): 65–92.

———. 2008. *The Bush Is Sweet: Identity, Power and Development among WoDaaBe Fulani in Niger*. Uppsala: Nordiska Afrikainstitutet.

———. 2009. "'Pure Manliness': The Colonial Project and Africa's Image in Nineteenth Century Iceland." *Identities: Global Studies in Culture and Power* 16: 271–93.

———. 2013. "Republishing 'Ten Little Negros': Exploring Nationalism and Whiteness in Iceland." *Ethnicities* 13(3): 295–315.

———. 2014. "Going to Eden: Nordic Exceptionalism and the Image of Blackness in Iceland." *African and Black Diaspora: An International Journal*. Special issue, *Nordic Reflections of African and Black Diaspora* 7(1): 27–41.

———. 2017. "Being 'The Damned Foreigner': Affective National Sentiments and Racialization of Lithuanians in Iceland." *Nordic Journal of International Migration* 7(2): 70–78.

———. 2019. *Crisis and Coloniality at Europe's Margins: Creating Exotic Iceland*. London: Routledge.

———. 2020. "An Alternative World: A Perspective from the North on Racism and Migration." *Race & Class*. https://doi.org/10.1177 percent2F0306396820948320.

Loftsdóttir, Kristín, and Lars Jensen. 2012. *Whiteness and Postcolonialism in the Nordic Region: Exceptionalism, Migrant Others and National Identities*. Farnham: Ashgate.

———. 2014. "Introduction: Crisis in the Nordic Nations and Beyond." In *Crisis in the Nordic Nations and Beyond: At the Intersection of Environment, Finance and Multiculturalism*, ed. Kristín Loftsdóttir and Lars Jensen, 1–18. Farnham: Ashgate.

———. 2016. *Whiteness and Postcolonialism in the Nordic Region: Exceptionalism, Migrant Others and National Identities*. London: Routledge.

Loftsdóttir, Kristín, Andrea L. Smith, and Brigitte Hipfl. 2018. "Introduction." In *Messy Europe: Crisis, Race and Nation-State in Postcolonial Europe*, EASA series, ed. Kristín Loftsdóttir, Andrea L. Smith, and Brigitte Hipfl, 1–30. New York: Berghahn Books.

Lo Sardo, Sébastien. 2010. "Faraway So Close: Presence and Absence among Hausa Migrants in Belgium and Urban Niger." In *Mobility, Transnationalism and Contemporary African Societies*, ed. Tilo Grätz, 34–43. Newcastle upon Tyne: Cambridge Scholars Publishing.

———. 2013. "Dan Belgique: The Making Of Hausa Transnational Spaces between Brussels and the Sahel." *Urban Anthropology and Studies of Cultural Systems and World Economic Development* 42(3): 305–31.

Lucassen, Leo. 2018. "Peeling an Onion: The 'Refugee Crisis' from a Historical Perspective." *Ethnic and Racial Studies* 41(3): 383–410.

Lunaček, Sarah. 2013. "Tuareg Travelling to Europe: Particularities and Continuities." *Studia ethnologica Croatica* 25: 159–82.

Lüthi, Barbara. 2017. "Agitated Times: Why Historians Need to Question the Rhetoric of the 'Refugee Crisis.'" *Histoire@Politique* 1: 55–63.

Lüthi, Barbara, Francesca Falk, and Patricia Purtschert. 2016. "Colonialism without Colonies: Examining Blank Spaces in Colonial Studies." *National Identities* 18: 1–9.

Lutz, Catherine A., and Jane L. Collins. 1993. *Reading National Geographic*. Chicago: University of Chicago Press.

Majcher, I., M. Flynn, and M. Grange. 2020. *Immigration Detention in the European Union*. Cham: Springer.

Manço, Ural, and Meryem Kanmaz. 2005. "From Conflict to Co-Operation between Muslims and Local Authorities in a Brussels Borough: Schaerbeek." *Journal of Ethnic and Migration Studies* 31(6): 1105–23.

Mann, Gregory. 2015. *From Empires to Ngo's in the West African Sahel*. Cambridge, UK: Cambridge University Press.

Martiniello, Marco. 2003. "Belgium's Immigration Policy." *International Migration Review* 37(1): 225–32.

Mau, Steffan, Fabian Gulzau, Lene Laube, and Zaun Natascha. 2015. "The Global Mobility Divide: How Visa Policies Have Evolved over Time." *Journal of Ethnic and Migration Studies* 41(8): 1192–1213.

Mavhunga, Clapperton Chakanetsa, Jeroen Cuvelier, and Katrien Pype. 2016. "'Containers, Carriers, Vehicles': Three Views of Mobility from Africa." *Transfers* 6(2): 43–53.

Mazzocchetti, Jacinthe. 2012. "Feelings of Injustice and Conspiracy Theory. Representations of Adolescents from an African Migrant Background (Morocco and Sub-Saharan Africa) in Disadvantaged Neighbourhoods of Brussels." *Brussels Studies* [Online] 63. http://journals.openedition.org/brussels/1123.

McClintock, Anne. 1995. *Imperial Leather: Race, Gender, and Sexuality in the Colonial Contest*. New York: Routledge.

McGregor, Andrew. 2007. "Mining for Energy: China's Relations with Niger." *ChinaBrief* VII(18): 8–9.

M'Charek, Amade, Katharina Schramm, and David Skinner. 2014. "Topologies of Race: Doing Territory, Population and Identity in Europe." *Science, Technology and Human Values* 39(4): 468–87.

McIntosh, Laurie. 2014. "Before and After: Terror, Extremism and the Not-So-New Norway." *African and Black Diaspora: An International Journal* 7(1): 70–80.

Meiu, G. P. 2016. "Belonging in Ethno-Erotic Economies: Adultery, Alterity, and Ritual in Postcolonial Kenya." *American Ethnologist* 43(2): 215–29.

Mielants, Eric. 2006. "The Long-Term Historical Development of Racist Tendencies within the Political and Social Context of Belgium." *International Journal of Comparative Sociology* 47(3–4): 313–34.

"Migrant Deaths and Disappearances." 2020. Migration Data Portal. Retrieved 19 June 2020 from https://migrationdataportal.org/themes/migrant-deaths-and-disappearances.

Miller, Todd, and Joseph Nevins. 2017. "Beyond Trump's Big, Beautiful Wall: Trump's Plan to Wall off the Entire US–Mexico Border Is Just One of a Growing List of Actions that Extend US Border Patrol Efforts Far Past the International Boundary Itself." *NACLA Report on the Americas* 49(2): 145–51.

Milne, Seumas. 2012. "If There Were Global Justice, NATO Would Be in the Dock Over Libya." *The Guardian*, 12 May. Retrieved 6 August 2017 from https://www.theguardian.com/commentisfree/2012/may/15/global-justice-nato-libya.

Mini-Europe. n.d. "Mini-Europe, Brussels." Retrieved 19 June 2020 from https://www.minieurope.com/wp-content/uploads/2015/11/Mini-Europe-UK.pdf.

———. 2019. "Mini-Europe. Brussels." Retrieved 25 June 2020 from https://www.mini europe.com/wp-content/uploads/2018/10/8390-MNE-Brochure-2019-UK-light-compressed.pdf.

Mini-Europe.brussels. n.d. "Spirit of Europe." Retrieved 25 June 2020 from https://www.minieurope.com/en/spirit-of-europe/description/.

Muehlebach, Andrea. 2018. "What Is a Life? On Poverty and Race in Humanitarian Italy." In *Messy Europe: Crisis, Race and Nation-State in Postcolonial Europe*, EASA series, ed. Kristín Loftsdóttir, Andrea L. Smith, and Brigitte Hipfl, 126–47. New York: Berghahn Books.

Naum, Magdalena, and Jonas Nordin. 2013. "Situating Scandinavian Colonialism." In *Scandinavian Colonialism and the Rise of Modernity: Small Time Agents in a Global Arena*, ed. Magdalena Naum and Jonas Nordin, 3–16. New York: Springer.

Norocel, O. C. 2013. "'Give Us Back Sweden!' A Feminist Reading of the (Re)Interpretations of the Folkhem Conceptual Metaphor in Swedish Radical Right Populist Discourse." *NORA-Nordic Journal of Feminist and Gender Research* 21(1): 4–20.

Olivier de Sardan, Jean-Pierre. 2011. "Local Powers and the Co-delivery of Public Goods in Niger." *IDS Bulletin* 42(2): 32–42.

Ostow, Robin. 2017. "Occupying the Immigration Museum: The *Sans Papiers* of Paris at the Site of Their National Presentation." In *Global Mobilities: Refugees, Exiles and Immigrants in Museums and Archives*, ed. Amy K. Levin, 265–87. London: Routledge.

Özyürek, Esra. 2005. "The Politics of Cultural Unification, Secularism, and the Place of Islam in the New Europe." *American Ethnologist* 32(4): 509–12.

Painter, Thomas M. 1987. "Bringing Land Back In: Changing Strategies to Improve Agricultural Production in the West African Sahel." In *Land at Risk in the Third World: Local-Level Perspective*, ed. Peter D. Little, Michael M. Horowitz, and A. Endre Nyerges, 144–63. Boulder: Westview Press.

———. 1991. *Approaches to Improving Natural Resource Use for Agriculture in Sahelian West Africa: A Sociological Analysis of the 'Aménagement/Gestion des Terroirs Villageois' Approach and Its Implications for Non-Governmental Organizations*. New York: CARE: Agriculture and Natural Resources Technical Report Series. No. 3. Agriculture and Natural Resources Unit, CARE.

Papastergiadis, Nikos. 2013. "'Why Multiculturalism Makes People So Angry and Sad.'" In *Space, Place & Culture*, ed. Helen Sykes, 47–71. Melbourne: Future Leaders.

Paret, Marcel, and Shannon Gleeson. 2016. "Precarity and Agency through a Migration Lens." *Citizenship Studies* 20(3–4): 277–94. https://doi.org/10.1080/13621025.2016.1158356.

Perchoc, Philippe. 2017. "Brussels: What European Urban Narrative?" *Journal of Contemporary European Studies* 25(3): 367–79. https://doi.org/10.1080/14782804.2017.1351928.

Pfeiffer, James. 2019. "Austerity in Africa: Audit Cultures and the Weakening of Public Sector Health Systems." *Focaal* 83: 51–61.

Philip, Alan Butt. 1994. "European Union Immigration Policy: Phantom, Fantasy or Fact?" *West European Politics* 17(2): 168–91.

Pilkington, Ed. 2018. "Crystal Mason Begins Prison Sentence in Texas for Crime of Voting." *The Guardian*, 28 September. Retrieved 3 March 2021 from https://

www.theguardian.com/us-news/2018/sep/28/crystal-mason-begins-prison-sentence-in-texas-for-of-voting.

Pinelli, Barbara. 2018. "Control and Abandonment: The Power of Surveillance on Refugees in Italy, during and after the Mare Nostrum Operation." *Antipode* 50(3): 725–47.

Ponzanesi, Sandra. 2016. "The Point of Europe: Postcolonial Entanglements." *Interventions* 18: 159–64. https://doi.org/10.1080/1369801X.2015.1106962.

Ponzanesi, Sandra, and Bolette B. Blaagaard. 2011. "In the Name of Europe." *Social Identities* 17(1): 1–10.

Ponzanesi, Sandra, and Gianmaria Colpani. 2016. "Introduction: Europe in Transition." In *Postcolonial Transitions in Europe: Contexts, Practices and Politics*, ed. Sandra Ponzanesi and Gianmaria Colpani, 1–22. Lanham: Rowman & Littlefield International.

Ponzanesi, Sandra, and Koen Leurs. 2014. "On Digital Crossings in Europe." *Crossings: Journal of Migration & Culture* 5(1): 3–22.

"Population." n.d. *BISA—Brussels Institute for Statistics and Analysis*. Retrieved 27 June 2020 from http://statistics.brussels/themes/population/population#.Xvfb8C2z1gd.

"Population, total—Niger." 2019. The World Bank. Retrieved 5 March 2021 from https://data.worldbank.org/indicator/SP.POP.TOTL?locations=NE.

Poulot, Dominique. 2015. "The Changing Roles of Art Museums." In *National Museums and Nation-Building in Europe 1750–2010: Mobilization and Legitimacy, Continuity and Change*, ed. Peter Aronsson and Gabriella Elgenius, 89–118. Oxon: Routledge.

Poushter, Jacob, and Russ Oates. 2015. *Cell Phones in Africa: Communication Lifeline*. Washington, DC: Pew Research Centre. http://www.pewglobal.org/files/2015/04/Pew-Research-Center-Africa-Cell-Phone-Report-FINAL-April-15-2015.pdf

Powers, Theodore, and Theodoros Rakopoulos. 2019. "The Anthropology of Austerity: An Introduction." *Focaal* 83: 1–12.

Puig, Oriol. 2015. "Nigerien Migrants Long for Pre-War Libya." *Euractive* [Originally published in El País—Planeta Futuro, translated by Sam Morgan]. Retrieved 26 September 2018 from https://www.euractiv.com/section/development-policy/news/nigerien-migrants-long-for-pre-war-libya/.

Pyrhönen, Niko, and Gwenaelle Bauvois. 2019. "Conspiracies beyond Fake News. Producing Reinformation on Presidential Elections in the Transnational Hybrid Media System." *Sociological Inquiry* 90(4): 705–31.

Rain, David. 1999. *Eaters of the Dry Season: Circular Labor Migration in the West African Sahel*. Boulder: Westview Press.

Rannard, Georgina. 2020. "Leopold II: Belgium 'Wakes Up' to Its Bloody Colonial Past." *BBC News*, 13 June. Retrieved 12 April 2021 from https://www.bbc.com/news/world-europe-53017188.

Rasmussen, Susan. 1992. "Disputed Boundaries: Tuareg Discourse on Class and Ethnicity." *Ethnology* 31(4): 351–65.

———. 1995. "Art as Process and Product: Patronage and the Problem of Change in Tuareg Blacksmith/Artisan Roles." *Africa* 65(4): 592–609.

———. 2005. "A Temporary Diaspora: Contested Cultural Representations in Tuareg International Musical Performance." *Anthropological Quarterly* 78(4): 793–826.

Rehman, Javaid. 2007. "Islam, 'War on Terror' and the Future of Muslim Minorities in the United Kingdom: Dilemmas of Multiculturalism in the Aftermath of the London Bombings." *Human Rights Quarterly* 29: 831-78.

"Resident Foreigners on 1st January—Citizenship: Lombardia." 2021. Immigrants.Stat. Retrieved 1 February 2021 from http://stra-dati.istat.it/Index.aspx?lang=en#.

Reynolds, Rachel R., and Scott M. Youngstedt. 2004. "Globalization and African Ethnoscapes: Contrasting Nigerien Hausa and Nigerian Igbo Migratory Orders in the US." *City & Society* 16(1): 5-13.

Roberts, Pepe. 1981. "'Rural Development' and the Rural Economy in Niger, 1900-75." In *Rural Development in Tropical Africa*, ed. Judith Heyer, Pepe Roberts, and Gavin Williams, 193-221. London: Macmillan Press Ltd.

Rochtus, Dirk. 2012. "The Rebirth of Flemish Nationalism: Assessing the Impact of N-VA Chairman Bart De Wever's Charisma." *Studies in Ethnicity and Nationalism. Special Features Section on Creating the 'Other' in Germany and Britain* 12(2): 268-85. https://doi.org/10.1111/j.1754-9469.2012.01174.x.

Rodriguez, Anne-Line. 2019. "European Attempts to Govern African Youths by Raising Awareness of the Risks of Migration: Ethnography of an Encounter." *Journal of Ethnic and Migration Studies* 45(5): 735-51.

Roes, Aldwin. 2010. "Towards a History of Mass Violence in the Etat Indépendant du Congo, 1885-1908." *South African Historical Journal* 62(4): 634-70. https://doi.org/10.1080/02582473.2010.519937.

Rosaldo, Renato. 1989a. *Culture and Truth: The Remaking of Social Analysis*. Boston: Beacon Press.

———. 1989b. "Imperialist Nostalgia." *Representations* 26: 107-22.

Rosen, Rachel, and Sarah Crafter. 2018. "Media Representations of Separated Child Migrants: from Dubs to Doubt." *Migration and Society* 1(1): 66-81.

Rothe, Delf, and Mariam Salehi. 2016. "Autonomy in Times of War? The Impact of the Libyan Crisis on Migratory Decisions." In *Understanding Migrant Decisions: From Sub-Saharan Africa to the Mediterranean Region*, ed. Belachew Gebrewold and Tendayi Bloom, 80-98. Abingdon: Routledge.

Rozanska, J. 2011. "Polish EU Officials in Brussels: Analysis of an Emerging Community." *Migracijske i etničke teme* 27(2): 263-98.

Rytter, Mikkel. 2019. "Writing Against Integration: Danish Imaginaries of Culture, Race and Belonging." *Ethnos* 84(4): 678-97.

Salazar, Noel B. 2011. "The Power of Imagination in Transnational Mobilities." *Identities: Global Studies in Culture and Power* 18(6): 576-98.

Salazar, Noel B., Alice Elliot, and Roger Norum. 2017. "Introduction: Studying Mobilities: Theoretical Notes and Methodological Queries." In *Methodologies of Mobility: Ethnography and Experiment*, ed. Alice Elliot, Roger Norum, and Noel B. Salazar, 1-24. New York: Berghahn Books.

Salazar, Noel B., and Alan Smart. 2011. "Anthropological Takes on (Im) Mobility." *Identities* 18(6): i-ix.

Sammon, Paul M. 2007. "Of Blade Runners, PKD, and Electric Sheep." In *Blade Runner (Do Androids Dream of Electric Sheep?)* by Philip K. Dick, 243-65. New York: Del Rey Books.

Schapendonk, Joris. 2008. "Stuck between the Desert and the Sea: The Immobility of Sub-Saharan African 'Transit Migrants' in Morocco." In *Rethinking Global Migration: Practices, Policies and Discourses in the European Neighbourhood*, ed. Helga Rittersberger-Tiliç, Aykan Erdemir, Ayça Ergun, and Hayriye Kahveci, 129–43. Ankara: KORA, METU & Zeplin Iletisim Hizm.

———. 2011. "Turbulent Trajectories: Sub-Saharan African Migrants Heading North." PhD diss., Radboud University Nijmegen.

———. 2017. "Afrostars and Eurospaces. West African Movers Re-viewing 'Destination Europe' from the Inside." *Etnografia e ricerca qualitativa* 10(3): 393–414.

———. 2020. *Finding Ways through Eurospace: West African Movers Re-viewing Europe from the Inside*. New York: Berghahn Books.

Schapendonk, Joris, Matthieu Bolay, and Janine Dahinden. 2020. "The Conceptual Limits of the 'Migration Journey.' De-Exceptionalising Mobility in the Context of West African Trajectories." *Journal of Ethnic and Migration Studies* 47(14): 3243–59. https://doi.org/10.1080/1369183X.2020.1804191.

Schär, Bernhard C. 2019a. "Introduction: The Dutch East Indies and Europe, ca. 1800-1930. An Empire of Demands and Opportunities." *BMGN—Low Countries Historical Review* 134(3): 4–20.

———. 2019b. "From Batticaloa via Basel to Berlin. Transimperial Science in Ceylon and Beyond around 1900." *The Journal of Imperial and Commonwealth History* 48(2): 230–62. https://doi.org/10.1080/03086534.2019.1638620.

Schmitt, Eric. 2018. "A Shadowy War's Newest Front: A Drone Base Rising from Saharan Dust." *The New York Times*, 22 April. Retrieved 19 October 2020 from https://www.nytimes.com/2018/04/22/us/politics/drone-base-niger.html.

Schoumaker, Bruno, Eleonora Castagnone, Albert Phongi Kingiela, Andonirinia Rakotonarivo, and Tiziana Nazio. 2018. "Congolese Migrants' Economic Trajectories in Europe and after Return." In *Migration between Africa and Europe*, ed. Cris Beauchemin, 217–38. Cham: Springer.

Schuermans, Nick, and Filip De Maesschalck. 2010. "Fear of Crime as a Political Weapon: Explaining the Rise of Extreme Right Politics in the Flemish Countryside." *Social & Cultural Geography* 11(3): 247–62.

Schwarz, Inga. 2016. "Racializing Freedom of Movement in Europe. Experiences of Racial Profiling at European Borders and Beyond." *Movements. Journal for Critical Migration and Border Regime Studies* 2(1): 253–65.

Sciurba, Alessandra. 2017. "Misrecognizing Asylum: Causes, Modalities, and Consequences of the Crisis of a Fundamental Human Right." *Rivista di Filosofia del diritto* 6(1): 141–64.

Seeberg, Peter. 2013. "The Arab Uprisings and the EU's Migration Policies—The Cases of Egypt, Libya, and Syria." *Democracy and Security* 9(1-2): 157–76. https://doi.org/10.1080/17419166.2013.747909.

Seligman, Thomas K. 2006. "African Arts." In *Art of Being Tuareg: Sahara Nomads in a Modern World*, ed. Thomas K. Seligman, Kristyne Loughran, and Edmond Bernus, 56–79. Los Angeles: Iris & B. Gerald Cantor Center for Visual Arts at Stanford University: UCLA Fowler Museum of Cultural History.

Shore, C. 2004. "Whither European Citizenship? Eros and Civilization Revisited." *European Journal of Social Theory* 7(1): 27–44.
Sigurþórsdóttir, Sunna Karen. 2018. "Íslendingar senda Mahad aftur til Noregs." *Fréttablaðið*, 30 April. Retrieved 19 October 2020 from https://www.frettabladid.is/frettir/islendingar-senda-mahad-aftur-til-noregs/.
Silverman, Debora L. 2015. "Diasporas of Art: History, the Tervuren Royal Museum for Central Africa, and the Politics of Memory in Belgium, 1885-2014." *The Journal of Modern History* 87(3): 615–67.
Smedley, Audrey, and Brian D. Smedley. 2005. "Race as Biology Is Fiction, Racism as a Social Problem Is Real: Anthropological and Historical Perspectives on the Social Construction of Race." *American Psychologist* 60(1): 16–26.
Smith, Nicole, Gabriel Canter, Austin Shipman, and Jason De León. 2020. "The Human Cost of Border Enforcement Policies." *Anthropology News* website, 16 November. Retrieved 19 April 2021 from https://doi.org/10.14506/AN.1537.
Snorek, J. 2016. "Contested Views of the Causes of Rural to Urban Migration Amongst Pastoralists in Niger." In *Understanding Migrant Decisions: From Sub-Saharan Africa to the Mediterranean Region*, ed. Belachew Gebrewold, and Tendayi Bloom, 59–79. Abingdon: Routledge.
Sorge, Antonio. 2018. "Navigating the Mediterranean Refugee 'Crisis': Alter-globalization Activism and the Sediments of History on Lampedusa." In *Messy Europe: Crisis, Race and Nation-State in Postcolonial Europe*, EASA series, ed. Kristín Loftsdóttir, Andrea L. Smith, and Brigitte Hipfl, 196–219. New York: Berghahn Books.
Spinelli, Maria-Lydia. 1995. *What's in a Theme Park? Exploring the Frontiers of Euro Disney*. Prepared for the Fourth Biennial Meeting of the European Community Studies Association. Charleston, South Carolina. Unpublished manuscript.
Stanard, Matthew. 2005. "'Bilan du monde pour un monde plus déshumanisé': The 1958 Brussels World's Fair and Belgian Perceptions of the Congo." *European History Quarterly* 35(2): 267–98.
———. 2011. "King Leopold's Bust: A Story of Monuments, Culture, and Memory in Colonial Europe." *Journal of Colonialism and Colonial History* 12(2): n.p.
Stoler, Laura Ann. 2008. "Imperial Debris: Reflections on Ruins and Ruination." *Cultural Anthropology* 23: 191–219. https://doi.org/10.1111/j.1548-1360.2008.00007.x.
———. 2013. "Introduction 'The Rot Remains': From Ruins to Ruination." In *Imperial Debris: On Ruins and Ruination*, ed. Laura Ann Stoler, 1–35. Durham, NC: Duke University Press.
Stoller, Paul. 2010. *Money Has No Smell: The Africanization of New York City*. Chicago: University of Chicago Press.
Stoller, Paul, and Jasmin Tahmaseb McConatha. 2001. "City Life: West African Communities in New York." *Journal of Contemporary Ethnography* 30(6): 651–77.
Storm, Eric, and Hans Vandevoorde. 2012. "Bierstuben, Cottages and Art Deco: Regionalism, Nationalism and Internationalism at the Belgian World Fairs." *Revue Belge de Philologie et d'Histoire* 90(4): 1373–88.
Sumiala, Johanna, Minttu Tikka, Jukka Huhtamäki, and Katja Valaskivi. 2016. "#JeSuisCharlie: Towards a Multi-Method Study of Hybrid Media Events." *Media and Communication* 4(4): 97–108.

Swift, Jeremy. 1984. *Pastoral Development in Central Niger*. Niamey: USAID.
Swyngedouw, Erik, and Guy Baeten. 2001. "Scaling the City: The Political Economy of 'Glocal' Development—Brussels' Conundrum." *European Planning Studies* 9(7): 827–49.
Sylvain, Renée. 2002. "'Land, Water and Truth': San Identity and Global Indigenism." *American Anthropologist* 104(4): 1074–85.
Taş, Hakki. 2020. "The Chronopolitics of National Populism." *Identities*. https://doi.org/10.1080/1070289X.2020.1735160.
Thedvall, Renita. 2007. "The EU's Nomads: National Eurocrats in European Policy-Making." In *Observing Government Elites: Up Close and Personal*, ed. R. A. W. Rhodes, Paul 't Hart and Mirko Noordegraaf, 160–79. London: Palgrave Macmillan.
Theodossopoulos, Dimitrios. 2010. "Introduction: United in Discontent." In *United in Discontent: Local Responses to Cosmopolitanism and Globalization*, ed. Dimitrios Theodossopoulos and Elisabeth Kirtsoglou, 1–19. New York: Berghahn Books.
Thorleifsson, Cathrine. 2019. *Nationalist Responses to the Crises in Europe: Old And New Hatreds*. London: Routledge.
Tinti, Peter. 2017. "The EU's Hollow Success over Migrant Smuggling in Niger." *The New Humanitarian*, 17 January. *Identities*. Retrieved 20 April 2020 from https://deeply.thenewhumanitarian.org/refugees/community/2017/01/17/the-e-u-s-hollow-success-over-migrant-smuggling-in-niger.
Tinti, Peter, and Tom Westcott. 2016. "The Niger-Libya Corridor Smugglers' Perspectives." *The Institute for Security Studies, ISS Paper* 299: 1–23.
Titley, Gavan. 2009. "Pleasing the Crisis: Anxiety and Recited Multiculturalism in the European Communicative Space." In *Manufacturing Europe: Spaces of Democracy, Diversity and Communication*, ed. Inka Salovaara-Moring, 153–70. Göteborg: Nordicom.
Torresi, T. 2013. "An Emerging Regulatory Framework for Migration: The Libya–Italy Agreement and the Right of Exit." *Griffith Law Review* 22(3): 648–65.
Tryggvadóttir, Helga Katrín, and Kristín Loftsdóttir. 2020. "The Word I Hate: Racism, Refugees and Asylum Seekers in Iceland." *Stjórnmál og stjórnsýsla* 16(1): 23–42.
Tsing, Anna L. 2011. *Friction: An Ethnography of Global Connection*. Princeton: Princeton University Press.
UNHCR. 2020. Figures at a Glance. UNHCR—The UN Refugee Agency, 18 June. Retrieved 26 June 2020 from https://www.unhcr.org/figures-at-a-glance.html.
United Nations Development Programme (UNDP). 1996. *Human Development Report 1996*. New York: Oxford University Press. Retrieved 26 June 2020 from http://hdr.undp.org/sites/default/files/reports/257/hdr_1996_en_complete_nostats.pdf.
———. 2020. *Latest Human Development Index Ranking*. http://hdr.undp.org/en/content/latest-human-development-index-ranking.
US Department of Health & Human Services. 2019. "Separated Children Placed in Office of Refugee Resettlement Care." Retrieved 26 June 2020 from https://oig.hhs.gov/oei/reports/oei-BL-18-00511.pdf.
van Dessel, J. 2019. "International Delegation and Agency in the Externalization Process of EU Migration and Asylum Policy: The Role of the IOM and the UNHCR in Niger." *European Journal of Migration and Law* 21(4): 435–58.

van Houtum, Henk, and Rodrigo Bueno Lacy. 2020. "The Migration Map Trap. On the Invasion Arrows in the Cartography of Migration." *Mobilities* 15(2): 196–219. https://doi.org/10.1080/17450101.2019.1676031.

Veronese, Guido, Alessandro Pepe, and Marzia Vigliaroni. 2019. "An Exploratory Multi-Site Mixed-Method Study with Migrants at Niger Transit Centers: The Push Factors Underpinning Outward and Return Migration." *International Social Work* January: 1–17.

Vertovec, Steven. 2004. "Cheap Calls: The Social Glue of Migrant Transnationalism." *Global Networks* 4(2): 219–24.

Vickers, Tom, John Clayton, Hilary Davison, Lucinda Hudson, Maria A. Cañadas, Paul Biddle, and Sara Lilley. 2019. "Dynamics of Precarity among 'New Migrants': Exploring the Worker–Capital Relation through Mobilities and Mobility Power." *Mobilities* 14(5): 696–714. https://doi.org/10.1080/17450101.2019.1611028.

Vieillard, Gilbert. 1932. "Notes sur deux institutions propres aux populations peules d'entre Niger et Tchad, le *soro* et le *gerewol*." *Journal des Africanistes* 2(1): 85–93.

Virkki, Tuija, and Satu Venäläinen. 2020. "Affective (Re)Orientations in Online Discussions on the Threat of Violence Posed by Migrants." *Social Identities* 26(3): 403–18. https://doi.org/10.1080/13504630.2020.1767055.

Vrăbiescu, Ioana. 2020. "Deportation, Smart Borders and Mobile Citizens: Using Digital Methods and Traditional Police Activities to Deport EU Citizens." *Journal of Ethnic and Migration Studies*. https://doi.org/10.1080/1369183X.2020.1796267.

Walther, Olivier, and Denis Retaillé. 2010. "Sahara or Sahel? The Fuzzy Geography of Terrorism in West Africa." *Ceps/Instead Working Papers* 2010-35.

Wardle, Huon. 2010. "A Cosmopolitan Anthropology?" *Social Anthropology* 18(4): 381–88.

"The Way In: Main European Migration Routes, Detection of Illegal Border Crossings, January–July 2015." 2015. *The Economist*, 29 August–4 September.

Weeber, Christine. 2020. "Why Capitalizing 'Black' Matters." *SAPIENS*, 29 July 2020. Retrieved 15 July 2021 from https://www.sapiens.org/language/capitalizing-black/.

Weisbord, Robert G. 2003. "The King, the Cardinal and the Pope: Leopold II's Genocide in the Congo and the Vatican." *Journal of Genocide Research* 5(1): 35–45. https://doi.org/10.1080/14623520305651.

Wekker, Gloria. 2016. *White Innocence: Paradoxes of Colonialism and Race*. Durham, NC: Duke University Press.

Werbner, Pnina. 2007. "Veiled Interventions in Pure Space: Honour, Shame and Embodied Struggles among Muslims in Britain and France." *Theory, Culture & Society* 24(2): 161–86.

Westin, Charles. 2010. "Identity and Inter-Ethnic Relations." In *Identity Processes and Dynamics in Multi-Ethnic Europe*, ed. Charles Westin, José Bastos, Janine Dahinden, and Pedro Góis, 9–51. Amsterdam: Amsterdam University Press.

Wilson, Valerie Plame, and Joe Wilson. 2013. "How the Bush Administration Sold the War—and We Bought It." *The Guardian*, 27 February. Retrieved 19 October 2020 from https://www.theguardian.com/commentisfree/2013/feb/27/bush-administration-sold-iraq-war.

World Heritage Convention, UNESCO. n.d. La Grand-Place, Brussels. Retrieved 26 June 2020 from https://whc.unesco.org/en/list/857.

Wright, Donald R. 1999. "'What Do You Mean There Were No Tribes in Africa?': Thoughts on Boundaries and Related Matters in Precolonial Africa." *History in Africa* 26: 409–26.

Wynne, Amelia. 2020. "Activists Remove a Statue of Belgium's King Leopold II in Brussels Days after Another One Was Taken Away in Antwerp Due to Anti-Racism Vandalism." *Daily Mail*, 12 June. Retrieved 26 June 2020 from https://www.dailymail.co.uk/news/article-8414819/Activists-remove-statue-Belgiums-King-Leopold-II-Brussels.html.

Xchange. 2019. "Agadez: Voices from a Historical Transit Hub Niger Report 2019 (Part One)." Retrieved 23 February 2021 from https://reliefweb.int/report/niger/agadez-voices-historical-transit-hub-niger-report-2019-part-one.

Xiang, Biao. 2013. "Multi-Scalar Ethnography: An Approach for Critical Engagement with Migration and Social Change." *Ethnography* 14(3): 282–99.

Youngstedt, Scott M. 2004a. "Creating Modernities through Conversation Groups: The Everyday Worlds of Hausa Migrants in Niamey, Niger." *African Studies Review* 47(3): 91–118.

———. 2004b. "The New Nigerien Hausa Diaspora in the US: Surviving and Building Community on the Margins of the Global Economy." *City & Society* 16(1): 39–67.

———. 2012. *Surviving with Dignity: Hausa Communities of Niamey, Niger*. Lanham: Lexington Books.

Youngstedt, Scott M., Sara Beth Keough, and Cheiffou Idrissa. 2016. "Water Vendors in Niamey: Considering the Economic and Symbolic Nature of Water." *African Studies Quarterly* 16(2): 27–45.

Zibouh, Fatima. 2011. "The Political Representation of Muslims in Brussels." *Brussels Studies* [online], Collection générale, no. 55, 5 December 2011. Retrieved 8 September 2020 from http://journals.openedition.org/brussels/1072; https://doi.org/10.4000/brussels.1072.

Index

Abu-Lughod, Lila, 32
Afghanistan, 28, 34
Afifi, Tamer, 77
AfricaMuseum, 119
Africans, 41, 46, 49, 58, 109
  West, 6, 41, 43, 47, 136–37
Agadez, 82, 83
Agamben, Giorgio, 19
Algeria, 80, 85, 94
Alidou, Ousseina D., 48, 77, 80, 89
Americans, 27, 89
Amnesty International, 140–41
Andersson, Ruben, 18, 19, 29, 34, 140
anti-muslim, 67
Apostolova, R., 35, 142
Appadurai, Arjun, 80
Arab, Arabic, 107, 125
Arab Spring, 17, 28, 34
Arizona, 24, 26, 29
Arlit, 87
artisanry, 95, 100, 103, 104
artists, 7, 53, 104, 111, 118, 134
assimilation, 64

backstage, 11, 41, 51, 56–57, 60–61.
  See also front stage
Bhambra, Gurminder K., 59
Bialasiewicz, L., 140
Bisbee, 24–25
Blainey, Marc G., 52, 61n2
Boko Haram, 85
borders, 11, 18–19, 27, 34–35, 41,
  137–38
  in Africa, 28, 78
  border control, 20, 29, 38, 68, 83,
    141
  border patrol, 25, 86–87, 105, 123,
    142

border protection, 23
borderland, 23, 52
deportation, 6, 38
Europe, 11, 19, 28–29, 69, 123, 129
externalization of European borders,
  8, 85, 139–41
fortification of European borders,
  3–4, 12, 34, 126
US/Mexico, 24–26
See also Frontex
Brachet, J., 85–86
Bruxpat, 55. *See also* Eurocrats; expatriate
Buettner, Elizabeth, 107–108, 127
Bunzl, Matti, 33–34
Burkas, 32. *See also* veils: national ban on
  veiling
Burkina Faso, 87, 98

Ceuppens, Bambi, 66–67, 111
Charlie Hebdo, 36
Chasin, Barbara H., 78
Chaudhuri, Shohini, 19, 141
Christou, Anastasia, 18
cloistered remembering, 111
Cologne, 36
colonial
  amnesia, 111, 136
  empire, 57, 76, 112–13, 127
  exhibitions, 109
  government, 77–78, 95
  imagination, 3, 94, 104
  legacies, 12
  past, 4–5, 60, 110–12
  powers, 45, 95–96
  violence, 111, 113–114
  See also history: colonial
colonialism, 5, 8, 64, 77, 91
  and Congo, 107, 110–11, 113, 118

history of, 12, 76, 107, 112–13, 135
and Iceland, 113–14, 135
and museums, 117–18, 126–27, 137
Nordic countries, 112–14
coloniality, 3
colonialization, 64, 76, 91, 95, 107
colonies, 19, 52, 107, 108, 114, 127
conflict zones, 85
Congo, 107–8, 111, 113–14, 118–19, 127, 134
migration, 53, 109–10
Congolese, 108, 110–11
migrants/diaspora, 53, 106, 110, 137
in Belgium, 53, 111
Convention on Controls on Persons Crossing External Frontiers, 28
cosmopolitanism, 4, 7, 18, 59–60, 105
Côte d'Ivoire, 85, 87
COVID-19, 135. *See also* pandemic
Crafter, Sarah, 35
crime, 38, 54, 68, 103, 108
criminality, 20, 132
criminalization, 27
criminals, 12, 27, 65, 68, 86, 142
crisis
crisis talk, 135–36
economic, 8, 34, 43, 46, 104, 134
humanitarian, 8, 34, 142
of multiculturalism, 5, 8, 32–34, 62, 64, 135–36
See also refugees: refugee crisis
Curtis, Mark, 19, 38

De Bruijn, Mirjam, 47
De Cesari, Chiara, 129, 137
De Cleen, Benjamin, 66
dehumanization, 11, 23
Demart, Sarah, 109
democracy, 60, 92, 120, 126, 142
Department of Homeland Security, 24
Deshingkar, Priya, 6
detention, 34, 54, 123, 139
detention centers, 24, 140, 142
detention facilities, 24, 54
See also Global Detention Project
development assistance, 78, 88
developscape, 76, 80–81
Deycard, Frédéric, 78
diaspora, 110

discrimination, 6, 12, 68, 110, 123.
See also UN Committee on the Elimination of Racial Discrimination
Dismaland, 12, 134–35, 137–38
Disneyland, 134–35, 143n1
diversity, 4, 18, 33, 53–54, 60
Djibouti, 23
docile agents/subjects, 36, 91
dualistic classifications/thinking, 18–19
Dublin Regulation, 23, 28, 30n2
Dutch, 114
empire, 52
identity, 52, 113
speaking, 67–68
Dutch East Indies, 112

Eastern European migrants, 18
economic migrants, 4, 31, 35, 76, 107
mobility, 41, 51, 54
Ekman, Mattias, 37
Elgenius, Gabriella, 32, 118
Elischer, Sebastian, 88
ethnicities, 9, 47, 77, 104
ethnicity, 9, 18, 48–49, 77, 94, 98, 100
brassage Sahélien, 77
ethnic group, 77, 90
WoDaaBe/Tuaregs, 9, 48, 78, 94–95, 102, 104
ethnography, 10–11
Eurocentric, 91, 124
Eurocontrol, 54
Eurocrat, 51, 55–57, 59, 118. *See also* Bruxpat; expatriate
Europe, project of, 4, 18, 105, 118, 128, 141–142
European Union (EU), 28, 54, 59, 82, 135, 140
Brussels, 41, 56, 118
the EU Trust Fund for Africa, 83
the European Commission, 88, 119
institutions, 40–57
legislation/policies, 19, 139
member states, 28, 34, 120, 140
and museums, 119–20, 126–28
and Niger, 83, 88, 85–86, 136
Europeans, 63, 92, 125–26, 128, 134
and Africa, 94–95, 107, 109, 126
in Brussels, 104
Europeanness, 118

mobility, 136
Ewans, Martin, 108
exclusion, 5-6, 20, 139
exhibition, 107, 109-10, 118, 120, 122, 128, 137
exotic others, 6, 12, 60, 93-94, 104
expatriate, 4
   in Brussels, 54-55, 57, 60
   in international aid, 18
   in Niger, 3, 80, 95-97, 99
   and privileged mobility, 24
   See also Bruxpat; Eurocrat
experts, 4, 24, 80-81
exploitation, 6-8, 20, 107, 124

Falk, Francesca, 112
Fekete, Liz, 28, 38
Flanders, 52, 66-67
Flemish, 52, 61n2, 66-67
Flemish language, 52, 65, 67-68
Flynn, M., 28, 139, 141
Fontanari, Elena, 17, 19, 29
Fox, Jon E., 20
France, 33, 49, 80, 124
   migration, 44-45, 53, 99
   uranium, 87-88
Franke, Richard W., 78
French
   the French, 49, 70
   speaking, 20, 45, 49, 52, 65, 67-68, 132
French colonial government/authorities, 77, 95
front stage, 41, 56-57, 60, 118. *See also* backstage
Frontex, 34, 83, 84, 85, 129
Fulani, 9, 48-49, 64, 77, 94
Fulfulde, 20, 64

Gaddafi, 8, 44-45, 83, 89
Gardaland, 1-2, 12, 29, 134, 137
Garner, Steve, 19
Gatti, Emanuele, 54-56
Gerewol, 96, 97, 99
Germany, 44, 99
ghetto, 58
Gibson, Sarah, 57, 60, 68
Glick Schiller, Nina, 34
global citizen, 11, 51, 59, 104

Global Detention Project, 140. *See also* detention
global politics, 12
globalization, 9, 32, 47, 61n6, 69, 97
   concept of, 3, 80
Goddeeris, Idesbald, 111
Goffman, Erving, 57
Grand Place, 57, 114, 134
Grange, M., 28, 139, 141
Greece, 28, 36
Greenpeace, 87
Grosfoguel, Ramon, 18-19
guest-workers, 53, 61n3
Günel, Gökçe, 11

Hamani, Djibo, 77
Hausa, 77, 91
   in Brussels, 9, 48-49, 58, 61n5, 70
   migration, 39, 47, 87, 104
Heyvaert, 58, 61n5
hierarchy, 18, 19, 29, 46, 55, 122
history, 62-63, 106, 119, 133
   Belgian colonial, 12, 51, 106-7, 111
   colonial, 19, 41, 91, 120, 126
   Europe, 13n2, 41, 56, 64, 124, 136
   in museums, 122, 126-29, 137
   Niger, 9, 12, 75-76, 86, 95-97, 104, 136
   See also colonialism: history of
Hochschild, Adam, 110
House of European History, 117, 126-29, 133n1
humanitarianism, 12, 118, 124-25
humanity, 19, 59, 91, 125, 141-42
Hussein, Saddam, 88

identity, 120
   Belgian, 104
   Dutch, 52, 113
   ethnic, 48, 67, 102
   Muslim, 100
   Nigerien, 9, 48, 78, 91, 101-2
Idrissa, A., 83, 85-86
illegality, 19, 35
immigrant, 4-5, 40, 53, 60, 65-67, 125
   African, 48, 68, 110
   illegal, 19, 38, 65
   illegal immigrants, 29, 35, 55, 59, 142

immigration, 5, 54, 129
  anti-immigration, 65, 67
  control, 19
  officers, 26, 28, 83
immobility, 2, 7, 34, 60
imperial nostalgia, 97, 137
imperialism, 76–77, 112–14, 135
Indigenous, 93–94, 96–98, 102
inequalities, 6, 10, 18, 61n4, 92n4, 129
  global, 11, 41, 49, 76
inferiority, 18, 34
instability, 8, 87
integration, 4, 7, 64, 80
international aid, 18, 77–78
international development organizations, 75, 88
International Monetary Fund, 80, 141
international protection, 28, 30n2, 31, 46, 139–40
invasion, 11, 35, 62, 88
invisible people, 57, 60, 68, 102, 128
IOM (International Organization for Migration), 84, 85–86
Iraq, 28, 34, 88
Islam, 13n2, 32, 48, 66, 94
Islamic radicalism, 27
Islamists, 37
Islamophobia, 34, 67
Italian, 20, 45–46

justice, 68, 70, 87, 124

Kanmaz, Meryem, 65
Kanuri, 77
Kel Tamashek, 94
Klein, Adam, 37
Knight, Daniel, 64
Kohl, Ines, 44
Kurdish-Syrian, 36

labor market, 6, 22, 29, 55, 65, 122
Lähdesmäki, Tuuli, 119, 122
Lampedusa, 45–46, 83
Larsen, Rasmus Kløcker, 88
Lentin, Alana, 32–33
Leopold II
  and Congo, 107-8, 110–11
  and monuments/memory, 111–12, 137
  and museum, 118–19, 127

Leopold Park, 57, 117, 129
Leurs, Koen, 37
Lewicki, Paweł, 55
Libya, 94, 104
  border control, 83, 140
  civil war, 8, 17, 45, 83
  escaping the war, 17, 28, 36, 44–45, 64
  Gaddafi's regime, end of, 8, 89
  migration from, 20, 22, 71, 85, 103
  migration to, 22, 44, 64, 80, 86
  refugees, 140–141
Lo Sardo, Sébastien, 48, 58, 61n5, 104
Lucassen, Leo, 27–28, 63
Lunaček, Sarah, 96, 102, 104
Lüthi, Barbara, 112

Maalbeck metro station, 129
Maghreb, 83
Majcher, I., 28, 83, 139, 141
Mali, 83, 85, 89, 94, 96
  Malien refugees, 85, 105
Mamosso, Christiane Alzouma, 88
Manço, Ural, 65
Mann, Gregory, 80–81
marginalization, 58, 60, 87, 95
Martiniello, Marco, 54
Mauritania, 98
Mazzocchetti, Jacinthe, 58–59, 68
media, 35, 37, 81, 100
  counter-media, 37
  crisis discourse, 32–34, 124
  events, 33, 36–37
  and migration, 21, 23, 35, 69, 75
  narratives, 3, 12, 41, 71, 132, 143
  Niger/WoDaaBe, 86, 88, 96
  and terrorism, 27, 36, 129
mediascape, 37, 63, 69, 125
Mediterranean, 20, 23, 36, 45, 62
methodology, 10, 106
Mexico, 24–25, 29
Middle East, 27, 34
Mielants, Eric, 53, 55–56, 65–66
migrant workers, 6, 64, 96
Milan, 21, 70, 89
  asylum seekers, 20, 45–46, 125
  and migration, 2, 9, 22, 29, 128
  research in, 1–3, 9, 17–18, 30, 40
Mini-Europe, 117–20, 121, 122–23, 126–28

mobile subjects, 11, 137
modernity, 5, 7, 134, 138–39
    Europe, 57, 124
    Niger, 12, 75–76
Molenbeek, 41, 58, 132
Morocco, 53
Muehlebach, Andrea, 46
Mueller, Lisa, 88
Muhammad cartoons, 33
multi-actor, 37
multicultural
    Europe, 11, 40, 63, 65
    society, 5–6, 63–64
multiculturalism, 11, 32, 41, 63
    metanarrative of, 64
    migration, 7
    See also crisis: of multiculturalism
museums, 106, 118, 128, 135, 137
    national museums, 118, 129
    The Royal Museum of Central Africa/
        Africa Museum, 109, 118–19
    See also House of European History;
        Mini-Europe

Naco, 24–26
Narayan, John, 59
National Museum of Immigration, 129
nationalism, 117–18
native, 69, 113
    Belgian, 53, 56, 58, 66
    Congolese, 108
NATO, 44, 54
neocolonialism, 91
neoliberalism, 6, 141
Netherlands, 33, 53, 105n1
New York, 32, 87, 98, 143
NGO (non-governmental organization),
    54, 81, 86, 99
Niamey, 80, 82, 90, 95
Nigeria, 77, 85, 87
Nigerians, 85
nomads, 3, 101
nomadism, 95
nonbeings, 11
non-European, 9
non-white, 1–2, 56
Nordic countries, 112–14
Northern Europe, 29, 43, 46, 59, 70,
    114n1
Norway, 23, 33

Olivier de Sardan, Jean-Pierre, 89
Oso, Laura, 18
Other, the, 4, 12, 27, 33, 66, 94, 118,
    129
    exotic other, 6, 60, 93–94, 104
    muslim, 3, 63, 67
    racialized, 27, 56, 141
Otherness, 12, 27, 68

Painter, Thomas M., 78
pandemic, 8, 135. *See also* COVID-19
Paris, 36, 49, 119, 123, 129
pastoralism, 80, 87
Place de la Bourse, 129, 130
Poland, 55, 122
policy, 81
    migration, 10, 24, 34, 61n3, 139
    See also SAP (Structural Adjustment
        Programs)
Polish expats/migrants, 55
Ponzanesi, Sandra, 37
populism, 141
    populist parties/groups, 5, 35, 37,
        143
    populist leaders, 136, 139–40
postcoloniality, 126
post-Fordism, 6
poverty, 31, 143
    ahistorical, 75–76, 91
    in Brussels, 42, 56
    and migration from Niger, 9, 63–64,
        70–71, 83, 87
    in Niger, 69–70, 76, 80, 82, 88–89,
        103, 134
precarious migrants, 8, 11–12, 117, 128
    backstage, 57
    in Brussels, 56, 104, 139
    mobility, 6, 18, 21, 23, 46
    from Niger, 3–4, 11, 21, 46, 75,
        103–4, 114, 123–24
    from other European countries, 55
    West Africa, 2–3, 6, 21
precarity, 22
    economic, 46, 104, 135
    and Global North/Europe, 8, 43, 47,
        70, 138–39, 141
    theoretical, 6
prisons, 24, 26–27, 38, 140
privileged migrants, 54–55, 57
Purtschert, Patricia, 112

race
    as category, 4–5, 19, 33, 58–59
    critical studies/science, 5, 13n1, 112
    racial classification, 5
racialization, 2, 5–6, 8, 11, 135
racism, 13n1, 19, 21, 77, 105, 113, 136, 141
    in Belgium, 66–68, 110–11, 124, 131
    institutional, 19–20
    labels, 5, 8, 18, 33
    and media, 37, 133
    mobility, 2, 7, 11, 46
    post-racism, 33
    structural, 33, 38, 68, 123, 135
Rain, David, 21
Rasmussen, Susan, 96, 98–99, 103
refugees, 5, 27, 63, 82, 126, 138
    category, 61n3, 106, 142
    danger, 37–38, 131, 140
    discourse, 8, 11, 31, 66, 125
    Iceland, 4, 9, 10, 123
    Niger, 86, 105n2
    numbers, 28, 46, 85
    refugee camps, 8, 85, 98, 140
    Refugee Convention, 141
    refugee crisis, 5, 8, 34–36, 62, 66, 124, 135–36, 139
    refugee status, 20, 46
regionalism, 118
regulations, 7, 19, 27–28, 87
religion, 8, 99
    as label, 4–5, 32–33
rights, 19, 35, 98
    civil/legal/political, 54, 95, 108
    human, 19, 63, 68, 88, 124–25, 140–42
    Human Rights Watch, 49n2
Rosaldo, Renato, 93, 97
Rosen, Rachel, 35
Rozanska, J., 55
ruination, 76, 91, 136
Rwanda, 108
Rydgren, Jens, 32

Sahara, 8, 87, 89
    and mobility, 29, 76, 83, 85–86, 95
    and Tuaregs, 78, 94, 96, 104
    See also Sub-Saharan Africa; terrorism: Trans-Saharan Counterterrorism Initiative

Sahel, 8, 21, 78, 81, 89, 94
    and EU, 82–83, 140
    and mobility, 76, 86, 95
    Pan-Sahel Initiative, 82
Salazar, Noel B., 7, 21, 34, 46, 60
SAP (Structural Adjustment Programs), 80
Schaerbeek, 41
Schapendonk, Joris, 7
Schengen, 84, 85, 123, 140
    visa to, 6, 12, 103
Schwarz, Inga, 123
Sciurba, Alessandra, 36
securitization, 4, 25, 132
segregation, 40, 58
Senegal, 20
Sicily, 20, 22
Silverman, Debora L., 119
smugglers, 71, 86–87
social capital, 45, 49
social Darwinism, 28
social networks, 18
Somalia, 23
Spain, 33, 43, 123
Spinelli, Maria-Lydia, 135
"Spirit of Europe," 122
stereotypes, 32, 98, 111
Stewart, Charles, 64
stigmatization, 68
Stoler, Laura Ann, 76, 91
Stoller, Paul, 98
Stora, Benjamin, 111
subordination, 20
Sub-Saharan Africa, 7, 23, 47, 68, 83, 110. *See also* Sahara
superior, 19, 77, 95
supranational, 85, 118
surveillance, 4, 7, 27, 131
Sylvain, Renée, 97
Syria, 28, 34

Tamashek, 94, 101
technology, 47, 80, 87, 134, 136
    and borders, 18, 142
    media/information, 37, 89
terrorism, 27, 33, 68, 82, 85
    Trans-Saharan Counterterrorism Initiative, 82
    See also War on Terror
terrorist, 5, 25, 32, 82, 89, 131, 135
    attacks, 36, 93, 100, 129, 132

theme parks, 1, 11, 17, 134, 137. *See also* Dismaland; Disneyland; Gardaland
Thorleifsson, Cathrine, 37
Tinti, Peter, 83, 86
Titley, Gavan, 32-33
Toubou, 9, 77
tourism, 40, 51, 103, 105
tourists, 4, 17-18, 24, 29
    in Brussels, 40, 51, 56-57, 59-60, 114, 118
    in Niger, 3, 95-96, 99, 103
transit zone/hub, 8, 83, 85-86
transnational movement/migration, 5, 8, 10, 21, 64
Trump, Donald, 24, 37, 141
Tsing, Anna L., 10
Tuareg, 77-78, 80, 85, 87, 93-105, 137
    Europe, 9, 42, 48-49, 110, 124
Turkey, 53, 140

Ukraine, 140
UN Committee on the Elimination of Racial Discrimination, 54
unassimilated others, 33, 63
undocumented migrants/workers, 22, 29, 35, 43, 84
    in Belgium, 41, 57, 124
    racism, 124
    resistance, 128-29
United Kingdom, 35, 49, 111, 139, 141
United States, 23, 27, 30n3, 37, 108, 143
    migration, 85
    Niger and, 47-48, 82, 89, 91

    post-racism and, 111
    Tuareg and, 94, 96, 98, 100
    US drone bases, 82
    US State Department, 82
    US/Mexico border, 24-25, 29
un-people, 19, 38
uranium, 8, 77, 87-89

Varma, Saiba, 11
veils, 33
    national ban on veiling, 33, 65
violence, 37, 91, 131, 142
    colonial, 111, 113-14
    migrants, 6, 31, 69

Wallonia, 52
Wallonians, 66-67
war on migrants, 23
War on Terror, 8, 23, 82
Watanabe, Chika, 11
we-ness, 67
Westcott, Tom, 83
WEU (Western European Union), 54
white privilege, 2, 54, 113
WoDaaBe, 9, 48, 90, 93-104, 137
    Europe, 3, 110
    exotic others, 3, 6
World Bank, 141
World Exhibitions, 110, 118, 120, 137

Youngstedt, Scott M., 47-48, 80, 91

Zarma-Songhay, 9, 48, 77, 131

www.ingramcontent.com/pod-product-compliance
Lightning Source LLC
Chambersburg PA
CBHW051549020426
42333CB00016B/2164